"It is a reasonable assumption that successful boards will share some common characteristics, as will failing boards. The challenge is to identify these factors before success or failure occur. This book, evidently based on Didier Cossin's years of experience with boards around the world, goes a long way in doing so. The Four Pillars of Board Effectiveness will be an inspiration for many boards and their directors, as they consider how they can further strengthen their governance, enhance their effectiveness and ensure their success."

– **Paul Bulcke**, Chairman of the Board of Directors, Nestlé S.A. (Switzerland); Vice-Chairman, Board of Directors, L'Oréal (France); Member, J.P. Morgan International Council

"Didier is one of the true leaders in academia on governance, with extensive practical experience from his engagement with many management teams and boards across the world. His Four Pillars of Board Effectiveness offers a simple yet practical approach to making the most out of the boardroom."

– **Robert Maersk Uggla**, CEO, A.P. Møller Holding A/S

An important distillation of Didier Cossin's insight and expertise on effective governance. As a long-time follower of his work, I am glad to see Prof Cossin publish this comprehensive guidebook to governance that transcends both geography and sectors. From stewardship of strategic objectives, to managing and structuring risk, the importance of board diversity and more, the lessons are at once practical and essential for any board member.

– **Peter Maurer** is the President of the International Committee of the Red Cross

"It is inspiring to read Professor Cossin's monograph, *High Performance Boards*. His conclusion for board governance – the Four Pillars of Board Effectiveness is classical, profound and impressive. The full time Non-Executive Directorship has enhanced the effectiveness of state-owned and -affiliated financial institutions in China. However, the Four Pillars remain the direction for us to achieve better performance and successful transformation just as all other organizations."

– **Xueling Huang**, Deputy Head, Comprehensive Management Department of Central Huijin Investment Ltd, China Investment Corporation; Executive Director, Central Huijin Asset Management Ltd

"This is the bedside book any board member should read and reread. Building on his extensive and deep experience, Didier pragmatically helps us to challenge our ways of interacting around the board table and establish a multi-dimensional frame in order to foster the best decision

making. Every page calls into question one's practice and pushes each of us to avoid biases and revisit his/her ways of thinking for the ultimate benefit of the company."
– **Barbara Dalibard,** Lead Independent and Chair of Compensation and Appointments Committee, Michelin Group

"Educational and refreshing to the brain, where page after page relate to something one has experienced. The themes are wrapped up and packaged in a very practical way. Overall, it is not a book to read once then shelve, it is something that directors need to read from time to time to ensure protection from drifting with personal habits."
– **H.E. Abdulsalam Mohammed Al Murshidi**, President, State General Reserve Fund of Oman

"Professor Cossin has got it spot on. His four-pillared 'temple' of board effectiveness is brought to life with the boardroom adventures of Joanne Marker. Indeed his construct has two outer buttresses that centre around people. Their quality, focus, dedication and also how they interact with each other dynamically to produce a governance culture of excellence. One hopes that right-minded and passionate directors or would-be directors will read this book and say 'I want to be a John or Joanne Marker when I grow up!'"
– **Teo Swee Lian**, Chairwoman, CapitaLand Mall Trust; Board Member of AIA, Singtel and Dubai Financial Services Authority; former Deputy Managing Director Monetary Authority of Singapore

"This book offers a complete and enlightening review of current board governance practices and challenges. The approach and framework it offers are as pertinent in the east as in the west in establishing high performing boards."
– **Hsieh Fu Hua**, Chairman, ACR Capital Holdings Pte Ltd; Board Member of GIC, Singapore and Grab Holdings, Singapore; Chairman of the National University of Singapore and National Gallery of Singapore

"The foundation of *High Performance Boards* is set in the Values and Character of its members. Didier brings this critical point front and center."
– **Ann M. Fudge**, former Chairwoman and CEO, Young & Rubicam Brands; Board Member of Novartis and Northrop Grumman Corporation, US; Chairwoman, WGBH Public Media, US

"Creating a culture of exchanges and constructive challenges among the board remains one of the most inspiring roles for a Chairman. Making sure that members feel accountable for the sustainable success of the firm must be the overarching purpose guiding this inspiration."
— **Michel M. Liès**, Chairman, Zurich Insurance; Board Member, Institute of International Finance (IIF)

"The book is a comprehensive and practical guide to key issues relevant for all boards aiming to improve their decision-making processes. There are many useful takeaways on how to increase the dynamics in the boardroom."
— **Olaug Svarva**, Chairwoman, DNB ASA (Norway); Chairwoman, Norfund; Board Member of Investinor and Institute of International Finance (IIF)

"Thank you, Dr Cossin. Board members needed this book for a long time. This work will assist board members to understand their responsibilities better."
— **H.E. Dr. Mohammed bin Hamad bin Saif Al Rumhy**, Minister of Oil and Gas, Sultanate of Oman; Chairman, Petroleum Development Oman; Chairman, OQ; Board Member, SGRF

"This book offers valuable insights on what it takes to be an effective board. It facilitates a deeper understanding of the range of challenges and dilemmas that boards are faced with and offers guidance and best practices for how these might be addressed. Didier's elucidation of board structures, processes and culture as key elements of quality board interaction and decision-making is timely and instructive. The checklist at the end of each chapter is a useful reminder of the many dimensions of board effectiveness and provides a quick tool for self-evaluation. This book is essential reference for boards navigating through today's era of uncertainty and greater operational complexity, with the attendant new areas of potential risks and accountabilities."
— **Tan Sri Zarinah Anwar**, Chairwoman, Institute of Corporate Directors Malaysia; former Chairwoman, Securities Commission of Malaysia

"I have known Didier Cossin for 14 years. He has always been close by during my executive and supervisory careers. The experience he has built, through academic research and real-life sharing with likes of "Joanne Marker," myself and others, have allowed him to develop and expand a top-of-the-class, practical and applied science of Corporate Governance. The IMD Global Board Center is today 'the' governance reference for current and potential board members, and this is Didier's greatest achievement.

Having managed a number of serious crisis during my supervisory career, I can only recommend Didier's book which is a very up-to-date inventory of the skills required to be an impactful board member or chairperson in today's challenging world."

– **Michel Demaré**, Deputy Chair, Louis Dreyfus Company; Board Member of Vodafone and Astra Zeneca; Chair of the Supervisory Board, IMD

"The free market system has created the largest aggregate economic growth in human history. However, the serious problems created by its excesses and structural limitations have become painfully apparent. Prof. Cossin's granular understanding and insights on enterprise governance, contemporary risks and challenges and, most importantly, his perspective on stewardship are extremely valuable in achieving the maximisation of long-term stakeholder value – the 'holy grail' of modern enterprise. This book is borne out of Prof. Cossin's extensive experience across sectors and geographies – a must-read for committed enterprise directors and trustees."

– **Francis Estrada**, Board Member, Philam Life (Philippines); Chair, Institute of Corporate Directors (Philippines)

"When reading this book, I recall the inspiring sessions conducted by Professor Cossin for Effective Board Practices. This topic is extremely attractive and well accepted by the boards who want to bring value to the company. The board is a publicly exposed body of the company, which is influenced from inside and outside. Diversity, board dynamics and culture on the one hand, and growing number of stakeholder interests, reconsideration of business purpose and economic trends on the other. The environment inevitably creates challenges for the board and the governance specialists."

– **Oleg Tsvetkov**, Managing Director - Corporate Secretary, Sberbank, Russia

"*High Performance Boards* is the most insightful book I've ever read on corporate governance. It is a brilliant, comprehensive and thorough practical guide that shows how boards do function, but it is also much more than that: it describes with vivid accuracy and real company cases and real-life anecdotes how boards should really function. A must-read for anyone who wants to look behind the curtain and learn about the actual dynamics in the boardroom and, in particular, about the relationship between the Chair and CEO – one of the most important aspects of Corporate Governance."

– **Pierre Vareille**, Chairman of the Board, BIC S.A.; Board Member of Etex SA, Ferroglobe plc and Outokumpu Oyj; Co-Chairman and Founder, The Vareille Foundation

"High Performance Boards is 'the companion' – the guide you need. Of course, you will find in this book all the dos and don'ts for your daily board work. Professor Cossin takes you well beyond the checklist. More than anything else you will be inspired by the leadership dimension – the moral compass. What you will see in these pages are your values in action as you serve in the boardroom."

– **Diane de Saint Victor**, Chairwoman of Compensation Committee, Altran; Chairwoman of Nomination Committee, Natixis

High Performance Boards

High Performance Boards

A PRACTICAL GUIDE TO IMPROVING AND ENERGISING YOUR GOVERNANCE

Didier Cossin

This edition first published 2020
© 2020 John Wiley & Sons Ltd.

Registered office

John Wiley & Sons Ltd, The Atrium, Southern Gate, Chichester, West Sussex, PO19 8SQ, United Kingdom

For details of our global editorial offices, for customer services and for information about how to apply for permission to reuse the copyright material in this book please see our website at www.wiley.com.

Wiley publishes in a variety of print and electronic formats and by print-on-demand. Some material included with standard print versions of this book may not be included in e-books or in print-on-demand. If this book refers to media such as a CD or DVD that is not included in the version you purchased, you may download this material at http://booksupport.wiley.com. For more information about Wiley products, visit www.wiley.com.

Designations used by companies to distinguish their products are often claimed as trademarks. All brand names and product names used in this book are trade names, service marks, trademarks or registered trademarks of their respective owners. The publisher is not associated with any product or vendor mentioned in this book.

Library of Congress Cataloging-in-Publication Data

Names: Cossin, Didier, author.
Title: High performance boards : a practical guide to improving and
    energizing your governance / Didier Cossin.
Description: Chichester, West Sussex : John Wiley & Sons, 2020. | Includes
    index.
Identifiers: LCCN 2019056741 (print) | LCCN 2019056742 (ebook) | ISBN
    9781119615651 (cloth) | ISBN 9781119615682 (adobe pdf) | ISBN
    9781119615699 (epub)
Subjects: LCSH: Boards of directors. | Corporate governance.
Classification: LCC HD2745 .C644 2020 (print) | LCC HD2745 (ebook) | DDC
    658.4/22—dc23
LC record available at https://lccn.loc.gov/2019056741
LC ebook record available at https://lccn.loc.gov/2019056742

Cover Design: Wiley
Cover Image: © sorbetto/Getty Images modified by Wiley
Author Photo credit: Headshot Pro, Christophe Senehi

Set in 11/13pt NewBaskerville by SPi Global, India

Printed in Great Britain by TJ International Ltd, Padstow, Cornwall, UK

10 9 8 7 6 5 4 3 2 1

Contents

About the Author

Didier Cossin is professor of governance at IMD, Switzerland. He is the founder and director of the IMD Global Board Center, the originator of the Four Pillars of Board Effectiveness methodology and an advocate of Stewardship.

Prof. Cossin works with sovereign wealth funds, large corporations, non-profit organisations, families and institutional investors on governance and stewardship issues. He is an advisor to central banks, regulators and international organizations across the world.

He is the author of other books such as Inspiring Stewardship, book chapters (such as Governance Risk: A Guide for Investors) and articles in the fields of governance, investments, risks and stewardship. He is also principal author of a proprietary methodology of investment selection on governance that is used in financial markets.

Prof. Cossin holds a PhD in Business Economics from Harvard University (Robert C. Merton chair), is a former Fulbright Scholar from the Massachusetts Institute of Technology and is a graduate from ENS, rue d'Ulm, Paris as well as of Sorbonne University and EHESS.

Acknowledgements

Many have contributed, directly and indirectly, to my work and to this book. Of those that contributed directly, I am particularly indebted to Sophie Coughlan and Abraham HongZe Lu. Both Sophie and Abraham have helped me directly in my practice and shaped several of the chapters of this book. This book would not be there without their contribution. I am also grateful for the many others that contributed to this work: Quentin Dufresne, Francesca Vitucci, Julie Poivey, Martin Kralik, Richard Eames. And for a personal collaboration that has addressed many of the issues hereby described, Loic Frank.

Of those that contributed indirectly, I owe a particular debt to the real actors of the governance world, board members, directors, government officials, investors, that have peopled my words and my ideas, for the better or for the worse! They probably are just as happy to not see their name mentioned here, as a chair of one of the largest financial institutions in the world wryly remarked once: "Being in Didier's writings tells you it's time to go!". I suppose that my critical eye has helped a few towards self-awareness J. For many though, they have been an inspiration of how to drive true governance, and many of them are chairpeople or board members of influential and powerful organizations. I am grateful for all those who shared intimate and confidential situations that make the reality of good and bad governance. Without them, I could not contribute to governance improvements that I know impact the world for the better (and sometimes dramatically and publicly so). The dedication, integrity, and altruism of many is commandable. Some are famous, some are unknown, and all support us towards a better governed world. And indeed I have rarely met individuals that did not want to do better, in all senses of the word better. We, as society, should always support the development and improvement of those that govern us and our organisations, and I hope that through my words, their contribution will be heightened. I am in many ways a go-between, putting in words and concepts what the very best-in-class are naturally doing. This book is simply a mapping and synthetization of what some gifted and dedicated individuals have endeavored to bring to society through their personal judgement skills.

Preface

Governance, or the quality of decision-making at the very top of an organisation, has become central to success. But although an effective board can be a huge asset in this regard, boards often fail their organisations – typically in the areas of risk management, strategy, the selection and support of the CEO and senior management, and integrity. Making boards more effective, therefore, is crucial to improving governance around the world.

My own interest in the subject began more than 30 years ago, when I studied the governance of risk. I was fortunate to have many inspirational teachers, including five Nobel Prize winners – one of whom, Robert C. Merton, chaired my PhD committee. In parallel with my mathematical work, I quickly became convinced that the human element is crucial to effective governance, and my interest in psychology, philosophy, and ethics increasingly shaped my approach.

In the decades since, I have worked with boards across the globe to assess and improve governance – in big global companies, sovereign wealth funds, government bodies, international organisations, non-profits, family businesses, and tech start-ups. Over the years, I have developed a systematic approach to increasing a board's effectiveness that rests on four pillars: the quality, focus, and dedication of individual directors; sophisticated information architecture; well-functioning structures and processes; and, healthy group dynamics and board culture. By focusing on continuous improvement across all four dimensions, my methodology has repeatedly shown its ability to transform boards for the better.

Diagnosing governance problems is often relatively straightforward, although in some rare cases the causes can be deep and hidden, especially with integrity failures. Improving governance, on the other hand, is often a longer-term process, requiring a gradual, sustained effort over several years.

This book covers both the diagnosis and treatment of governance problems, and aims to provide directors with a practical guide to making their boards more effective. Part I introduces the Four Pillars of Board Effectiveness methodology that my team and I use to assess governance health. Readers may wish to think of this section as a check-up process. Part II addresses the most common areas of governance failure, and how boards can guard against these. Finally, Part III is a compendium of best-in-class governance practices, with each chapter covering a specific aspect of board work.

My colleagues at IMD business school, and especially the team at the IMD Global Board Center, have contributed hugely to the content of this book. So, of course, have the thousands of board members whom I have had the pleasure of working with. I pay tribute to them in this book by describing the board experiences of a character called Joanne Marker (not her real name). The real Joanne, an exceptional woman of great energy and dedication, has softly (and sometimes not so softly) impacted the governance of three of the world's most iconic large-cap companies and one of its most influential philanthropic organisations.

As Joanne's experiences illustrate, good governance is about balance, responsibility, and genuine personal accountability. I therefore hope the following chapters will inspire you and your organisations to even better governance and further success.

Didier Cossin
Lausanne, January 2020

PART I
The Four Pillars of Board Effectiveness

Joanne Marker and Board Service

*O*ctober 2018: At age 69, Joanne Marker had been a senior independent director for over 20 years on the boards of many different companies and public organisations.

The previous year, Joanne had taken early retirement from her job as head of global marketing at Connect, a major US telecommunications company, where she had worked for more than two decades. Hers had been a rewarding and challenging career, of which she was proud.

Joanne now derived a different kind of satisfaction from her board service at three very different companies: Connect, international pharmaceutical company Ziogen, and engineering multinational SNB. In recent months a few other organisations had extended invitations, and she was currently evaluating each of them.

One morning, an email from her nephew Thorsten popped up on her screen.

Dear Aunt Joanne,

Exciting news! I just received an invitation to be on the board of Kloetzel & Brothers! First board meeting is next month. I wanted to pick the brain of my favorite board member! Can I take you to lunch at Mario's when you're in town next week?

Yours,
Thorsten

Thorsten was an ambitious, capable, and educated young man working in investment banking on Wall Street. Joanne had no doubt that he would make a fine board director; his knowledge of the financial markets and banking regulation would certainly be helpful to Kloetzel, a global financial services company. He was bright, energetic, and hardworking – and from what she had heard, had earned a reputation in banking as a name to watch. Still, she found herself remembering a few incidents that made her wonder whether he had the maturity and self-possession needed for boardroom discussions. She checked her calendar and emailed Thorsten, confirming the lunch.

***

Joanne cast her mind back to a chilly afternoon in March 1992. She had been in her office thinking about how to improve a distribution partnership for WeCare, the multinational consumer goods company she worked for at the time, when her phone rang.

It was her old friend from business school, Burt Goodman, who was now a mover and shaker at GCD, a major consulting firm. Goodman invited Joanne to join him for the Henry Street Settlement dinner in New York City. 'I'm just not cut out for big gala events, Burt', she had protested.

'Oh come on, it will be good for you', Goodman said. 'Sometimes even an MBA and over 20 years of experience in a major multinational can't match the magic of one lucky dinner conversation'. So Joanne decided to go.

At the dinner, she was seated next to Jordan Wise, the CEO of Amsterdam-based Virtuous Ventures, a major international conglomerate. Their conversation touched upon Joanne's family and career journey to date, and Wise asked her advice on the pros and cons of joint ventures in different emerging markets. Joanne shared her key learnings about each market, as well as the main strategic and industrial dimensions that needed to be considered.

'But doesn't it depend on your partners in the end?' Wise wanted to know. Joanne described the different partnerships that WeCare had developed locally, depending on the distribution channels in place (or not) in different markets.

Two days later, Wise called her with a proposal that took her by surprise. 'How would you like to be on the Virtuous board, Joanne?' he asked her. She had always aspired to board service at some point in her career – but she was only 44, surely far too young to be a director.

Wise explained: 'We're expanding internationally into a new retail business, and we need your international marketing expertise. You can bring in solid knowledge about distribution networks and consumer insight too'. Now Joanne's interest was piqued. She began to ask questions. Wise soon ran out of answers.

Her first meeting with Virtuous Ventures' Chairman Gerald Grossheim was over lunch at the famous Charlie Trotter's restaurant in Chicago's Lincoln Park. Over their first course, Grossheim explained how the company's 11-member board worked, how often it met (four times a year), and his relationship with Jordan Wise (almost daily contact, yet with a certain necessary distance). He also discussed other members of the top team.

Grossheim asked Joanne about the kinds of challenges she had encountered when negotiating with local distributors during international expansions, and about how she had developed an understanding of customers in different markets. Joanne happily described her extensive travels in India, Bangladesh, Thailand, China, and Egypt to talk to WeCare's local sales teams. She had accompanied them on visits, discussing their frustrations and where they saw opportunities, in order to get a sense of the reality on the ground.

Joanne had some questions of her own. While Grossheim sipped his coffee, she asked him:

- *Who was on the Virtuous board? How dedicated were they? What did each bring – and what was his or her unique contribution?*
- *How did board directors ensure they had the information they needed to make decisions? What were the board briefing papers like? Were there other sources of information?*
- *What kind of processes and structures did the board have in place to ensure it was doing things efficiently and professionally? How did it ensure directors have a sufficient board-level view of risk? (Here, Joanne recalled the WeCare board's inability to understand how their growth strategy had exposed her own company to key vulnerabilities.)*
- *What was the Virtuous boardroom culture like? What kind of dynamics were at play? How would the other directors view the contribution of a much younger woman?*

Together, they formulated questions for Grossheim to ask Virtuous Ventures' President of Marketing, including what additional information he could ask for that would be helpful in assessing the company's current global marketing plan.

Outside, they shook hands and agreed to speak again in the coming weeks. 'I hope to be seeing a lot more of you, Joanne', Grossheim said, smiling at her.

Three months later, after a series of discussions and a formal panel interview by the nominations committee, Joanne was appointed as an independent director and began eight years of board service with Virtuous.

***

The following Tuesday, Joanne walked into Mario's and kissed her nephew Thorsten on the cheek. It had been 18 months since she had last seen him. While Joanne sipped her iced tea, Thorsten told her how his favourite professor from business school, Sam Cragnolino, was on the board of Kloetzel and was approaching retirement.

As a member of the nominations committee, Cragnolino had seen the board's needs analysis, which had identified a gap in the area of finance – and investment in particular. The head of the committee had developed a skills and competency matrix, which specified that the candidate should also be young (between 30 and 40), and had then issued an invitation to executive search firms. He also asked the other board members if they had any candidates to nominate. Sam had recommended Thorsten.

James Caspar, Kloetzel's chair, had also screened the candidates proposed by the search firms, and invited Thorsten for a panel interview. The young man's expertise in securing and structuring deals with a series of major clients had attracted Caspar's attention as being something missing from the board's existing skillset – and something they very much needed. Thorsten had made the shortlist and passed the due diligence process, and then met the full board. He had been impressed by the ambition of its members to contribute to transforming Kloetzel.

'I really like what they're doing', Thorsten said to Joanne. 'James seems active and engaged, yet not overbearing. Everyone I talked to seems serious about really building something'. Joanne smiled at his enthusiasm.

'That's great, Thorsten', she said. 'Board service is one of the most rewarding experiences any professional can have during their career, and I think you stand to gain a lot. But tell me', Joanne said, putting down her fork and looking intently at the young man, 'what is it about your experience that leads you to think you could make a meaningful contribution to Kloetzel?'

'I know how companies are thinking about the costs and benefits of major transactions', Thorsten said. 'I could help Kloetzel think about whom they

could approach and with what messaging to expand in major markets, which is part of their strategy'.

Joanne asked him about Kloetzel's current performance, and whether there were discrepancies across major markets. Thorsten shook his head. He didn't know the details. He dug in his pocket for a pen to make a note.

She pointed out the difference between board service and an executive director role. 'You're not there to tell management how to do their job', she said. 'You're there to challenge them on the strategy to make sure it's a good one, and to help them to get what they need to be able to do it, and then to check that they actually do it'.

Then Joanne asked Thorsten the following questions:

- *People: Who were Kloetzel's current board members? What kind of skills, background, personality, and expertise did they have? How many other independent, non-executive directors were there? What kind of diversity and breadth of experience did they have? And how committed were they?*
- *Information architecture: What kind of information did he have access to that would help him to support Kloetzel in delivering its strategy and monitoring its risks? Who in his network could help? What kinds of social media was he following?*
- *Structures and processes: What kind of structures and processes did the Kloetzel board have in place? How were these helping it to stay ahead of regulation trends in the financial services industry? Did the board have a risk committee? An investment committee? Would Thorsten be able to serve on either of these?*
- *Dynamics: Had he spent enough time with the chair of Kloetzel? Did he like him and his style? What about the other directors? How were the interactions? How did the board engage with the firm's senior executives? And how much passion about the firm could he feel?*

'With all due respect Aunt Joanne, aren't you ahead of yourself?' Thorsten asked. 'Won't I have time to figure this out once I'm on the board?'

Joanne thought back to a board she had sat on – an Indian tech company, where she had submitted her resignation after just six months. She wished she had done her due diligence exercise better before joining that board.

'Fundamentally, Thorsten, it comes down to two questions', Joanne said. 'The first is: is this a good board which I want to be part of?' He nodded with vigour. 'The second is: am I good for this board?'

Joanne smiled at the young man. 'Saying no to the wrong board appointment is just as important as saying yes to the right one', she said. 'If you don't think you will be able to usefully contribute, do yourself a favour and save yourself from a world of frustration and pain'.

'Thanks Aunt Joanne', Thorsten said, slumping a little in his chair. 'I guess I have some homework to do'.

CHAPTER 1

The Four Pillars of Board Effectiveness

Over the past decade, we have witnessed dramatic and unprecedented developments in business, politics, and society. The main upshot of this has been the growing realisation that governance is the determining factor behind the success and failure of organisations. And with fresh evidence of abdication of duty in the corporate and policy-making spheres emerging on a weekly basis, there are growing demands for better governance in different countries, and for all types of organisations – businesses, governments, NGOs, and many others.

When we refer to governance, we mean the quality of decision-making and implementation at the top of organisations – and the processes to ensure these. Increasingly, boards are seen as having a key responsibility and role as the 'owner' of governance in an organisation. It is their competence, structures, and integrity, and their interactions with CEOs and management teams, that shape the governance DNA of organisations.

Until a few years ago, governance and boards were considered to be well understood, and operating along standard and predictable lines. As a result, the subject attracted relatively little attention from researchers. But the situation changed significantly as more stories of corporate malfeasance appeared in mainstream media, industry publications, and academic journals, inevitably accompanied by the question 'Where was the board?'

Indeed, events during the past decade have made it clear that boards can fail in various ways. They have failed to manage risks, failed to contribute proactively to firm strategy, failed to identify the 'right' team, and, in some cases, failed to deal with integrity issues and possibly outright fraud. We will discuss board failures and challenges in more detail in Part II.

Partly as a consequence of these much-publicised and damaging failures, today's boards are eager to improve their performance and to continually fine-tune their effectiveness. They have become more cognisant than ever of their role in supporting their organisations' long-term success by aiming for world-class governance.

So, if business as usual is not an option for boards, what are the main dimensions to target when trying to make a board function better? How do we distil the key factors that contribute to board effectiveness?

In our work over the years inspiring the boards of organisations around the world toward greater success, my team and I have identified four discrete pillars of board effectiveness (see Figure 1.1).

THE FOUR PILLARS
OF BOARD EFFECTIVENESS

GOVERNANCE EXCELLENCE

BOARD EFFECTIVENESS

People	Information Architecture	Structures & Processes	Group Dynamics & Governance Culture
Quality, Focus & Dedication	Internal vs External		
	Formal vs Informal		

Figure 1.1   Governance Excellence Rests on Four Pillars

These are people quality, focus, and dedication; information architecture; structures and processes; and group dynamics and board culture. We will explore each of these pillars in detail in Chapters 4 to 7.

This simple framework for assessing a board's effectiveness has a deep-rooted underlying rationale, and its practical application has helped to transform boards for the better in many different contexts. These include large publicly traded companies, family owned businesses, non-profit organisations, governments, and other bodies, across all geographies, and in both developed and developing contexts.

The four-pillar methodology, focusing on systematic and continuous improvement along each dimension, has proven to be a strong asset for all types of organisation.

The First Pillar: People Quality, Focus, and Dedication

A boardroom is a social place, as is business in general. Therefore, the first of the pillars that support a board's effectiveness consists of the people who socialise, interact, learn, make sense of situations, and reach decisions in the boardroom. Their quality, focus, and dedication are often what makes or breaks a board's ability to perform effectively.

The quality of the board's composition and functioning is crucial. For starters, members of the board and its committees are expected to have the necessary and relevant knowledge. Boards are typically composed of experienced, accomplished individuals from a variety of backgrounds, including top managers, public officials, and education experts. Yet these backgrounds do not automatically give them the knowledge they need to contribute effectively to the work of a specific board.

As we have seen time and again in recent years, having limited knowledge hinders a board member's effectiveness. Whenever a major corporate initiative has run aground, the board members' technical and other specialised knowledge has come under scrutiny. Effective boards therefore ensure that performance and knowledge standards are articulated and tailor-made for individual directors, with the help of matching learning modules and other opportunities. Board members' performance can then be evaluated against those standards.

The quality of the board is further enhanced by its diversity of gender, personality, and opinion. (For a fuller discussion of diversity, see Chapter 23.) In particular, high-quality boards are typically successful at managing their mix of personalities. How many times have we read news stories attributing boardroom confrontations, showdowns, and dramatic exits to a 'clash of personalities', 'incompatible personalities', or, to use a euphemism, 'strong personalities'? The example of Steve Jobs being fired by the board of Apple is just one of many such cases.

To avoid becoming one of these headlines, a board needs to map out, understand, and learn to work with the range of personalities on it. As in all such exercises, this requires tools or 'cognitive handles' that help to capture not only the composition of personalities and the risks involved, but also the configurations which, with a bit of planning and effort, can help to infuse the board with additional vibrancy and strength of performance.

Boards can productively employ and draw on a number of taxonomies in this regard. For instance, personality diagrams highlight board members' introversion or extroversion, their abstract 'big picture' thinking or orientation to detail, their level of emotional reactivity, and the emphasis they put on competition as opposed to harmony. The well-known NEO Personality Inventory framework describes the 'Big Five' dimensions of personality: emotionality, introversion/extroversion, openness to experience, agreeableness, and conscientiousness (see Chapter 13 on Group Dynamics and Board Culture).

As important as skills and quality are, directors must also be focused and dedicated. Yet these attributes are often missing, in varying degrees, from the boardroom.

Dealing with ambiguities in decision-making is inevitable – in fact, it is a sign that the board is addressing real issues. But when directors misunderstand their roles and functions, their focus suffers. To sharpen and re-energise it, boards would do well to establish their own statement of purpose (often codified as a board charter statement) and define their role in a way that adds value to the company's activities. Boards need to reflect regularly on their involvement and strive to make it firstly distinctive, so that they do not replicate the efforts of other parts of the organisation; and secondly additive, whereby the board builds upon decisions made by the firm.

Well-focused boards know how to distinguish between contexts. From there, they determine whether they should perform a supervisory role or rather offer support to management. Such boards are ready to be proactive and jump into pre-emptive action when they see signs of risk and recognise that oversight is needed. In other situations, such as during a crisis when the organisation's reputation is at stake, they are just as efficient in identifying and acting on the need to communicate the firm's strategic objectives. In addition, a board's focus can be strengthened by having the right agenda: one that looks more towards the future than the past, and that aims to capture long-term issues while managing short-term matters.

But even high-quality, focused boards will underperform if their members are not fully dedicated to their work and to the organisation. Directors frequently tell me that their board meeting discussions reflect a level of preparation that was 'basic' and 'not in great depth'. A minority of them do report rich and diverse preparation, where board members have diligently read the relevant documentation and obtained external information where necessary. But all too many describe the board members in their organisations as typically 'not very well prepared'. The percentage of directors who have regularly witnessed great preparation for board meetings, with members actively consulting outside sources and analysing information in depth, is in fact small.

A similar picture emerges when we ask board members how many hours of preparation time one hour of a board meeting requires from each director. Typically, more than half of them estimate one to three hours of preparation, around 25% report three to seven hours, and only a minority report seven to ten hours. It is rare to hear of directors spending more than ten hours preparing for each hour of a board meeting. Worryingly, in fact, a few say that less than one hour of preparation time is required – even though most responsible individuals believe that a director should not sit on more than five boards at once anyway. Is this what board work has come to?

A director's sense of dedication should entail precisely what the word implies: giving freely of one's self, and not just because of the high-powered networking, access to industry information, and higher social status and income that come with the position. And, indeed, there are many directors whose main motivation for joining a board is their desire to contribute to the company's success, and who consider it an honour to serve in this capacity. These are the types of dedicated individuals that boards need to attract and empower: people of integrity, character, and conviction who are ready to speak up and voice their concerns for the greater good of the organisation.

The Second Pillar: Information Architecture

Sophisticated information architecture is key to successful boards. Although this design does not necessarily need to be complex, it should inform the board about all the company's essential activities and the issues facing it, both now and in the future. When considering information design, directors should have three rules of thumb.

First, board members should have as much information on external issues as they do on internal matters. Boards typically think of information as coming from management. Ideally, this will be brief, well focused, prioritised, and strategic, with executive summaries, key issues to tackle, and options to consider. But directors should also be fully informed regarding external issues, such as reputation analysis, the competitive landscape, customer knowledge, an understanding of shareholders, and technological evolution. Often, however, this is not the case, resulting in boards that do little more than go through the motions. Clearly, there is significant room for improvement.

Second, directors should have both formal and informal information channels. Formal internal information should be jointly designed by the board and management, with briefings that include financials with forecasts, a CEO report, risk and opportunity maps, analysis of the management gene pool, and a summary of financial analysts' views. In addition, regular communication between management and the board, for example via management letters between meetings, provides further efficient and timely information. Board committee reports are also fundamental in building the depth of knowledge required by directors in specific areas – as long as such reports include analysis of the issues and not just recommendations. It is critical that the board is actively involved in designing the information, including whether that design should change along with the firm, its environment, and its strategy.

At the same time, informal channels of information are key, and need to be cultivated. These channels should be diverse and well structured, giving board members access to employees and stakeholder networks, links to fellow directors outside board meetings, and connections with management. This might be through a Sunday afternoon barbecue, a coffee during the week, or an early evening call, depending on the board member. Such interactions must strike the right balance, providing board members with greater freedom and inspiration without infringing on management's role.

Third, dedicated directors should aim to receive as much information from independent sources as they do from management. Rather than relying solely on management information, these board members see it as their duty to track down the most useful social media posts, market information, and other sources.

The Third Pillar: Structures and Processes

As governance becomes more sophisticated, its structures have likewise evolved greatly. Board effectiveness is hugely influenced by the quality of the structures and processes organised by the board secretariat and steered by the chair. It is imperative that boards regularly benchmark these against the ideal situation and act to address any divergence.

In the most basic structural terms, the size of the board should be carefully examined, in addition to the necessary number and effective functioning of board committees. The main goal is to ensure that the board's committee structure is pertinent to the current reality of the organisation. There are a number of innovative and inspiring examples in this regard, such as HSBC's committee on Financial System Vulnerabilities, which addresses one of the primary strategic issues in banking today. In addition, board innovation committees are becoming increasingly common at companies operating in industries at high risk of disruption. Both Procter & Gamble – a global giant in fast-moving consumer goods – and UK-based bank RBS have a Technology and Innovation Committee on their respective boards, for example.

As we mentioned earlier, beyond its structural 'hardware', a board should radiate a well-managed diversity of personality, experience, gender, and opinion. The independence of board members is crucial too – but so is their structured access to the right individuals. For example, in some organisations the chief risk officer has a dotted reporting line to the chair of the risk committee, or to the chair of the board.

Along with structures, a number of processes need to be in place to ensure that the board systematically addresses the issues within its remit. The list of processes that truly matter includes agenda setting, reviewing and monitoring management performance, CEO succession, stakeholder engagement, audit, regulatory compliance, risk, strategy, ongoing board improvement, and many others.

A strong board will integrate these processes smoothly within its yearly agenda. Below, we briefly discuss four of them: strategy, agenda setting, evaluation, and CEO succession. We then examine board structures and processes more closely in Chapter 6 and other parts of the book.

The board's strategy process is critical to increasing its effectiveness. Strategic board involvement occurs along three dimensions – co-creation, supervision, and support – and good processes will enrich all three. Typically, regular board meetings will complement retreats, and external presentations will add to internal ones. Focused, decision-oriented meetings will complement boards' long-term strategic understanding of the company and its industry. A well-designed board strategy process strengthens the firm's strategy by helping to define it, aligning it with objectives and ensuring commitment. Ultimately, this enables boards to efficiently assess the company's strategic risks and opportunities. We will discuss the board's strategic role in more detail in Chapter 15.

Setting the agenda is another key board process. This necessarily involves a number of balancing acts, such as board-management interaction, consideration of stakeholder issues, clear prioritisation, a focus on key issues, and time management. A strong agenda-setting process will be both strategic, by providing a high-level setting for the next two years, and tactical, by ensuring the board spends its time on the most critical issues.

A third decisive process is board evaluation. When directors are not performing to the standards set by the board, they need to receive feedback clearly indicating this. A poor evaluation process contributes to governance failure, which is why thriving boards engage in a formal assessment procedure. This might be self-assessment or external assessment, and should cover individual directors' roles, dynamics, and performance. A good practice is to utilise technology. Using smartphones or tablets to evaluate board sessions during meetings, for example, provides results in real time and offers an opportunity for careful and dynamic scrutiny in between annual evaluations.

Finally, CEO succession is a critical process that requires ongoing attention and planning. Whether based on an internal or external 'horse race' or search, the process of identifying leadership talent and candidates should focus on the transparency of selection criteria, the fit with the organisation, the quality of the on-boarding process, and the smoothness of the transition.

Hewlett-Packard (HP) provides a good example of difficult successions creating real governance risk. In a period of six years, HP fired three CEOs, resulting in corporate turmoil that negatively affected the company's brand reputation. In one of the cases, the HP board did not meet the new CEO before proceeding with the nomination. This raises questions regarding the process in place, and the implied failure of the board to identify a candidate who would fulfil the company's strategic vision.

The Fourth Pillar: Group Dynamics and Board Culture

The three board effectiveness pillars we have examined so far include focused, dedicated people accessing different types of information and applying this to increasingly sophisticated structures and processes. In keeping with this strongly social, people-centric snapshot, the dynamics within this group of people constitute the final pillar in our edifice. This pillar concerns how board members interact as a group, and what they individually bring to and collectively take away from their discussions. Over time, these dynamics give rise to a specific board culture: a set of customs, practices, and often unspoken rules about 'how we get things done around here'.

As with any group, it sometimes doesn't take much for a board to go down the path of inefficiency and dysfunction. Sleepy, low-energy boards are sadly quite common. And in some cases, dysfunctional dynamics are intentionally used to set a board up for governance failure – for example, through late distribution of meeting documents and not making relevant information available. But some of the more benign board pathologies can be just as destructive. These include the presence of disruptive or dominating members on the board, or a tendency to group-think, where board members avoid any paths less travelled in an effort to ingratiate themselves with the group.

These dysfunctions are often symptoms of a deeper issue, such as a lack of trust or overlapping roles. Governance is enriched by directors' different opinions and constructive dissent; having a critical view of assumptions makes for an effective strategy. Yet some firms appoint directors who are close associates of the company's founder or CEO. They may be prominent figures in their respective industries, but their role on the board is circumscribed by their relationship with a dominant figure in the company.

Interactions between the board and senior management are an important aspect of this pillar. BlackBerry (formerly Research in Motion) once thrived on the long-running partnership and friendship of its two co-CEOs. Once they stepped aside, deep divisions surfaced within the company and the board regarding its flagship product, key technology alliance, and planned China expansion, with the new CEO actively canvassing behind the scenes to kill off some of these flagship initiatives. BlackBerry's share price then plummeted, and its product offerings were considered late to market.

Although conflict is important for an open exchange of views, boards are more effective when discussions remain productive. This can only be achieved if a board makes its rules of engagement clear to all its members and promotes their equal participation and mutual respect. Functional board dynamics can help to avoid conflicts of interest, especially if the board culture emphasises accountability towards relevant stakeholders and is based on openness and constructive dissent (see also Chapter 13). And a culture that ensures board members are connected to reality also reduces the likelihood of them being overconfident.

The chair's role is key in developing a successful board culture. This can be partly formalised in writing in order to be easily shared and understood. An awareness of discussion styles (such as fast thinking, influencing, and the 'false yes') and decision styles (whether autocratic, consensual, or indecisive) is similarly essential in managing group dynamics. We will look at these in more detail in Chapter 7.

Even more fundamentally, boards are now increasingly discussing their common values, and the level of stewardship they want to provide to the organisation. Do board members share the same long-term perspectives? Do they have a common view of their contributions to society, and of their impact on employees, customers, and other stakeholders? This will form the focus of Chapters 27 and 28.

Board effectiveness requires constantly sustaining the four pillars we discussed in this chapter. A board cannot neglect the quality, focus, and dedication of its members. Information architecture needs to be carefully designed in order to optimise its effectiveness. Successful boards continuously improve their structures and work processes as they become more sophisticated. Finally, effective board dynamics, based on a culture that promotes quality discussion, greatly contribute to the strategic coherence of the firm.

Excellence in these areas makes for sustainable success in board practices. Although the four pillars do not constitute a foolproof guarantee against board or company failures, they provide a solid foundation for good governance and help to make organisations more resilient. And as we will see in Chapter 2, good governance is becoming increasingly vital around the world.

2

Governance Challenges around the World

Governance is the ability to take the right decisions at the top of organisations, and it is fast becoming a competitive differentiator. In an increasingly chaotic, rapidly changing environment, good governance is vital to giving organisations the resilience they need to withstand shocks. Governance drives organisations' efficiency, integrity, and social impact, all of which are necessary for sustainable success. Yet today, there are numerous examples of poor governance around the world, in the corporate, public, non-governmental, and inter-governmental domains.

The case of Volkswagen (VW) shows how a rift between the chair and CEO can result in major governance failures. In April 2015, VW Chair Ferdinand Karl Piëch, the 78 year-old grandson of Ferdinand Porsche (who founded Porsche), made the following comment to *Der Spiegel* without forewarning the board: 'I am distancing myself from [VW CEO Martin] Winterkorn'. This caused tension among the board members, who began to speculate whether it would be the chair or the CEO leaving the company. VW's executive committee (as well as supervisory board member Wolfgang Porsche, also a grandson of Ferdinand) urged Piëch to soften his statement, and publicly reiterate his support for Winterkorn. Piëch agreed – allegedly on the condition that the committee recommend that he once again be elected chair of VW's supervisory board when his contract expired in April 2017.

Winterkorn, the company's CEO since 2007, had joined VW subsidiary Audi in the 1980s and had been hand-picked by Piëch, himself a former VW CEO. Piëch initially batted away suggestions that his wife Ursula might replace him at the head of the supervisory board, saying that the position was earmarked for somebody with an engineering background. A panel of six board members that had been established during the crisis concluded that 'in the light of the past weeks, the mutual trust necessary for successful cooperation was no longer there'. Piëch, a representative of the family controlling 52% of VW shareholder votes, resigned from the supervisory board and was replaced by an interim chair.

This infighting was a red flag that foreshadowed the subsequent governance failure at VW. It also revealed the very human side of governance, with the frailties and flaws of the individuals involved.

Later in 2015, the cover up of VW's diesel emissions scandal was made public. The company had installed software in engines just so that they could pass laboratory emissions tests – a practice orchestrated at very senior levels of the organisation. The head of VW's US compliance team, Oliver Schmidt, had briefed executive management about the software in July 2015, and told them that US regulators were not aware of it. But he had been instructed to persist in the deception. NGOs in Europe and then in the US had suspected the problem much earlier than that, and it was apparently known about within VW for probably two years. The scandal led to an investigation and estimated costs of $18 billion. According to Alexander Juschus, director at German proxy advisor IVOX, 'The scandal clearly also has to do with structural issues at VW...There have been warnings about VW's corporate governance for years, but they didn't take it to heart and now you see the result'.[1]

By 2019, the emissions scandal had cost VW roughly €28 billion ($31 billion). In addition, the US Department of Justice had appointed Larry D. Thompson, a former US Attorney General who worked on the prosecutions of Enron executives, to monitor the company. According to the VW website, Thompson would ensure that the Volkswagen Group was fulfilling the conditions of the company's settlement agreement with the US government. These

---

[1] Bryant, C. and R. Milne (2015). Boardroom Politics at Heart of VW Scandal. *Financial Times* (4 October 2015). https://www.ft.com/content/e816cf86-6815-11e5-a57f-21b88f7d973f

include compliance-enhancing measures, reporting and monitoring mechanisms, and the implementation of an enhanced compliance and ethics programme at the company. Thompson would also be tasked with certifying that VW's compliance programme is able to detect issues such as that involving diesel emissions, and to prevent anything similar from happening again.

In 1920, the average lifespan of a company in the S&P 500 Index was 67 years – longer than average human life expectancy, which then stood at 54 years. But by 2010, things looked dramatically different. Whereas people's life expectancy had increased from 54 to 76, the average lifespan of S&P companies had fallen to just 15 years.[2]

There are of course much older businesses, some of them hundreds of years old, or even a thousand years in a small number of cases. But many of them are small businesses facing few competitive challenges, such as hotels, wineries, or funeral homes. By contrast, global firms that are more than 300 or 400 years old are extremely rare.

The strong process of natural selection in the business world has spread to non-governmental organisations – and possibly to government bodies as well. That process is probably at the heart of the success of the capitalistic market system. And in that world of accelerated natural selection, modern governance has become crucial to long-term success.

Scientific Lessons from Natural Selection

Older companies tend to underperform. In order for a company to survive and actually thrive in the long term, it must apply the Darwinian principles of variation, selection, and replication. Just like in the natural world, the most successful firms evolve constantly to adapt to changing conditions, while those that fail to do so become extinct.

It is worth considering variation and replication in a governance context, because of the many different models around the world. In terms of ownership structure, for example, there are publicly traded companies; family owned, private-equity owned, and government-owned firms; non-profits, members' associations, and so on.

---

[2] The calculation and methodology is given by Innosight in the 'Corporate Longevity Forecast' available on www.innosight.com.

One interesting case is how the Communist Party of China governs the country's state-owned assets, and in particular its publicly listed state financial institutions, through the sovereign wealth fund CIC and its dedicated division, Huijin. CIC has developed governance practices that might be useful for large, complex organisations elsewhere. These include having full-time non-executive directors in parallel to Western-style independent directors, and strongly aligning perspectives in the governance of holding groups and subsidiaries. It might well be an inspiration in other parts of the world from a technical governance standpoint, and beyond the political dimension. For example, is it possible that large global financial institutions have become too complex to be governed by part-time independent directors mostly and would professional full-time board members make sense?

Yet the current global focus on excellence in governance has only been possible because of earlier success in other important areas: administration, management, and leadership. High-quality administration was developed and systematised as early as the eighteenth century by organisations such as the East India Company. Then quality management to ensure efficiency and better results was systematised in the first part of the twentieth century by business leaders such as Alfred Sloan and Henry Ford. Business schools were then established to educate leaders in management. The second part of the twentieth century saw the systematisation and theorisation of leadership – the ability to engage and energise people at a higher level – through theories developed in the 1970s.

Today, organisations need to go to the next level. Moving from A to B, and energising people towards achieving this result, requires organisations to develop the ability to choose the right objectives and make the right decisions. And this is the essence of governance. With public trust in corporations and leaders at an all-time low, quality governance will be one of the competitive advantages of the future.

At the same time, today's governance successes and failures stem from the reliance on leadership within organisations.

What is Transformational Leadership?

Of the many types of leadership that have emerged over the past century, transformational leadership is one of the most recent. In the 1970s, James MacGregor Burns defined this in both a

WHAT IS
TRANSFORMATIONAL LEADERSHIP?

Figure 2.1   Transformational Leadership Principles

political and business context as leadership that enables leaders and followers to raise one another to higher levels of motivation and morality. The more active such leadership is, the more effective it is (Figure 2.1).

In general, transformational leaders:

- empower followers and nurture them through change;
- become a strong model for their followers;
- create a vision for the organisation;
- act as change agents for a new direction within the organisation; and
- become social architects.

Should We Trust Leaders?

The transformational leadership model relies strongly on trust, and in particular on employees trusting their leaders. Yet many inspiring and transformative leaders have changed their organisations for the worse instead of for the better. And in recent years, trust in leaders has been affected by a string of events that have negatively impacted many people's lives and well-being.

One example is the nuclear leak in 2011 at the Fukushima plant of the Tokyo Electric Power Company (TEPCO). Back in 2007, an earthquake had caused a small nuclear leak, and the company's president, Tsunehisa Katsumata, was asked to retire. However, Katsumata then became chair of TEPCO, despite his previous failure to adequately manage this risk.

Another case concerns Chinese company Sanlu, which raised protein levels in baby milk by using chemicals including melamine. The firm's top management was aware of this and informed the board, which included directors from New Zealand. Hundreds of thousands of babies were affected, and Sanlu's board voted to recall all the products in question. However, because the crisis happened just before the 2008 Beijing Olympic Games, the company's chair at the time reversed the board's decision in an attempt not to harm China's reputation. Six babies subsequently died after consuming the milk. After being informed by the New Zealand government, the Chinese authorities intervened. At the time of writing, the chair is in jail and the company no longer exists.

Many other large organisations have been hit by scandals related to governance risk in recent years. They include Volkswagen, Boeing, BP, Olympus, Goldman Sachs, Adecco, Lehman Brothers, and Oxfam, to name just a few.

Little wonder, then, that many people are increasingly reluctant to trust leaders and their decisions. According to the Edelman Trust Barometer, employees have grown more distrustful and sceptical of institutions and leadership. Nearly one in three don't trust their employer. And more than two-thirds feel that CEOs are too focused on short-term performance. As a result, employees are far less likely to say positive things about the company they work for.[3]

In addition, economic shifts mean that leaders' unwise decisions can now hurt their organisations even more than previously. These days, the market value of companies is mostly based on intangible assets such as knowledge, goodwill, brand, and R&D (Figure 2.2). The quality of decision-making at the top is therefore critical. Intangible assets are typically more sensitive to decision-making than tangible, hard assets are.

---

[3]http://www.edelman.com/insights/intellectual-property/2016-edelman-trust-baro meter/state-of-trust/employee-trust-divide/.

COMPONENTS of
S&P 500 MARKET VALUE

Intangible Assets   Tangible Assets

Figure 2.2   Components of S&P500 Market Value.

Source: Ocean Tomo LLC

The Governance DNA

Corporate governance requires a balance in decision-making between different bodies in order to provide a good counterweight to leadership. The governance DNA entails balancing decision-making power between an organisation's leader, board, and owners at the heart of the triangle (Figure 2.3) and ensuring the quality of decision-making through the participation of all three parties. Any decision that is taken at one corner of the triangle, in isolation from the others, is poorly governed. Decisions should ideally be located at the triangle's centre of gravity.

Another principle of governance effectiveness is clarity of roles. The board sets the tone, culture, and objectives; it often chooses the leadership team; and it aims to ensure objectives are reached by supervising and supporting the team in place. There are differences in the board's role, of course. In China, for example, the boards of state-owned enterprises do not select the leadership team. Rather, this is the job of the Central Organisation Department, the HR arm of the Communist Party, which also nominates key government

LINES OF ATTACK
THE GOVERNANCE DNA

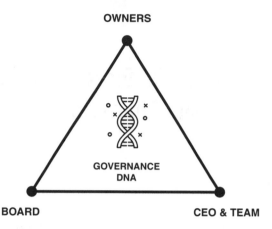

Figure 2.3   The Governance DNA

leaders including ministers. But even in this environment, balance is key to quality decision-making, and with clarity of roles, is the essential element of governance.

Good decision-making at the top is the key to governance success, and the underlying force beneath the four pillars. The integrity of decisions is therefore particularly important. This can be reinforced by board members' independence, as well as by overcoming the various conflicts of interest that arise naturally in an organisational context. Diversity, having an open mind, and being able to combine a range of perspectives are vital for quality organisational decision-making in many contexts. But there is much more to a successful director than that. And this is what we explore in the next chapter.

CHAPTER 3

The Successful Director: Values and Character

Board decisions concern large amounts of resources, and impact people within the organisation as well as external stakeholders. This means board directors wield tremendous power. It is key, therefore, that they adhere to a culture underpinned by fundamental values. In turn, they need to uphold board values, and ensure that their behaviour reinforces the board culture.

Along with their power, board members must accept and embrace their responsibility toward the company they serve. This requires having total clarity regarding their role, and the conscientiousness to perform it to the full. Directors need to acknowledge that the board has a duty to oversee the organisation's success. It must also supervise risks that are important for the organisation and impact employees and their families, customers, and society as a whole, often into the next generation.

Accountability is another key value. Board members must be prepared to explain and justify decisions that have been taken, and to be answerable to the company's stakeholders. Being a board director also requires moral authority – the adherence to a set of principles founded on a correct course of action.

Finally, while diverse opinions and constructive dissent need to be heard in the boardroom, it is essential that directors embrace the 'one-voice principle' once a decision has been taken. In other words, they must fully respect the decision and support it within and outside the boardroom. This voice is usually expressed by the chair (although it may not necessarily represent his or her private views).

A board's values set expectations regarding directors' behaviour, and also define what is unacceptable in this regard. Directors should demonstrate independence and integrity, and be committed to enhancing their own knowledge through external support and continuous education. Discussions should be characterised by equal participation and mutual respect, as well as openness and constructive dissent. Zero tolerance for imprudent, unlawful, or unethical behavior must also be embedded in board culture (see Figure 3.1).

Specific expectations regarding a board member's contributions and responsibilities may vary, partly depending on whether he or she is an executive director, independent director, or a shareholder or employee representative. An independent director of a publicly

BOARD CULTURE

PRIMARY VALUES

Responsibility
Accountability
Moral Authority
One Voice Principle (no single director authority)

DIRECTORS' BEHAVIOURS

Independence and Integrity
Equal Participation/Mutual Respect
Openness and Constructive Dissent
Knowledge Acceleration
External Support & Continuous Education

UNACCEPTABLE BEHAVIOURS

Imprudent
Unlawful
Unethical

Figure 3.1   Reinforcing Board Culture

traded company has different responsibilities than an owner representative and full-time employee on the board of an oil and gas joint venture, for example.

Nonetheless, all directors need to successfully fulfil their two mandates: the duty of care, whereby they undertake their role and responsibility with care, diligence, judgement, and skill; and the duty of loyalty, or putting the interests of the company and its shareholders ahead of their own. Board members therefore need a combination of core attributes, including relevant skills and competence, a detailed knowledge of their legal responsibilities, and dedication and focus.

Duty of Care

Good judgement is essential for directors to fulfil their duty of care. When this is lacking, the quality of decision-making suffers. Judgement comes from knowledge and intuition, both of which can be improved.

First, individuals must have the necessary knowledge – acquired through education and experience – to make good, considered decisions. Education gives us the technical knowledge to understand complex problems. Curiosity helps individuals to complement their formal education and continue learning, thereby enabling access to a memory bank of information and details that may be relevant to the present.

People also use their individual experiences to draw lessons from the past and apply them to the future, in an integrative process. In some situations, either weak signals or true shocks may prompt us to realise that our knowledge is insufficient, and that we require additional input to evaluate situations effectively.

Specifically, a board member develops an integrative view – in terms of the executive world, he or she may generally put a premium on analysis, when in fact it is synthesis that is badly needed in many contexts. Because a board needs to address many stakeholders toward the long term and the next generation, a certain skill in deriving the essential from many pieces of information is key to board quality.

Intuition is the second key driver of good judgement and depends on individual personality and values. According to the Swiss psychologist Carl Jung, personality consists of both the ego – how we identify ourselves – and the unconscious or shadow side that we are not aware of and have suppressed early in life.

Emotions play an important role in intuition. They affect how we respond to crises, for example – whether we remain calm and hopeful, or suffer anxiety and panic. The other component of intuition is values. These are drawn from our sense of ethics – the moral principles that govern our behaviour – as well as individual integrity. Good judgement is a function of the interplay between internal variables and external factors, summarised in Figure 3.2.

For experienced and well-prepared board members, good judgement often materialises as a well-informed 'gut feeling', or right intuition. This in turn comes from lengthy preparation, going through the right materials, having the right balance, not putting too much ego into the discussions and decisions, being aware of one's weaknesses, and having both the right ethical values and the integrity

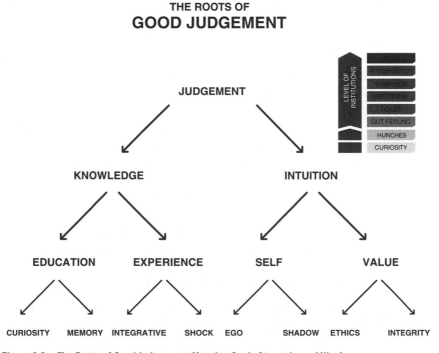

Figure 3.2   The Roots of Good Judgement: Mapping One's Strengths and Weaknesses

to withstand pressure. All this feeds into discussions among peers in a confidential and protected setting that result in a collective board decision.

Good judgement is especially important today, as boards face increasing external pressures and may have to deal with crises that challenge their decision-making skills. We will discuss crisis management in more detail in Chapter 12.

Duty of Loyalty

Conflicts of interest are rampant in today's world. They arise when directors lose impartiality because of either material interest or a conflict of roles. When directors are in a position that may benefit them, or someone close to them, in any way, then they can no longer make impartial decisions; this is a material conflict of interest. A conflict may also result from one director having different roles, so that their obligations to one company are compromised by those to another. Directors who sit on multiple boards may therefore have a potential conflict if two of these organisations form any kind of relationship.

Another source of conflict is self-interest. When directors focus primarily on maintaining their position, comfort, and income rather than on what is best for the company, they are likely to be highly biased. They may also become compliant and not wish to be unpopular. Again, they lose their impartiality.

Sometimes directors fail to acknowledge conflicts of interest – even to themselves. It is critical that directors think about this honestly, because it has a direct impact on board service. All of us are conflicted, and figuring out these conflicts is part of our duty. We explore the four tiers of conflicts of interest facing boards in Chapter 13. A good rule of thumb is for board members to have a list of their own conflicts of interest: time, money, effort, friends, relationships, financial interests, reputation, social network, and more.

Integrity: A Key Characteristic of Board Directors

Directors need to know what is right and have the courage to stand up for it. They also need clarity about their role. In times of crisis, confusion may obscure the right course of action, making individuals vulnerable to mental biases. But board members with integrity devote themselves to doing the job for which they were hired, and conscientiously equip themselves with the necessary knowledge and skills. As such, integrity is a keystone of successful directorship.

For some, integrity means fully adopting the values one believes are right. This requires authentic deliberation about individual values through deep personal reflection, rather than a simple acceptance of social norms. Maintaining integrity means being able to resist engaging in self-deception about whether individual actions are the logical outcome of personal values or some other force (such as fulfilling psychological needs).

Another definition of integrity is the ability to be clear about the boundaries of what is acceptable, and the commitment to stand by these regardless of the consequences. In other words, integrity is the way in which individuals support projects and then loyally commit to them. This is the case with artistic integrity, for example, when artists demonstrate loyalty to their vision and pursue their path, rather than conforming to what others think is right or acceptable or commercially valuable.

There is also a social dimension to integrity.[1] Having integrity means not only standing up for what you believe and defending it, but also recognising that others have their own judgements and convictions. Bullying and coercion are therefore antithetical to integrity, whereas compromise and ambivalence might not be.

Table 3.1 summarises the key behaviours of successful directors.

Board members' specific legal responsibilities depend on the nature of the organisation and the jurisdiction within which the board operates. But clearly, successful directors need to have good judgement and the integrity to stand by what they believe. During crises, directors need to rise to the occasion, simplify the situation, and have the courage to do what is right.

We will return to the subject of board leadership and values in Chapter 17. But now we will look more closely at the first pillar of a board's effectiveness: people quality, focus, and dedication.

---

[1] Calhoun, C. (1995). Standing for something. *The Journal of Philosophy* 92(5): 235–260. http://links.jstor.org/sici?sici=0022-362X%28199505%2992%3A5%3C235%3ASFS% 3E2.0.CO%3B2-G

Table 3.1 Behaviours of Successful Directors – A Checklist

Independence and Integrity
1. Do I say what I mean and mean what I say?
2. Do I speak up when I fundamentally disagree with what someone has said – even if it may result in confrontation or ridicule?
3. Am I clear about my role and legal responsibility as a director? Can I clearly and simply articulate my mandate and responsibility?
4. How do I demonstrate accountability as a director?
5. How do I feel about holding other directors accountable?
6. Am I clear on what personal moral and ethical boundaries I will not cross, no matter what the consequences?
7. Do I feel that I bring a fresh perspective to discussions – a different viewpoint or knowledge set – from the other directors?

Equal Participation/Mutual Respect
1. Do I contribute to the best of my ability in the boardroom?
2. How curious am I about the company, what it does? How much time do I spend asking questions and seeking answers to these questions?
3. Do I actively listen to others' contributions and respect their opinion, even if it is very different from mine?
4. Can I understand the perspective of others – even if I don't agree with them?

Openness and Constructive Dissent
1. Am I willing to express my viewpoint, even if I know it will be unpopular?
2. Am I able to land sharp remarks in a positive and respectful way?
3. Are there times when I hold back, due to a fear of how I may be perceived by the other directors?
4. How do I ensure that I am not simply conforming with the group, but checking that my evaluation of issues is sound?
5. How do I feel when others challenge my view?
6. How actively do I challenge others' perspective and underlying assumptions?

Critical Thinking and Framing
1. How do I ensure I am not falling prey to my own biases?
2. Do I consistently reframe decisions presented in relative terms in absolute terms?
3. Do I fear someone or something on this board?

Conflicts of Interest
1. Have I thoroughly considered my different business relationships and roles and how they influence one another (if at all)?
2. How important is the income and status of this board seat? Does it affect my willingness to speak up?

Knowledge Acceleration
1. Do I seek external support when I feel that I need more knowledge in a certain area?
2. How do I ensure that I continue to educate myself on topics that enable me to make an effective contribution, including professional service?
3. Do I actively seek feedback from the Chair or other directors as to my knowledge and competence – and fill in necessary gaps?
4. Do I have a firm grasp on the corporate governance code, pertinent regulations, and social expectation?
5. Do I meet with key stakeholders?
6. Do I regularly meet with other directors, beyond board meetings?

CHAPTER

4

The First Pillar: People Quality, Focus, and Dedication

The quality, focus, and dedication of board members is critical. Directors need to be committed, competent, and qualified, possessing both the expertise and the willingness to contribute. A board that lacks the right composition, does not focus on the most important issues, or whose directors are insufficiently dedicated, is at risk of major failure.

A case in point is the Toshiba accounting scandal, where individual and institutional corruption at the 140 year-old Japanese electronics conglomerate went undetected by its board of directors.

Quality

Expertise and competence are essential attributes of any high-quality board. In this regard, skill maps are a useful tool for not only assessing the range of competencies of the current directors but also for specifying the skills, attributes, and even personalities required for effective board work – and for addressing any gaps between the board's current and ideal composition. The fit between the skillset of each member and the board's requirements is what counts. There is no ideal skill map, and typically it should extend beyond professional experience to include personal attributes and personality traits, as exemplified in Table 4.2 at the end of the chapter.

Case study: The Toshiba Accounting Scandal

In 2015, Toshiba admitted to having used accounting irregularities to inflate its profits by 151.8 billion yen ($1.22 billion) between 2008 and 2014. This overstatement represented approximately one-third of Toshiba's pre-tax profits during the period. The revelations, which came just six weeks after the introduction of a corporate governance code in Japan, were a surprise to many because Toshiba had long been lauded for its ethical culture and corporate governance practices. In the early 2000s, the company had hired outside directors and moved to a 16-member board, which was best practice in Japan at the time. But although the company's governance structure looked good on paper, it was ineffectively monitored – as the accounting scandal showed.

Toshiba established an external committee to probe the fraudulent accounting. Its report found that the company's problems resulted from top executives putting intense pressure on subordinates to meet increasingly difficult profit goals, even as demand for Toshiba's products fell during the 2008 global financial crisis. Pressure from senior management often came before the end of a quarter or fiscal year, which may have pushed lower-level employees to postpone losses, push forward sales, and understate costs on long-term projects. Toshiba's auditor, Ernst & Young ShinNihon LLC, failed to detect the improper accounting practices because these were not isolated incidents but rather a systematic practice carried out by employees across the company.

The report found that Toshiba's three most recent CEOs were complicit in inflating the company's operating profit. In the wake of the scandal, chief executive Hisao Tanaka immediately resigned. The two previous CEOs, Atsutoshi Nishida (2005–2009) and Norio Sasaki (2009–2013), were forced to resign from the positions that they retained at the company. In total, 8 of the 16 board members resigned.

In the wake of the scandal, Toshiba cut thousands of jobs and sold parts of its semiconductor, medical equipment, and consumer-electronics businesses. In September 2015, the Tokyo Stock Exchange put Toshiba on its watch list, the heaviest punishment short of delisting, to pressure the manufacturer to strengthen internal controls.

Continuing to reel from these events, Toshiba cut its workforce further and continued to spin off troubled assets during the following years. The company's aim was to reduce the potential for future losses and win back the investor confidence it had lost as a result of the scandal.

Table 4.1 Traditional Board Competencies (Rating From 1 to 10, With 10 Full Expertise and 7 Proficiency)

Experience/skill	DIRECTOR									CANDIDATE				
	1	2	3	4	5	6	7	8	9	1	2	3	4	5
Accounting/financial expert														
Governance experience														
Strategic planning														
Innovation and technology														
Digitalisation														
Partnering experience														
Value creation														
Regional experience														
Business transformation														
Prior audit committee experience														
Prior nomination committee exp.														
Other committees														
Industry experience														
Investments														
Capital formation														
Capital markets														
Financial services														
Information technology														
Legal & regulatory compliance														
Asset management														
Risk management														
Securities analysis														
Joint venture management														
HR														
Cross-culture experience														
Geopolitics														
Turnaround experience														
Other outliers as required														

Sources: Multiple.

Diversity – of industry, professional background, gender, personality, and opinion – also improves the quality of board decisions, in particular when creativity and innovation are required. By bringing in a range of specific types of expertise, diversity can enhance the board's ability to consider different solutions and reframe issues.

Diversity in terms of personality is important on a board, but can be uncomfortable. (One instrument for understanding differences in personality is the NEO-PI, which we discuss in greater detail in a later chapter on diversity.) Gender diversity is also important; boards with more women are likely to explicitly identify criteria for measuring strategy, monitoring its implementation, and developing and monitoring a code of conduct, for example.[1] However, poorly managed diversity can sometimes lead to communication difficulties and decreased trust, which are disruptive. Boards therefore need to develop processes to leverage and manage diversity well. We explore how to achieve effective diversity in Chapter 23.

Focus

Even an excellently composed board will underperform if it does not focus on the most important issues. Because their time is limited, boards need to be strategic about their work for the organisation. This means figuring out what matters most, rather than simply having a precooked agenda meeting after meeting. Relying on the charter's definition of the role of the board is therefore not enough. In fact, being proactive in defining the board's role can help directors decide on their priorities. The ability of board members to clearly understand the role of the board in the organisational context, to focus on the right issues, and to prioritise is crucial.

Figure 4.1 below,[2] which is based on the board of a sovereign wealth fund, outlines the classical roles of the board and the nature

---

[1] See, for example, Terjesen, S., R. Sealy, and V. Singh (2009). Women directors on corporate boards: a review and research agenda. *Corporate Governance: An International Review* 17(3): 320–337. There is of course a large literature on the topic.
[2] This very useful process for determining board focus is adapted from Paul Strebel (2004). The Case for Contingent Governance, Sloan Management Review, MIT.

WORKING ON
THE ROLES OF THE BOARD

Figure 4.1   The Roles of the Board. Source: Adapted from Strebel (2004)

of its corresponding involvement. In general, a board may concentrate more on internal or external issues. Many boards that used to be highly focused on internal matters, including audit and performance review, now spend more time addressing external issues such as regulatory trends and geopolitics. Another dimension to consider is whether the board's primary task is to support the success of management, or to supervise and monitor it. This will depend on the maturity of the management as well as the context of the organisation.

Boards need to achieve on all fronts, of course, but because of time constraints will prioritise what matters most to the organisation. Often, board members will have different views in this regard. By working along a graph like the one below, they can understand their differences and build alignment. In the example underneath, members of one board – including three government ministers and other leading chairpersons – put a star in the quadrant they saw as

AN EXAMPLE OF
TYPICAL BOARD TASKS

INVOLVEMENT	TASKS
INTERACTIVE	Essence, culture, and core values
INTERACTIVE	Strategic direction and objectives
	Selection of an effective management team, particularly:
INTERACTIVE	• Managing director
SUPERVISORY	• Top management and General management
SUPERVISORY	• Management processes
APPROVING	Policy formulation
SUPERVISORY	Policy application
APPROVING	Organisational Structure
INTERACTIVE	Assuring the availability of financial resources and their proper allocation, financial soundness, long-term success and survival
EXECUTIVE	Effectiveness and continuity of the Board
INTERACTIVE	Monitoring of all facets of operations
INTERACTIVE	Protection and promotion of reputation
INTERACTIVE	Analysis and interpretation of environmental influences
INTERACTIVE	Assuring socially responsible corporate behaviour
INTERACTIVE	Ethical Code and Code of Conduct

Figure 4.2   An example of typical board tasks

the board's top priority and possibly a second one in their second priority. The exercise revealed a lack of alignment among directors as to where the board should focus its priorities. This was resolved through a session dedicated to improving focus.

Once it has achieved a certain alignment regarding its role, the board can focus on elaborating a list of main tasks. These will then be incorporated into a two- to three-year action plan that will guide the board's work more productively than a traditional passive agenda could. Figure 4.2 below highlights some of the typical tasks that boards undertake, while Figure 4.3 summarises the action plan of that sovereign wealth fund board.

AN EXAMPLE OF
ACTION PLAN

SHORT-TERM IMPLEMENTATION	WITHIN 1 YEAR	TO BE CONSIDERED
More active knowledge about our investments (invite other boards & investors) More information about top executives (succession, selection, development) Self-assessment, evaluation of effectiveness of board Structure of board meetings (4+2 lengthy for purpose meetings)	Revisit our business transformation strategies (and have we implemented them properly?) More brainstorming sessions between the board & management Stronger monitoring of our subsidiary companies Clarity of essence, culture, values, social responsibility principles	Board size / Diversity Committee transformation: Nomination / Succession / Governance

Figure 4.3   A board action plan from a sovereign wealth fund

Dedication

The most effective board members are more than simply competent and conscientious – they are individuals with genuine passion, energy, and dedication who are not motivated solely by the financial or social rewards of board membership. Board members must spend enough time keeping up to date on relevant issues and preparing for meetings, including through conversations with fellow directors. Norms in terms of preparation time have increased dramatically; according to a KPMG survey, for large organisations, one hour of board meeting requires 17 hours of preparation. As we saw in Chapter 1, many directors spend much less time than this. But the best board members always go the extra mile in their preparation.

The first pillar of board effectiveness is about people, and in particular their quality, focus, and dedication. All three of these dimensions are important, and none are ever perfect, of course. The board's composition needs constant adjustment, by understanding members' weaknesses and addressing them through education and other means. A smart board will seek a strong, dynamic focus on the right issues, and will set a yearly agenda that prioritises and caters for these. Finally, dedication needs to be watched constantly, because some are good at faking it. Good board work requires some skin in the game, and not necessarily in a financial sense.

As well as the right people, boards also need to have the right information in order to be fully effective. This is the focus of our next chapter.

Table 4.2 Example of Board Skill Map

The Board Skill Map provides you with a simple tool with which to assess the knowledge level and personal attributes of your directors across various board critical dimensions. It can be used whether the board has a choice of directors or not (owners' representatives). Personal attributes matter as much as skills. *Note that the personal attributes in this skill map could be used in other organisations, including for profit corporates, technology, oil and gas, financials, etc.* This document is meant to be used for your self-assessment purposes and should be adapted to the organisation. Through administering it will offer you an overview of your board's competency, personality, and attribute gaps. This specific skill map was established for a non-profit: a sports organisation specialising on the fight against doping. Any skill map needs to be adapted to the characteristics of the organisation.

	Board members								
HIGH LEVEL SKILL MATRIX	1	2	3	4	5	6	7	8	9
Status (e.g. ED/ NED/Independent)									
Director since									
Age									
Board of Director Experience (Y/N)									

KINDLY RATE THE BELOW SKILLS

1 No Knowledge	2 Some Knowledge	3 Good Knowledge	4 Strong Knowledge	5 Expert

SECTOR EXPERIENCE	1	2	3	4	5	6	7	8	9
Sports direct									
Sports related									
Medical direct									
Medical related									
Government/regulatory direct									
Government/regulatory related									

(continued)

Table 4.2 (continued)

GROUP TECHNICAL SKILLS I	1	2	3	4	5	6	7	8	9
Management									
Accounting									
Legal									
Chemical/biology									
Human resources management									
Communication									
Core technical									
General technical									
Scientific									
GROUP TECHNICAL SKILLS II	1	2	3	4	5	6	7	8	9
Sector – commercial									
Funding									
Government and regulatory affairs									
IT/ Digital									
Legal – anti-doping									
Legal – general									
Marketing									
Risk management									
Strategic planning									
Human resource management									
Financial management/audit									
Other expertise									
PERSONAL ATTRIBUTES	1	2	3	4	5	6	7	8	9
Clear communication skills									
Leadership competencies									
Strategic agility									
Political astuteness									
OTHER ATTRIBUTES	1	2	3	4	5	6	7	8	9
Proactiveness									
Clear moral or ethical boundaries									

(continued)

Table 4.2 (continued)

Credible as independent voice

Honesty

Directness

Ability to challenge

Embracing ambiguity and coping
effectively with change

Ability to present the truth in
helpful ways

Network of contacts

CHAPTER 5

The Second Pillar: Information Architecture

October 2016: Joanne Marker was up late in her home office, preparing for a board meeting the following week at Cynched, a telecommunications company.

After going over her notes from the previous quarter, made on the basis of news clippings and her daily Google alerts, Joanne opened the information package from the board portal on her iPad. She highlighted key figures and elements of the firm's strategy, typing her questions as notes into the document. The past quarter's financial results were there, including all the breakdowns, along with notes on broader market trends.

Joanne then clicked open a podcast from the CEO and made a few notes: closure of a plant in Malaysia, possible acquisition of a small social media firm in Berlin, possible restructuring. She read the risk report in detail, questioning whether the provision set aside for a cyber-security breach was sufficient.

A digest of relevant tweets, Facebook posts, and LinkedIn comments also caught her eye – she saw on Glassdoor that a few bitter former employees were badmouthing a product release as being poor quality. Joanne concluded by going through her Hootsuite and checking on RelSci whether she had a direct connection to some of the complainers. She made a note to call her contact in marketing – as approved by the board – to see what the internal chatter was. Saving her notes directly into the document, she logged off the portal.

Joanne remembered receiving her first board package as a new director of Virtuous Ventures back in the early 1990s. It had been a heavy tome of more than 400 pages that had arrived by DHL three days before the meeting. She soon realised it was simply a copy of directors' reports, with in-depth figures from all the country offices. It had taken her days to make sense of the information, and even then she was missing key analysis that would enable her to understand the potential issues. There was nothing on competitors, trends, customer insights, or reputation. The package covered only internal matters, mostly financial, with nothing on culture. And there were no executive summaries of the main documents, nor any prioritisation or summaries of major decisions to be taken.

What a contrast to the crisp, well prioritised, and thorough package on internal and external issues from Cynched that Joanne had enjoyed working on for the past few hours.

***

For a board to function optimally, directors need to be informed about developments relevant to the business and its key value drivers. They should receive such information through both internal and external channels, and through formal and informal routes.

Board members must continually monitor competitive trends, regulatory and technological changes, and stakeholder developments that may be strategically relevant for the company. To do this, they need to effectively utilise external sources, such as stakeholders and social media, and not rely solely on information they receive internally through the company.

Directors also need to cultivate informal sources of information, for example through conversations with stakeholders, other board members, and management. Some make a point of visiting subsidiaries or local facilities when they travel, in order to develop relationships with the firm's local operations. Through conversations with people in the field, directors can learn a great deal about how strategy is being implemented, for example. Figure 5.1 below provides a quick checklist of some of these information channels and sources.

How Complete is Your Information?

Typically, information architecture is designed by management, who often fail to understand the type of inputs needed to make board decisions. Executives often want to provide too much data, often of

HOW COMPLETE
IS YOUR INFORMATION?

	INTERNAL	EXTERNAL
FORMAL	• Management presentations • Financial reports • Risk reports • Budgets • Strategy documents • Employee engagement surveys • Leadership pipeline assessment	• Analyst reports • Social media analysis • Industry analyses • Investor reports • Customer visits • Competitor benchmarking • Media reports
INFORMAL	• Conversations with top management and others • Field visits • Breakfast with top talents	• Customer feedback • Social media mentions • Regulatory and governmental network • Industry blogs • Conference on industry trends • Informal meetings with key stakeholders (goverment officials, regulators, unions, etc.)

Figure 5.1   Mapping Board Information Completeness

an operational nature. For sure, information for directors should be comprehensive, covering the company's essential activities and the main issues facing the organisation. But it should remain sufficiently high level to allow the board to have an informed discussion without getting lost in the detail.

Boards are increasingly using board portals to streamline information and materials. But although technology is an enabler for communication, it should not be the driver. It is essential that information design be aligned with the board's mandate – which is support and supervision.

Boards should start the process of information design by identifying the conversations they want to have, and then design the architecture accordingly. Strategy, performance, and governance should then each be addressed from the perspectives of steering and supervision, respectively, including by asking key questions:

1. Do we have the right strategy?
2. Is our strategy on track?
3. How can we work smarter?

4. What culture and policies do we foster?
5. Will we hit this year's targets without sacrificing our long-term ones?
6. Are we working in the 'right' way?

The aim is for boards to have more focused and productive conversations by ensuring they receive the information they need. To enable this, board packs should be shorter, more focused, and well prioritised on what matters so that directors can read their pack and fulfil their duties. To ensure that the pack achieves this while still being comprehensive, report writers must produce succinct papers that respond to the board's key questions.

A good board pack will include executive summaries, key decisions to be made, options for the different decisions, priorities in the materials (with a potential ranking from A to C), a summary of former discussions and materials distributed for each decision, elements of external information, and information on softer issues (personal perspectives on culture and conduct from key managers).

Typical components include the following:

- A board briefing that is jointly designed by the board and management and includes, on a yearly rotating basis:
  - circa five to ten pages of financials with forecast;
  - a one-to-three-page CEO report with personal views of key issues;
  - risk/opportunity analysis (three to five tools including maps, sensitivities, scenarios);
  - a brief on gene-pool analysis;
  - culture survey and trends;
  - a summary of financial analysts' or external views;
  - employee/customer surveys;
  - evolution of the customer proposition.
- Management letter in between meetings.
- Director outreach summary (plants/technology/audits, individual and group visits).
- Committee reports, including analysis and insights as well as a recommendation.

In my experience, it is common practice for management to take the lead in designing board packages with some input from the board, or even to design them alone. As a result, the board often receives incomplete information regarding external issues such as reputation analysis, customer knowledge, stakeholder understanding, and technological evolution.

Although the board is responsible for ensuring that it has complete information, it is still very rare for a board to co-design a package with management. However, such cooperation is essential to produce strategic packages that give the board a suitably high-level perspective and lead to meaningful boardroom discussion.

The primary purpose of board meetings is for directors to have productive conversations with regard to company strategy and people, and to supervise key risks, enabling them to make decisions to create long-term wealth for the company. Too often, however, boards spend the majority of their meeting time – frequently between 50% and 80% – listening to management presentations. Although such presentations serve an important function by exposing the board to talent in the management pipeline, they should never take up more than 30% of a meeting (and ideally far less). Having the CEO or CFO prepare podcasts in advance of board meetings, for example, would help the board to use its face-to-face time with management more efficiently.

Limiting presentations to fewer than seven slides and less than seven minutes is certainly good practice. One board I know has cancelled all *in situ* presentations by management to the board. Instead, presentations are sent to directors a few days before, and responsible managers are present at board meetings for direct questions and answers. To encourage this, the board secretary has organised a seating plan in which each manager present sits next to an external board member. On another board, to ensure a rejuvenation of information exchange, one of the independent external board members was asked to present specific views on a key dimension to the management, rather than the reverse. Finally, a third board interviews young recruits (typically 20 to 25 year-olds) to get a sense of how company culture is perceived by the younger generation, and to get a feel for the atmosphere. There is thus plenty of room for creativity and originality in reaching a best-in-class information-sharing process.

Information architecture is the crucial second pillar of board effectiveness. But to benefit fully from a rich flow of strategic information, boards also need to have high-quality structures and processes in place. These will be the focus of Chapter 6.

CHAPTER 6

Board Structures and Processes

*T*en days after her lunch with Virtuous Chair Gerald Grossheim, Joanne Marker had been formally invited to an interview with the nominations committee. Three months later, she had attended her first board meeting at Virtuous. Joanne enjoyed the mental challenge of mapping problems from her work at WeCare onto Virtuous, and figuring out the implications for the company's strategy and marketing efforts. As a member of Virtuous' strategy committee, she also enjoyed challenging the CEO on his strategic direction and any risks she thought he had overlooked – such as changing consumer trends and tastes in different geographies.

Joanne soon noticed that certain items were frequently left to the end of the discussion and somehow dropped off the agenda. She therefore suggested to Grossheim that he introduce a two-year agenda-setting process and also institute a standalone board secretary function. The latter worked well on another board Joanne was on, by helping its members to retain focus and have more disciplined discussions.

'A board secretary?' Grossheim said. 'But Gary (the chief legal officer) does this well'.

Joanne explained the value of having a dedicated board secretary who would ensure the quality of all board processes, support the chair in preparing meetings, and provide directors with synthetic overviews that would provide context and set the stage for effective discussion. Grossheim nodded his approval. He was fed up with having to use valuable discussion time *explaining and re-explaining things to directors who lacked the necessary background knowledge. He could also see that the board was not running as smoothly as it could. 'OK Joanne, done. What else?'*

She suggested an annual strategy retreat to address long-term megatrends, the competitive landscape, opportunities, and threats. She then asked Gross-heim to introduce 360-degree evaluations and feedback sessions for directors.

'That's not going to be very popular – especially with a few board members', laughed Grossheim.

Joanne didn't smile. 'Precisely my point', she said.

******

Effective structures and processes enable boards to deliver on their mandate of supervision and support. Indeed, high performance boards go a step further, innovating and refining these to a more sophisticated level. A relevant committee structure and a good board secretary can be influential in improving the quality of the board's work, while lead directors are playing an increasingly important role.

Processes

Boards must master a wide range of processes in order to be highly effective. A well-designed strategy process, for example, is critical to a board's strategic support function, as we will see in Chapter 15. We also discuss essential risk processes in Part II of the book. Tracking the effectiveness of the board's decisions is important, along with best practices in recruiting, onboarding, educating, and evaluating directors. CEO succession planning is vital too, yet boards often lack expertise in this area and thus avoid discussing it on a regular basis, especially as this is often a sensitive topic.

Below is a non-exhaustive list of key processes for boards. All directors – not only the chair – should have a good sense of how well the board is mastering them.

- Agenda setting and board session organisation (including decision recording and minutes).
- Management performance review.

- Audit (including board, committee, and management formal relation thereof).
- Regulatory compliance.
- CEO succession.
- Risk thinking, including risk identification, assessment, management, and appetite.
- Strategy.
- Ongoing board improvement process, including evaluation and education.
- Nominations.
- Gene-pool analysis.
- Organisational culture oversight.
- Conduct and ethics oversight.
- Crisis management.
- Onboarding and outboarding.

In addition, digital transformation is becoming a board process for many organisations. A family business may well have a family–board interaction process. In general, a well-specified process for management consultation by board members is also useful.

Board members should ask themselves the following questions:

- How do I feel about each of these processes? Do I have a clear view of each? Is each process complete and detailed enough?
- Do we have the right committees, with the right people on them?
- Are the reporting lines foolproof?

Committee Structure

Having mapped the processes, directors need to consider the implications for committees. They should also consider the legal requirements for committees, as well as their ideal composition in order to shape selection criteria. Committees should always inform board discussions rather than replace them. Although they are tasked with going into greater depth on audit, risk, nominations, technology, or other critical issues such as sustainability, committees do not have decision-making authority. Instead, they systematically report back to the board to help it make better, more informed decisions.

The committee structure needs to be closely aligned with organisational strategy and other requirements. Table 6.1 below provides examples from three large organisations.

Table 6.1 Examples from Three Large Organisations

HSBC
- Group Audit Committee
- Group Risk Committee
- Financial System Vulnerabilities Committee
- Group Remuneration Committee
- Nomination & Corporate Governance Committee.[1]

Coca-Cola
- Audit Committee
- Compensation Committee
- Directors and Corporate Governance Committee
- Executive Committee
- Finance Committee
- Management Development Committee
- Public Issues and Diversity Review Committee.[2]

Singapore Airlines
- Executive Committee
- Audit Committee
- Compensation and Industrial Relations Committee
- Nominating Committee
- Safety and Risk Committee.

Board Secretary

The secretary's role is to support the chair in ensuring the smooth functioning of the board. As a minimum, he or she should ensure that board meetings are called and organised in accordance with organisational requirements (such as the articles of association), and that minutes are accurately recorded and kept on file. The secretary may also need to make sure that the organisation complies with company law requirements, particularly regarding procedures for annual and extraordinary general meetings.

Other secretarial responsibilities include:

Meetings: sourcing agenda items from the chair and board members; circulating agendas; and circulating decisions made (ideally within 48 hours after the meeting ends).

Records and administration: keeping up-to-date contact details for the board members; filing minutes and reports; maintaining a database of names and addresses that are useful to the organisation; recording the organisation's activities and tracking future activities.

---

[1] https://www.hsbc.com/our-approach/corporate-governance/board-committees.
[2] https://www.coca-colacompany.com/investors/committee-charters.

Legal requirements: safeguarding the organisation's constitution and other company documents; monitoring legal requirements and organisational compliance in governance.

Communication and correspondence: responding to and filing all board correspondence; keeping an archive of all company publications; and keeping stakeholders informed of the organisation's governance activities.

In 2008, Abu Dhabi Commercial Bank (ADCB) appointed Simon Copleston, a UK-trained lawyer, as its first-ever group general counsel and board secretary. Copleston was then instrumental in making the bank a recognised regional leader in corporate governance.

ADCB clarified certain roles between the board and management and revised the board's composition. It took steps to improve the coordination of risk management throughout the bank and restructured the board and management committees. The bank also changed particular shareholder policies and improved their disclosures to put it on par with the highest international standards.

In particular, ADCB:

- adopted a target of one-third independent directors;
- appointed five new board members, including the CEO and directors with additional banking experience;
- clarified the distinction between board and management, emphasising the board's role in monitoring management performance;
- removed directors from the combined executive committee;
- adopted a revised committee structure including Audit, Risk, Nomination/ Remuneration, and Corporate Governance committees;
- developed clear terms of reference (TORs) for each, removed management duties (e.g. loan recoveries), and ensured adequate independent composition;
- set three-year terms with the possibility of re-election to ensure healthy turnover of directors;
- established a formal process for identifying and nominating appropriate directors for approval by the AGM, led by the Nominations Committee;
- introduced a formal annual evaluation process (internal and external) to assess the board's performance.

In May 2019, as part of a regional wave of consolidation in financial services, ADCB merged with Union National Bank and acquired Al Hilal Bank. The enlarged ADCB is now one of the three largest banks in the United Arab Emirates, with around $114 billion in total assets and a 15% market share.

Analysts say that the success of the merger will depend on whether ADCB can ensure that its strong corporate governance remains a core part of the merged bank's culture, including in the structure and processes of the new board.

Most importantly, the board secretary oversees all the above-mentioned processes, including evaluations, and thus ensures that the board functions smoothly in addition to satisfying legal requirements.

Lead Director or Vice Chair

The lead director role initially emerged in the US, in particular on boards where the chair and CEO roles were combined. The idea was that this board member would serve as a leader for independent directors and act as a counterweight to the chair–CEO. Many corporate boards inside and outside the US now have lead directors or vice-chairs, who typically contribute to improved corporate performance in four areas.

First, they take the initiative for improving board performance, often building on evaluations of individual directors and the chair. In addition, they aim to build a productive relationship between the board and the CEO – smoothing what is sometimes a tense relationship between the chief executive and the board – and to ensure the quality of the CEO–chair relationship where these roles are separated.

Third, lead directors provide leadership in crises when the chair is unable to, such as in a conflict-of-interest situation. Finally, they chair meetings of independent directors (they usually have the authority to call executive sessions), especially when the chair is not independent. This is particularly important when the roles of CEO and chair are combined, and also in family businesses where the chair is a member of the family and the CEO is an external professional. Typically, a lead independent director or vice-chair can help infuse governance in a setting where the family can dominate the board.

As we have seen in the last three chapters, people, information, and structures and processes are all essential to board success. But the dynamics and culture in the boardroom are ultimately crucial. We therefore conclude Part I by looking at this fourth and final pillar of board effectiveness.

CHAPTER

7

Group Dynamics and Board Culture

The quality of board members' interactions is crucial to board success. Traditionally, analyses of board dynamics focused on the individual director as a key building block, examining his or her demographic attributes, personality type, and emotional and cultural intelligence. But although these are of course important, a board is primarily a high performance work group and a social institution. We therefore need to know more about the board's collective processes and behaviours in order to understand and predict the quality of governance, and the resulting impact on the organisation's performance.

People create meaning through interactions with each other. The effectiveness of their decisions depends on their ability to productively exchange views and challenge one another. As such, board dynamics are an essential foundation for good governance. These include: the ways in which the board handles differences; generates trust; creates the right context for discussions and decision-making; manages conflict; and sets up leadership roles. In addition, directors' participation and contributions during board meetings are key factors in board effectiveness.

Boards need to present a unified front to the outside world in accordance with the 'one voice principle'. Nonetheless, that single voice must be reached after building on true differences in perspectives. These will arise from differences in background, personalities, or simply dynamics. Building on structural arrangements and cultural understandings, the system of interaction between board members must allow for productive exchanges in order to reach agreement on how to move forward.

Executives moving to a director role need to understand the significant change in communication and behavioural style required at board level, because this will be critical to their success in building a portfolio of directorships in the future. Board members must be able to observe and analyse the dynamics at play within a board and understand what kinds of discussion styles and non-verbal behaviour may be resulting in dysfunction.

How do boards exert power and influence? In joining the board, people have their own personal histories, motivations, and agendas to build on and pursue, and specific sets of stakeholders to represent. In this light, the board is a rich slice of not only business and industry but human community and society in general. Whether these dynamics induce dysfunctions, and how strong these dysfunctions are, is key to board work. Red flags as shown underneath are a good way to start from consequences and grow awareness of a board's problematic dynamics.

Understanding Group Dynamics

As with any group, board members don't convene just to sit in a room and be together. They immediately develop dynamic tensions and start forming alliances, whether consciously or semi-consciously. Upon entering the boardroom, we can instantly observe some of this emergent tension, and start reflecting on the rules, distances, and authority that are playing out. Are they formal, informal, or culturally defined? Do they follow some unconscious but clearly visible patterns?

The dynamics evolve greatly during a board member's tenure. A sign of health is the ability to transform these dynamics depending on the context or the issue being considered. A solidified fragmentation of the board into groups is one of the most difficult governance situations to resolve.

Table 7.1 Red Flags

Red Flags should trigger your Early Warning System as a board member. Below are some of the most common indicators of board dysfunction, which frequently point to deeper issues.

BOARD MEETING DISCUSSION STYLE	Yes, this happens frequently	Yes, this has happened	No, this never occurred
⚑ Inappropriate allocation of time to critical issues	☐	☐	☐
⚑ Sense of pressure to get through the agenda	☐	☐	☐
⚑ Rationalisation of poor decisions	☐	☐	☐
⚑ Executive debate tending to 'Yes I agree BUT'	☐	☐	☐
⚑ Little discussion on how debate could be improved	☐	☐	☐
⚑ No opportunity to consider 'What could we do differently next time?'	☐	☐	☐
⚑ Difficult issues not sufficiently discussed	☐	☐	☐
⚑ Debate becomes personalised, not issue-focused	☐	☐	☐
⚑ Dissenting voices marginalised	☐	☐	☐
⚑ Special insights not used	☐	☐	☐
⚑ Stereotyping of third parties	☐	☐	☐
⚑ Consistent lack of contribution	☐	☐	☐
⚑ Focus narrowly on 'own world view'	☐	☐	☐

INTERACTION WITH MANAGEMENT	Yes, this happens frequently	Yes, this has happened	No, this never occurred
⮌Management team is defensive/ aggressive	☐	☐	☐
⮌Long management presentations	☐	☐	☐
⮌Executive presenting answers rather than options	☐	☐	☐

When people first meet to discuss key issues, the initial, awkward orientation phase is marked by anxiety, the search for a 'safe spot', and attempts at pairing up with a peer (Phase I). A board member then goes through the exploratory phase, often marked by conflict, where they make sense of others', and their own, sense of power, authority, and status, and start to outline the first contours of competition (Phase II). The final phase is a state of cohesion, where board members finally allow themselves to settle into a fully-functioning group that builds on a sense of engagement, challenge, intimacy, and communicative disclosure (Phase III). For a board to be functional, each member should proceed as swiftly as possible on this path. As the stakes rise and issues become more complex, that process may need to be renewed.

For Uber, Travis Kalanick was the ambitious, tenacious co-founder and CEO who had made it possible for the company to report gross revenue of $37 billion in 2017, after only eight years of existence. However, the same attributes created a company culture built on a 'hustle at all costs' approach, which resulted in a spate of serious high-profile lawsuits and scandals and ultimately led to Kalanick's ousting as CEO. This dysfunctional, toxic culture was at the core of Uber's troubles – both within the company and its leadership team, and on the board.

In 2017, Uber commissioned an independent investigation led by former US Attorney General Eric Holder, following the publication of a scathing blog by former employee Sarah Fowler that outlined instances of harassment and discrimination at the company. The subsequent report strongly advocated improved boardroom dynamics in addition to reform of top management. The report sought to improve the board's oversight by ensuring its independence, and advised the board to create an Ethics and Culture Committee 'to oversee Uber's efforts and enhance a culture of ethical business practices, diversity and inclusion . . .'.

Uber's board of directors voted unanimously to adopt all the report's recommendations. The months that followed saw several steps towards implementing these – the largest being the replacement of Kalanick with Dara Khosrowshahi, the external CEO brought in to clean up the mess at the company.

Throughout these experiments and attempts to settle into an organic structure that is not yet defined but is starting to function, we never lose sight of our faculty of social comparison. Whether we admit it or not, what can drive some of our interactions with our new set of peers is an innate desire to define ourselves versus the others; for example, as superior, to feel 'better than you', or simply as truly distinctive.

Human dynamics are critical to understanding the complexities of how people function and interact with one another.[1] Our role in groups often starts with family dynamics – how we compete, learn, communicate, relate with family members, and develop as human beings. We often carry this 'valency' into other groups throughout our lifetime, which may unconsciously draw us into unproductive dynamics of dependency or dominance. It is important for any director to be aware of what is beneath the surface level of the group – unspoken power struggles or competition, for example – and to confront these dynamics if they begin to block effective exchange or critical thinking.

By applying an understanding of human dynamics to board work, directors can enrich relationships, communicate more effectively, and work together more productively. However, by the same token, competition and comparison is also an inevitable part of these interactions, because people generally want to feel good about themselves through winning. Within a board, this typically means that directors could well be striving to be:

- closest to the chair;
- the one most seen, most heard, most recognised;
- the cleverest board member;
- the most influential board member; or
- better than their predecessor/successor.

Coalitions Within a Board Are Inevitable – and they Feed into Politics

If things do not go according to plan in these competitive situations, someone will attempt to pinpoint a specific reason behind the board's lack of success. More often than not, a failure is attributed

---

[1] For a good example of how to analyse and overcome, see Manzoni, J-F. (2014) Dysfunctional dynamics behind boardroom conflicts. *SID Directors Bulletin* 4.

COALITIONS WITHIN A BOARD
ARE INEVITABLE

Figure 7.1   Mapping Board Alliances

to a scapegoat, because every group needs someone to blame when things do not go well (Figure 7.1). To avoid being the scapegoat, people form alliances. When these groups form, or shift suddenly, like in a game of musical chairs, the odd one out will be the scapegoat. The diagram below synthesises directors' perceptions of their own grouping on the board.

A common presumption in the management world is that when points of difference arise, they should be considered objectively; everyone should work together in a non-partisan way to deliver the chosen outcome. In this equation, the categories of power and politics are conspicuous by their absence. Yet cogent understandings of politics predate management theory – they have long been developed in disciplines such as philosophy, sociology, literature, and political science. In addition, postmodern theory has taught us to read between the lines, be comfortable with ambiguity, and also listen to what is *not* being said. Meanwhile, management theory and business education for the most part seem to maintain that within organisations, there are no out-of-bounds markers that we cross at our own peril. By contrast, sociology has long embraced the idea of all human interaction involving continual contestation of impulses drawing on science, intuition, and politics.

When executives fail in their new positions, the key factors are the culture and politics they stumbled upon in the new environment – and often not experience, nor even leadership capability. Politics means understanding that we are involved in processes of struggle for limited resources, not simply material or financial, or even power, but struggles for attention, respect – for time and the ability to be listened to carefully in a boardroom discussion, for example; nothing more and nothing less than that.

In healthy boards, such subgroups are floating and never solidified, and members can easily shift from one to the other depending on the issue. In practice, however, splitting up coalitions can often prove to be a challenge – especially if a board's culture needs to be reformed.

As boards become socially differentiated, their politics can give rise to cliques and factions, where several members align in opposition to the rest of the group. Sometimes an elite 'inner board' will form around the CEO or chair. This can be quite common in boards with ethnic, linguistic, political, or tribal differences, for example.

Language is a natural factor around which in-groups converge. On one Swiss board that my team worked with, the chair surrounded

---

Ecobank Transnational

In 2014, the board of directors of pan-African lender Ecobank Transnational (ETI) put an end to a protracted, nine-month battle with the bank's management by ousting the chief executive, Thierry Tanoh. Shortly before this, a shareholder meeting had discussed allegations, first brought to light by the *Financial Times,* that Tanoh had in 2012 agreed a pay rise and a 400% bonus increase with the former ETI chair. Additionally, Tanoh's appointment of the bank's internal auditor in a dual role as his special advisor represented a conflict of interest.

With a presence at the time in 35 countries and assets of more than $20 billion, ETI had been seen as one of Africa's business success stories. The campaign for Tanoh to step down had been launched by ETI directors, senior managers, former chairs, and possibly South Africa's Public Investment Corporation, a large shareholder. Coupled with Tanoh's denial of any culpability, the resulting developments weakened market confidence in the bank and led to a temporary outflow of deposits.[2] Tensions among different groups of directors (between French and English speakers, and between Nigerians and South Africans, for example) contributed greatly to the board's difficulties in handling the situation. Alleged malpractice by the ETI chair, which made the front pages of international papers, deepened the crisis and increased the board's fragmentation.

---

[2] www.ft.com/content/a51ad338-a93c-11e3-b87c-00144feab7de.

himself with fellow German-speaking Swiss (many of whom were also high-ranking military officials), leading to a sense of exclusion among the French-speaking members. The German-speaking Swiss didn't realise this, because they made it a point to always speak French, but the in-group was still perceived as a cultural one.

Although we live in a global era, the tendency to invest social meaning and trust in concepts, structures, and systems is largely a Western tradition. Other national cultures, by contrast, may find more meaning in face-to-face interactions.

The owner of a family business in Southeast Asia, for example, may see many governance structures, including the board itself, as little more than 'window dressing'. The dynamics of his or her national and family culture may dictate that the ties of kinship, religion, and ethnicity trump all other structures, under any circumstances. Even members of this cohort who have willingly set out to take their company public will freely admit that they struggle with the idea of heeding the advice of an independent director, when 'we are the ones who spent the past ten years building this enterprise from scratch'.

Boards Fall into Traps[3]

Because of the high stakes involved, and the overlapping factors of responsibility, seniority, and loyalty, boards risk falling into behavioural traps. These may be tough for a new board member or an outsider to identify, and can be highly damaging to the company and the people involved. Dysfunctional discussion and decision styles can lock boards into three common traps in particular:

- the argumentative/broken relations trap – trust breaks down, and the board becomes dysfunctional;
- the happy family/support trap – everyone is too supportive and does not raise red flags;
- the leader control trap – one or two board members have disproportionate influence.

The checklist below can help board members to diagnose some of these dysfunctions and the resulting traps.

---

[3] This section as well as the table on discussions styles and decisions styles is strongly inspired by Paul Strebel's work and notably his co-authored article 'How boards get trapped and what to do about it': Paul Strebel, Denise Kenyon-Rouvinez, and Phil Whiteley, Working Paper, IMD 2018.

Table 7.2 Boardroom Discussion and Decision Styles

Boardroom discussions sometimes fall prey to dysfunctional dynamics, often leading to suboptimal boardroom decision styles.

Have you experienced any of the following during your board meetings?

DISCUSSION STYLES	Often	Occasionally	Never
Uncompromising no Members stay closed to the opinions of others, refusing to yield in any way.	☐	☐	☐
Perpetual maybe Discussion never moves beyond possibilities to a point where a clear path of action is adopted.	☐	☐	☐
Failure to reach closure Discussions fail to lead to a clear decision point, remaining entrenched in opposing viewpoints.	☐	☐	☐
Group narcissism/denial Individuals have an inflated love of the board as an in-group, and are often blind to any possible mistakes or shortcomings.	☐	☐	☐
Group think/false yes An excessive desire for harmony and conformity prevents the group from engaging in critical thinking.	☐	☐	☐
Manipulation/influencing One or two group members steer the board toward supporting their personal agenda, exerting influence and other tactics to prevent constructive debate.	☐	☐	☐
Fast thinking Board members move too quickly through the agenda items, not giving sufficient time to considering all angles of an issues; individual members may lack the opportunity to contribute their perspective.	☐	☐	☐

What kinds of decisions does your board tend to make? Have you ever experienced any of the following during board meetings?

DECISION STYLES	Often	Occasionally	Never
Blocking One or two members consistently disagree, finding a reason why a specific course of action won't be successful.	☐	☐	☐
Inaction The board discussion fails to engender a clear decision to pursue a course of action.	☐	☐	☐
Indecisive Further information is needed and more studies conducted before a decision can be taken.	☐	☐	☐

Table 7.2 (continued)

DECISION STYLES	Often	Occasionally	Never
Unanimous consensus A desire to avoid conflict suppresses dissenting board member voices from being expressed or heard.	☐	☐	☐
Majority coalition A majority subgroup forms a dominant alliance, influencing decision outcomes that may be suboptimal.	☐	☐	☐
Rapid/autocratic Excessive dependence on one or two individuals to make decisions – usually quickly.	☐	☐	☐

Given our discussion styles and decision styles, might any of the underlying dysfunctions be at work on our board?

DISCUSSION STYLES	DECISION STYLES	UNDERLYING DYSFUNCTION
– Uncompromising no – Perpetual maybe	– Blocking – Inaction	→ Broken relations
– Group narcissism/denial – Group think/false yes	– Indecisive – Unanimous consensus	→ 'Happy family' syndrome
– Manipulation/influencing – Fast thinking	– Majority coalition – Rapid/autocratic	→ Dominated by a strong leader

Do you have further thoughts on discussion or decision styles on your board?

Table 7.3 NEO PI-R: NEO Personality Inventory – Revised[4]

The NEO PI-R is a measure of the five major domains of personality as well as the six facets that define each domain. Taken together, the five domain scales and thirty facet scales of the NEO PI-R facilitate a comprehensive and detailed assessment of normal adult personality. The NEO PI-R is recognised internationally as a gold standard for personality assessment. Today, reputable developers of personality tests for the occupational market will as a matter of course publish data on the relationship of their tests with the five-factor model using one form or another of the NEO as the benchmark. The total amount of recent data from high level academic journals concerning the NEO PI-R underpins its quality.

Description of the domain and facet scales

Neuroticism/emotionality: identifies individuals who are prone to psychological distress.
1. Anxiety: level of free-floating anxiety.
2. Angry hostility: tendency to experience anger and related states such as frustration and bitterness.
3. Depression: tendency to experience feelings of guilt, sadness, despondency, and loneliness.
4. Self-consciousness: shyness or social anxiety.
5. Impulsiveness: tendency to act on cravings and urges rather than reining them in and delaying gratification.
6. Vulnerability: general susceptibility to stress.

(continued)

4   Costa P.T. (Jr.) and R.R. McCrae. The NEO Personality Inventory – Revised. Hogrefe Ltd. The Test People, Oxford.

Table 7.3 (continued)

Extraversion: quantity and intensity of energy directed outwards into the social world.
1. Warmth: interest in and friendliness towards others.
2. Gregariousness: preference for the company of others.
3. Assertiveness: social ascendancy and forcefulness of expression.
4. Activity: pace of living.
5. Excitement seeking: need for environmental stimulation.
6. Positive emotions: tendency to experience positive emotions.

Openness to experience: the active seeking and appreciation of experiences for their own sake.
1. Fantasy: receptivity to the inner world of imagination.
2. Aesthetics: appreciation of art and beauty.
3. Feelings: openness to inner feelings and emotions.
4. Actions: openness to new experiences on a practical level.
5. Ideas: intellectual curiosity.
6. Values: readiness to re-examine own values and those of authority figures.

Agreeableness: the kinds of interactions an individual prefers from compassion to tough mindedness.
1. Trust: belief in the sincerity and good intentions of others.
2. Straightforwardness: frankness in expression.
3. Altruism: active concern for the welfare of others.
4. Compliance: response to interpersonal conflict.
5. Modesty: tendency to play down own achievements and be humble.
6. Tender-mindedness: attitude of sympathy for others.

Conscientiousness: degree of organisation, persistence, control, and motivation in goal-directed behaviour.
1. Competence: belief in own self-efficacy.
2. Order: personal organisation.
3. Dutifulness: emphasis placed on importance of fulfilling moral obligations.
4. Achievement striving: need for personal achievement and sense of direction.
5. Self-discipline: capacity to begin tasks and follow through to completion despite boredom or distractions.
6. Deliberation: tendency to think things through before acting or speaking.

Drawing Strength from the Board's Potential

All the board dynamics we have outlined so far are driven by powerful human forces. Rather than letting these roam free, directors and boards need to learn to manage such influences and prevent them from becoming destructive.

Individual board members should train themselves to follow some basic rules. The chair can facilitate this process by compiling and distributing a common set of 'rules of engagement', or 'ground rules' to help directors channel and conduct discussions in the boardroom.

For instance, board members need to differentiate clearly between a person and his or her opinion, rather than summarily dismissing both because they do not agree with the other's point of view. Our brains use every opportunity to take shortcuts and latch onto 'cognitive handles' that break down, simplify, and help us digest reality. Although these handles help the brain to use information more efficiently, they also come with pitfalls, such as the urge to label and stereotype others.

As a result, we tend to fall back on the duality of the human mind, which produces the 'paradox of the missing middle', transforming subtle differences into dramatic, black-and-white distinctions. In other words, once we categorise, we also polarise. And given how strongly we are invested as individuals in feeling different or superior, we truly see what we want to see. From there, we are also quick to judge – and more often than not, we judge the entire person, not only their behaviour or argument.

The Biblical verse about looking at the speck of sawdust in one's brother's eye while paying no attention to the plank in one's own is not just a moral message – it is a profound observation on human nature. One successful chair I know, for example, urges his fellow board members to always assume the best intentions from each other, and has made this one of his three golden rules in chairing the board.

In addition, directors need to remain clear about their function in the boardroom, and frame discussions accordingly. When problems are framed positively, by presenting options as certain (or absolute) gains, individuals tend to focus more on risk aversion. But with negative framing, which looks at the relative likelihood of losses, individuals are more likely to make riskier choices. Directors have a responsibility to remain vigilant to framing and to challenge the board members to reframe the discussion in absolute terms, rather than relative terms.

Developing Self-Awareness

Individual directors also need to ensure that they are not falling prey to flawed thinking, which can result from cognitive biases or from self-deception rooted in a lack of self-awareness. Self-deception leads to individuals refusing to acknowledge a conflict of interest – even to themselves. Honing self-awareness requires regular and honest reflection, as well a commitment to seeking honest feedback from others to identify one's own blind spots. Tackling cognitive biases, meanwhile, requires awareness and vigilance to maintain rationality in the face of various pressures, and a certain discipline in order to frame problems correctly.

Cognitive Biases: Groupthink

Although many individuals may exercise good judgement in most aspects of their life, cognitive biases may sometimes cloud their thinking and lead them to take decisions or actions in an illogical manner. One major cognitive bias is the psychological phenomenon of groupthink, in which members of a group fail to critically evaluate different viewpoints or courses of action, in order to preserve harmony and minimise conflict.[5] The in-group tends to overrate its own decision-making abilities (or has an 'illusion of invulnerability'), and underestimates those of the out-group. An example of groupthink is the decisions that led to the launch of the Challenger space shuttle, and the subsequent disaster.

Individual directors need to remain vigilant toward possible symptoms of groupthink. According to the American psychologist Irving Janis, these include an inflated sense of the group's power or morality; closed-mindedness (rationalising potential challenges to the group's assumptions, and stereotyping anyone opposed to the group, for example); and pressures toward uniformity (including illusions of unanimity, suppressing dissent, or framing dissent as disloyal).

Reintroducing productive interpersonal dynamics into the boardroom   When faced with a dysfunctional situation, directors can take steps to reintroduce productive interpersonal dynamics into the boardroom. The key is to align the individual board members' objectives in a constructive fashion, through commitment and shared responsibility. This will involve pre-empting and diffusing polarisation while stimulating healthy and constructive exchanges, even managed conflict.

On political boards, for example, the chair and/or individual members can assume the role of a cultural and political 'translator', bridging opposing views on a particular issue. They can also break up factions by separating political allies when assigning members to activities such as site visits, external meetings, and research projects. It's also useful to poll individual board members occasionally, with

---

[5] Janis, Irving L. (1971). Groupthink. *Psychology Today* 5: 84–89.

external consultants administering this if necessary. And remember that good governance is creative: one Finnish board I know sings together and has a great time. Another leading chair plays the cello and sometimes brings the board together around music.

Similarly, contained conflict can serve as a productive platform to 'get things out in the open' and obtain clarity on individual perceptions and objectives. When properly channelled and managed, this may allow board members to feel strong by making themselves vulnerable. The process will also enable directors to further their technical knowledge (about products, markets, and technologies), cultural awareness (about norms, values, and assumptions), and political sense (regarding alliances, power, and influence).

The leaders in the boardroom are those who can identify the dynamics, conflicts, and emotions and harness them for the betterment of the organisation they serve. They should ask themselves the following questions:

- How well is our board addressing the political issues that should engage its attention?
- How much does the board encourage effective challenging within the board itself?
- How successful has it been in creating a sense of commitment and shared responsibility?

Finally, boards need effective mechanisms for identifying what kinds of challenging discussions are taking place at different levels of the business, including in the board itself. These can be supported by mentoring or coaching processes that draw out effective performance in all three of the scientific, intuitive, and political dimensions.

If boardroom interactions are healthy and guided enough to produce meaning, then board members will react accordingly. Instead of 'selling their time and expertise', which is impersonal and calculative, they will show creativity, resilience, and caring.

Board Culture

As we saw in Chapter 3, directors have a duty to clearly embody and reinforce board culture through their values and behaviour. The following checklist will help board members assess the health of their own board's culture – essential for setting the tone at the top.

Table 7.4 Reinforcing Board Culture

To what extent do you agree with the following statements with regard to your own board?

No, not at all.	To a limited extent.	I'm not sure.	Mostly, with some exceptions.	Yes, this is true.
1	2	3	4	5

(1) PRIMARY VALUES:
Each individual on our board is highly committed to these values:

	1	2	3	4	5
a. Responsibility	☐	☐	☐	☐	☐
b. Accountability	☐	☐	☐	☐	☐
c. Moral authority	☐	☐	☐	☐	☐
d. One voice principle (no director authority)	☐	☐	☐	☐	☐

What other values are fundamental for our boards?

(2) DIRECTORS' BEHAVIOURS:
Our directors' unequivocally demonstrate the following behaviours:

	1	2	3	4	5
a. Independence and integrity	☐	☐	☐	☐	☐
b. Equal participation/mutual respect	☐	☐	☐	☐	☐
c. Openness and constructive dissent	☐	☐	☐	☐	☐
d. Knowledge acceleration	☐	☐	☐	☐	☐
e. External support & continuous education	☐	☐	☐	☐	☐

What other behaviours does your board deem to be critical for its directors?

Table 7.4 (continued)

No, not at all.	To a limited extent.	I'm not sure.	Mostly, with some exceptions.	Yes, this is true.
1	2	3	4	5

(3) UNACCEPTABLE BEHAVIOURS/EXECUTIVE LIMITATIONS:
There is zero tolerance for these behaviours by individual board members. We are all clear that any evidence of these behaviours will result in removal from the board.

	1	2	3	4	5
a. Imprudent	☐	☐	☐	☐	☐
b. Unlawful	☐	☐	☐	☐	☐
c. Unethical	☐	☐	☐	☐	☐

Are there additional behaviours which are unacceptable for your board members?

```



```

In Part I, we have introduced the four pillars of board effectiveness and discussed each of them in turn. The toolkit on the following pages contains checklists for each pillar that will enable directors to measure the health of their board.

In practice, of course, many boards fail, and almost all face major challenges at some point. These failures and challenges will be the focus of Part II.

Summary table to Part I: The four pillars of board effectiveness toolkit.

At the forefront of organisations, boards have a key role to play. Governance is a critical driver of success – or failure. In order to assess the health of a board, it is useful to examine the strength of each of its four pillars:

1. people quality, focus, and dedication
2. information architecture
3. structures and processes
4. group dynamics.

Are you, as a board, delivering to a high standard on these four dimensions? Checklists on each of these dimensions are provided below, to help you evaluate each pillar in turn.

No, not at all.	To a limited extent.	I'm not sure.	Mostly, with some exceptions.	Yes, this is true.
1	2	3	4	5

Checklist on People Quality, Dedication, and Focus

	1	2	3	4	5
1. The company is close to the heart of every board member.	☐	☐	☐	☐	☐
2. Where do I truly add value to this board?					
3. I am confident in my board colleagues to steer our company in the right direction.	☐	☐	☐	☐	☐
4. Our board has a good level of diversity in terms of abilities, personalities, and competencies.	☐	☐	☐	☐	☐
5. I am clear about the role of our board.	☐	☐	☐	☐	☐
6. I am clear about the role of each committee.	☐	☐	☐	☐	☐
7. The agenda has enough focus on the future.	☐	☐	☐	☐	☐
8. My knowledge is on a par with that of the ideal board member for this company.	☐	☐	☐	☐	☐

No, not at all.	To a limited extent.	I'm not sure.	Mostly, with some excep- tions.	Yes, this is true.
1	2	3	4	5

Checklist on Information Architecture

	1	2	3	4	5
1. I know and intimately track business and its key value drivers.	☐	☐	☐	☐	☐
2. I am well informed of competitive trends, including regulatory changes, technological changes, and stakeholder evolution.	☐	☐	☐	☐	☐
3. I have enough information independent from management available for my judgement.	☐	☐	☐	☐	☐
4. I have strong informal information processes.	☐	☐	☐	☐	☐
5. I was involved in designing the information architecture, and so were my fellow board members.	☐	☐	☐	☐	☐

Checklist on Structures and Processes

	1	2	3	4	5
1. How well managed are these processes for your board?	☐	☐	☐	☐	☐
a. Strategy	☐	☐	☐	☐	☐
b. Evaluation	☐	☐	☐	☐	☐
c. CEO succession	☐	☐	☐	☐	☐
d. Risk	☐	☐	☐	☐	☐
e. Board education	☐	☐	☐	☐	☐

	1	2	3	4	5
f. Stakeholder engagement	☐	☐	☐	☐	☐
g. Audit	☐	☐	☐	☐	☐
h. Regulatory compliance	☐	☐	☐	☐	☐
i. Onboarding/outboarding	☐	☐	☐	☐	☐

2. When I think about the other processes that are truly important for this board, they are:

	1	2	3	4	5
3. I have a clear view of each of these processes, which is complete and detailed.	☐	☐	☐	☐	☐
4. We have the right committees and the right people on them.	☐	☐	☐	☐	☐
5. The reporting lines are foolproof.	☐	☐	☐	☐	☐

No, not at all.	To a limited extent.	I'm not sure.	Mostly yes.	Yes, this is true.
1	2	3	4	5

Checklist on Group Dynamics

	1	2	3	4	5
1. My board is energetic.	☐	☐	☐	☐	☐
2. I feel that the contribution of the different board members is strong.	☐	☐	☐	☐	☐
3. The culture of my board provides for well-managed meetings and 'equal participation' in discussions.	☐	☐	☐	☐	☐

	1	2	3	4	5
4. I genuinely listen to the opinions of others and challenge them, respectfully but without conceding, while keeping the personal relationship.	☐	☐	☐	☐	☐
5. I make points when I have knowledge or a judgement to offer. My points are short and to the point.	☐	☐	☐	☐	☐
6. I need to talk to the chair about something that we do not address well, possibly even in his or her own role.	☐	☐	☐	☐	☐

PART II
Board Failures and Challenges

CHAPTER

8

Four Areas of Board Failure

Boards are not infallible: they can fail the organisation that they are in charge of protecting and helping to thrive. My teams and I estimate that 90–95% of organisational failures due to board work occur in the following four areas:

1. Identifying, assessing and managing risks.
2. Strategy.
3. Non-executive to executive relations and especially CEO and team selection/support.
4. Integrity.

Board leadership in these areas is particularly important, and failures typically lead to terrible organisational damage. Boards therefore need to be particularly alert to their governance abilities in these domains. The following high-profile examples illustrate the four areas of failure.

A failure to adequately assess and manage risks: In 2008, global financial services giant UBS was the Swiss bank hit hardest by the sub-prime crisis. Due to its risk exposure, the bank wrote down around US$40 billion. The UBS board – which was ultimately responsible – was one of the highest paid in the world and included some of the most influential corporate leaders. Yet it was largely unaware of the risks and unable to deal with them, and its Chair, Marcel Ospel, was removed. For example, the board did not have any knowledge of UBS's exposure to the responsible instruments (concentration metrics on the derivatives of choice at the time, so-called collateralised debt obligations or CDOs), despite their contributing 40% of the bank's pre-crisis profits. UBS had a better risk positioning than most investment banks before the crisis (thanks to its massive wealth management outfit). But its lack of risk abilities at board level killed the bank (which was subsequently rescued by the Swiss National Bank).

Strategic failure: The board of Nokia, the Finnish multinational communications company, dismissed the first iPhone as a toy and did not see it as a strategic threat. The firm decided to allocate scarce resources to developing new phones that responded to previous market needs, instead of making devices and an operating system to compete with Apple and the smartphone revolution.

CEO and team selection/support issues: From 2007 to 2012, US technology company Yahoo went through a turbulent period with frequent changes in its leadership. Yahoo co-founder Jerry Yang took over as CEO in 2007, but was replaced by Carol Bartz in 2009 after he rejected a lucrative offer from Microsoft to buy the firm. Bartz was fired in 2011 and replaced by interim CEO Tim Morse. Former PayPal President Scott Thompson took over as chief executive the following year, but lasted only four months before being replaced in mid-2012 by Marissa Mayer, a former Google engineer.

Integrity failure: US federal prosecutors pursued criminal investigations into corruption at FIFA, football's international governing body, leading to the indictment of nine FIFA officials in 2015 for offenses related to illegally pursuing personal gain. Despite receiving independent recommendations to reform its governance policies, FIFA did not adopt time limits on board membership, introduce independent directors, provide transparency into its election processes, or adopt best practice conflict-of-interest policies.

Using the checklist below, directors can assess their own board's abilities in each of these four key areas.

The following chapters in this part of the book focus on two of these areas of failure: risks and integrity. We examine the board's role in strategy, and its relations with the CEO and management team, in Part III, in the context of board best practices.

Table 8.1 The Danger Zone: Board Failures

When board failures occur, they are typically the result of four different sources of breakdown in board work. Do you recognise any of these in your board?

Non-existent	Weak	Average	Strong	Best Practice
1	2	3	4	5

TECHNICAL RISKS
Extraordinary risks – such as economic risks, societal risks, and technology risks – are a reality. What are some of the significant risks we may not be considering?

How would we evaluate our board's technical expertise in identifying, assessing, and supervising risks and their mitigation?

| 1 | 2 | 3 | 4 | 5 |

STRATEGY
The board's ability to assess and engage on strategy is critical. What are some of the areas of threat to the strategy that the board needs to consider?

How would we evaluate our board's commitment and ability to engage on strategy with the executive team?

| 1 | 2 | 3 | 4 | 5 |

CEO AND TEAM SELECTION/SUPPORT
A frequent area of board failure is its inability to select the right CEO. On many occasions it is not handled proactively or systematically, and left until the last minute.

How would we assess the sophistication of our CEO selection process? How would we rate our board's capability to manage this as an ongoing process?

| 1 | 2 | 3 | 4 | 5 |

INTEGRITY
Integrity failure is another key area of failure, and a very common one. Have we had any recent failures in ethics? If not, we probably aren't looking hard enough! How central is integrity in our board discussions? Any challenges?

How would we rate the strength of our board's commitment to compliance and ethics?

| 1 | 2 | 3 | 4 | 5 |

CHAPTER 9

Risks and Ensuring the Right Board Risk-Philosophy

Risks are a primary board responsibility, and a strong risk philosophy will help boards to be a secure base in this area. The board provides risk backstops for management and also drives the risk appetite of the organisation. In addition, the board makes major choices regarding mergers and acquisitions, culture, and strategy that drive the fundamental risks of the business. Thus, a well-anchored risk philosophy is important, especially as the world becomes more chaotic and the risks ever more challenging.

As the value of goodwill features more prominently on companies' balance sheets, their responsibilities for managing risk – and especially reputational risk – increase greatly. Not handling this issue properly can have substantial implications, as the case of US theme park chain SeaWorld illustrates.

All boards should keep the following six principles in mind regarding risks, whether these concern people, markets, operations, safety, demand, or other parts of the organisation's activities.

Risks are everywhere! Many business leaders think about risk too narrowly. True business risks go far beyond the technical risks that risk departments or chief risk officers focus on. They can be external, related to the industry, competitors, customers, the environment, and the economy, or internal, stemming from operations, leadership and decision skills, and personal ethics. Risks can be hard

In 2013, a US documentary called *Blackfish* was released that criticised Sea-World's treatment of killer whales. It received much media attention and caused a public outcry against the company. The US Securities and Exchange Commission (SEC) later began investigating fraud charges against SeaWorld for misleading investors about the impact of the documentary on the company. In 2018, the SEC announced that SeaWorld, and its former CEO and Vice President of Communications, would pay more than $5 million to settle the charges. 'This case underscores the need for a company to provide investors with timely and accurate information that has an adverse impact on its business', said Steven Peikin, Co-Director of the SEC Enforcement Division. 'SeaWorld described its reputation as one of its "most important assets," but it failed to evaluate and disclose the adverse impact Blackfish had on its business in a timely manner.' [1]

and quantifiable or soft and qualitative. They may be well defined or ambiguous. Risks are connected to strategy, and to the levels of complacency, discipline, and creativity in the organisation. Boards must therefore develop a specific view of risks, and not rely solely on a management risk report.

Risk techniques will fail. Indeed, they are bound to do so, because if we knew exactly what the risks were, they would not be risks anymore. The goal of risk techniques is thus not to determine precise risk results, but to understand the complexity and sophistication of current risks in order to respond intelligently. This is why 'black box' risk models don't help boards in their risk work.

For every risk there is an opportunity. Success is about navigating risks, whether the goal is to make money, treat customers and employees well, or cater to shareholders or governments. A challenging wind can in fact carry a well-managed organisation further, while blowing others off course.

The deepest risk is the one within us. Ultimately, it is the ability to decide and steer a business in the right direction that matters the most. Each individual has their own risk responsibility, and every board member, manager, and employee owns his or her own risk decisions. This responsibility requires awareness, which in turn drives true success. The biggest risk is not external; it is our own ability to decide in the face of all the other risks.

---

[1] https://www.sec.gov/news/press-release/2018-198.

Risk is positive. What takes you down can take you up. Life is risk. Business is risk. Without risk, there is no movement, opportunity, challenge, or growth. Risk is what makes us choose the right path and the right decision. It is what sends us to the acme of success. The only thing more beautiful than risk itself may be the strength and ability to avoid the risks we choose to avoid, to take the risks we choose to take, and the wisdom to know the difference.

There is no single best way to measure risk. Risk techniques do have value. Sensitivity analyses, stress tests, volatilities, scenarios and Monte Carlo simulations all look for simple solutions to risks. But any model has deficiencies – from simple (extreme versus moderate risks) to complex (linkages between risks) – that make it incomplete and thus wrong. There is no complete and perfect mathematical measure of risks. These risk measurement tools can provide guidance and may support executive thinking. But they can fail too, so boards should remain somewhat sceptical.

Because risk measures do not always work, boards should have several frameworks to think about risk. Preparing for risks is more useful to a board than measuring them (or believing it has done so). And developing the right risk culture, with a balance of appetite and aversion, is most useful of all. Risk awareness should be ingrained in the behaviour of everyone within the organisation, with as great a sense of ownership as possible.

With these principles in mind, the next chapter offers practical ways for board members to think about risk.

10

A Board Member's Practical Guide to Risk Thinking

Risk thinking used to be reserved for the back office, and risk reports used to put board members to sleep. Not anymore. The complexity and impact of risk have increased dramatically, and those companies that have developed special skills, flexibility, and acumen in this area have gained a terrific advantage.

We find that best practices in risk are aligned along the following four dimensions:

- **Physical health check** – What are we exposed to?
- **Mental health check** – Are we capturing the right problems?
- **Strategic risk check** – Are we making the right moves?
- **Governance risk check** – Are we well-structured for continued awareness?

Boards must focus on all four dimensions, because slippage on any one of them may doom the organisation to failure or underperformance. When times were good, underperformance was often acceptable because everybody was doing well. But not in today's more difficult conditions. Money has become scarce, the generosity of fund providers is waning, and the competition is becoming tougher. Yet fortunes are often made during precisely these periods when only the fittest survive. And adequate risk fitness is crucial in this regard.

The Physical Health Check: Technical Risks

First and foremost, a physical health check is necessary. Every board should be aware of where the organisation hurts. Ideally, it will also know where major clients and suppliers are feeling pain, which individuals are most vital to the organisation's success and resilience, and which input prices have the biggest impact on the business. In short, a board should know which risks matter most.

I am puzzled by companies that almost seem surprised when they encounter difficulties as a result of volatility in well-known risk factors such as interest rates, currencies, and the prices of oil and other commodities. The high variance of these has long been demonstrated, and the past 30 to 40 years highlight their incredible uncertainty.

Suddenly, risks are converging, interconnecting and complicating each other. For example, bankers' traditional view of risk as residing in markets, credit, or operations has been blown to pieces (and the efficiency of regulations such as the Basel Accords are threatened as well). In the oil and gas sector, falling oil prices create ripple effects that go beyond revenues and even the organisation itself, touching suppliers, clients, countries, and geopolitics. Furthermore, culture and integrity may now have become a bigger risk than equity markets to any organisation.

In today's world, nothing should surprise us anymore. Boards therefore need to revisit their old risk assumptions, open their minds to all risks, and prepare as best they can. This will help to frame minds so that the organisation can react faster, better, and stronger when risks materialise. With that goal in mind, boards should consider adopting a four-step process for mastering technical risks: identify, assess, manage, structure.

Identify your Risks

Identifying risks is too important to be just a bottom-up process, because employees – whether a single person or a department – will often miss the big picture. When one well-known family packaging business started risk reporting to the board, it conducted a large survey of most of its employees. The survey suggested that the major risk – meaning the one consistently rated as having a high impact on each employee – was VAT compliance, which was hardly a major corporate risk. Without input from senior management, therefore, employees' views of major risks may not result in a good view of risk for the whole organisation.

However, the bottom-up approach, and listening to different viewpoints, is still important and should be supported by open lines of communication in the organisation. In April 2007, a risk manager at UBS reported difficulties in the valuation of subprime structured products to his boss. This could have been a strong signal to top UBS management and the board. But the chair's office did not take the signal, closed the trader's outfit, and integrated it in UBS's investment bank with little proper risk identification. And, as we saw in Chapter 8, we all know how that ended.

Old ways of identifying risks also need to be revisited. The board needs to engage on this; for example, by having an annual session – with management not present – where directors discuss major risks. These could result in simple maps that go beyond risks identified by management, to include risks related to the CEO, as well as cultural, social, geopolitical, and complacency risks.

Assess your Risks

Once the board has identified major risks, it must assess and gain a better understanding of them. Even nonquantifiable risks can be assessed. The assessment does not need to be exact. After all, if risks could be fully assessed, they would not be risks. Rather, the aim is to grow awareness and develop a common language that can be used to communicate and prepare for these risks.

There are many risk-assessment tools, and I recommend that boards use several for large or sensitive investments. Sensitivity analyses (tornado diagrams or spider diagrams), scenarios, and Monte-Carlo simulations are all useful tools, with different levels of granularity and ease of use. Verbal assessments by those closest to risk are also helpful. A simple scoring system will help the board agree on priorities and address differences in risk perceptions between members. The goal is not to increase paperwork, but rather to raise awareness of the potential impact of the identified risks. We will discuss advanced risk techniques for board members in more detail in the next chapter.

Manage your Risks

Managing risks does not mean eliminating all of them. Organisations may at times be too conservative, and in those cases management's concern with board prudence is justified. Investors and stakeholders expect risk-taking in pursuit of success. Organisations should eliminate only those risks that are not core, or that are too negative, and then manage the remaining risks with full transparency.

For example, a gold-mining company that does not fully disclose its price hedging may be misleading investors that bought the stock for its gold-price exposure. The best risks to manage technically (with hedging) tend to be those that create more downside than upside. A good example is airlines' exposure to fuel costs, because an airline has more to lose when oil prices are very high than when they are very low. Southwest's remarkable move to hedge fuel costs at about \$25 per barrel from 2004 to 2009 was the major reason for its continued profitability at a time when all other US airlines were in the red – and gave it a strategic advantage. This shows that hedges can have a strategic dimension. An easy rule of thumb for assessing whether a hedging programme can be valuable is to ask whether the risk is asymmetric: Is there more to lose than gain from the underlying risk, or vice versa?

Thus, for any risk management programme, boards should ask two questions. First, does it truly create value for shareholders, or rather create comfort for managers? Second, does the risk management programme depend on the timing of its implementation? If it does, then it is speculative. In that case, the board should ask management how good they are at speculation.

Structure your Risks

Finally, organisations have had considerable success in recent times with structuring – or sharing – risks. This entails identifying different risk exposures in a company's network of relationships (including with investors, clients, and suppliers) and agreeing to share the risks with those least sensitive to them, to create value for all. This principle has often been used in joint ventures and acquisitions (with earn-outs), as well as in commercial contracts. It has become part of digital transformation and of business transformation more generally.

For example, Syngenta, one of the world's largest producers of fertilisers and pesticides, has boosted its Latin American business by providing farmers in the region with yield guarantees. The high-risk farmers (who typically default in bad times) are thus able to pass on some of their risks to the company. Syngenta, in turn, can have its aggregated exposures hedged via a commodity trader. In this way, the company obtains more business, with less credit risk (since the 'insured' farmers will probably be more likely to pay), and typically at higher prices for its products. The company has since applied this practice to the US, Eastern Europe, and Russia. In today's turmoil, with parties so sensitive to risk, smart risk structuring can make an important difference.

Once the board has completed its physical check of technical risks, it needs to address the mental, strategic, and governance steps of the risk process. We discuss these briefly in this chapter, and in more detail later in the book. It is important to note that deep investigation in these areas can also create much value.

The Mental Health Check: Behaviours

> *'Real knowledge is to know the extent of one's ignorance'.*
>
> *Confucius (551–479 BCE)*

Boards are at the heart of risk governance. By their nature, risks cannot be fully and exactly measured. The real question proficient directors should ask, therefore, concerns the board's *attitude* to risks.

Market sentiments, fads, and even so-called global trends have taken many by surprise; these are well-known risk factors nowadays. Markets may be somewhat irrational, but they are simply a reflection of people, possibly even of ourselves. Can boards, therefore, look at their own failings?

As we saw in Chapter 7, we now have a good view of typical behavioural risks related to dysfunctional group dynamics and board culture. As an exercise, board members should assess and test themselves for the following nine behavioural risks. These are the ones I see most frequently on boards (many others are available in the general literature on mental biases):

- **Herd behaviour and groupthink:** Is your organisation following the herd? Are you as a board member doing the same and engaging in groupthink? There is something biological about living in agreement with others. It is typically much safer to be wrong with others than wrong alone. But although this behaviour may be safe for the individual (look at those who profited from the pre-financial-crisis era, for example), it does not contribute to the organisation's long-term performance and social responsibility. Boards should therefore revisit past decisions, successful ones as well as failures, in this light. Much governance work is about overcoming this classical mental bias, including through diversity in all its forms.

- **Optimism:** Senior management tends to comprise individuals with an optimistic bias. Indeed, optimism is typically better liked and more successful socially. It also supports modern leadership practices of motivating and energising employees. Finally, optimism helps resilience in the face of difficulties typically faced by top management. The ideal board member, by contrast, could well be slightly paranoid. In both cases, a reality check may be warranted.

- **Overconfidence:** The best professionals acknowledge that predicting oil prices is close to impossible. The same can be said for currencies or markets. Yet many of us start believing our own views. Do we truly know how little we know? Perhaps not surprisingly, most of the senior managers and board members, including government ministers, with whom my teams and I have administered a simple test of overconfidence tend to show strong overconfidence. This is not negative per se, because overconfidence may bring strong motivation and energy to an organisation. One does not lead others without a certain level of confidence. But when crucial decisions are taken, it is best to hold overconfidence in check. Governance concerns key decisions for the organisation, including strategy and mergers and acquisitions. Board members should therefore check themselves for possible overconfidence.

- **Dunning–Kruger Effect:** People with substantial, measurable deficits in their knowledge or expertise lack the ability to recognise these (see Figure 10.1). The Dunning–Kruger effect illustrates that people tend not to recognise their lack of ability at first, basking in a form of illusory superiority, but become more aware of it as their knowledge increases. As a result, board members may think they are performing competently

DUNNING–KRUGER EFFECT

Figure 10.1   The Dunning–Kruger effect.

Source: Based on data from https://www.optimalpbs.co.uk/the-risks-of-the-dunning-kruger-e_ect/

when they are not. This is particularly problematic for board members who are asked to make key decisions on matters beyond their expertise. Cultural diversity in the boardroom can help to overcome this effect, because the effect varies across cultures, as long as competency in the boardroom remains a priority.

- **Belief perseverance or Tolstoy effect:** This is well expressed by the great Russian writer's quote: 'The most difficult subjects can be explained to the most slow-witted man if he has not formed any idea of them already; but the simplest thing cannot be made clear to the most intelligent man if he is firmly persuaded that he knows already, without a shadow of doubt, what is laid before him.' Have you figured out the business or the world in such a smart way that you find it hard to challenge your views, despite the large shifts that are happening? If so, are your views steady or rigid? Most of us do not adapt fast enough; we do not have the flexibility. We have developed sophisticated heuristics to understand the systems we work in, which have probably been successful so far. But as the environment changes, these heuristics become obsolete and our decisions become challenged. How fast can you adapt to the new environment we are facing? Do we still expect the old times to come back? If so, it's time for a reality check.

- **Confirmation bias:** Our thoughts, opinions, beliefs, and worldviews are based on years of experience, reading, and rational, objective analysis. Unfortunately, these years of sampling information may have been subject to confirmation bias. We may always have implicitly paid more attention to information confirming our implicit views on ambiguous topics – such as what constitutes a great CEO, effective compensation structures, and the social impact of business.

- **Hindsight bias:** There is a tendency to overestimate one's ability to have predicted an outcome that was not easy to predict, once that event has happened. This manifested itself clearly after the financial crisis of 2008; few had foreseen it accurately, yet many subsequently thought they had done. Are you the type that tends to think 'I told you so. I knew it'? If so, are you looking back in time truthfully, or are you second-guessing how you would have reacted based on today's situation?

- **Anchoring:** Do you tend to anchor to values and numbers, even unconsciously? This bias particularly affects key decisions such as acquisitions, when board members may hold on to one number despite having a better understanding of synergies, integration challenges, or changes in context. Directors may intellectualise these changes and differences, but still typically come back to their original 'anchor' values.

- **Representativeness:** Giving a shape to highly uncertain processes also reassures the mind. Relying on patterns is the last of the typical biases we are most concerned with. It happens notably in cyclical activities (but aren't they all?). Do you believe that markets will come back up because they always do? Do you believe the cycle is four to five years, as it traditionally has been? Are you looking for some pattern to repeat itself? This may not be productive. Sometimes, life-altering changes happen – such as the Russian Revolution or the development of artificial intelligence – and change the world in such a way that past patterns do not return.

All of these behavioural patterns limit directors' awareness of risks and opportunities. Good governance can overcome these mental biases through the best practices described elsewhere in this book. These include boardroom diversity, effective processes, and good dynamics among directors, as well as between management and the board. Having a diversity of perspectives is particularly important to overcome limiting behavioural factors such as these, as we will see in Chapter 23.

The Strategic Risk Check

As major shifts happen, strategies need to be revisited. Holding on to past strategies does not make sense. But developing new ones, or adjusting passively to the markets, can be challenging. Strategic thinking is complex, and building strategies requires much work, such as improving client and competitor awareness and building on the organisation's core distinctiveness. Nonetheless, there are ways for boards to test strategic choices for their pertinence and thus overall risk.

Typical Strategies

Categorising strategies can help. Ohlsson and Strebel's framework,[1] for example, puts all big strategic moves into five categories:

- Going for growth, such as when rolling out a product.
- Restoring profitability, as when a company needs restructuring.
- Finding a new game, when a company attempts to reinvent itself.
- Relaunching growth, when a company levers its distinctiveness to differentiate itself from competitors or substitutes.
- Realignment, when a company realigns its value proposition to its customers through a revised value chain, with capability development; for example, with process efficiency.

Strategic Risk Assessment

Once the strategic move is well identified, whether along the dimensions proposed above or others (and this can be done for clients and

---

[1] Strebel, Paul and Anne-Valerie Ohlsson (2010). *Smart Big Moves*. FT Prentice Hall.

suppliers as well), the board needs to question whether the strategy is the right one. Overall, the right moves will confront three key strategic risks:

- Strategic Risk 1: Does the strategy lever the company's distinctiveness, i.e. its objectives, values, culture, and capabilities, in terms of skills and resources; and lever its resources, in terms of assets, clients, and partners, as well as match its social footprint?
- Strategic Risk 2: Does the strategy fall into psychological traps, including beliefs such as 'we can beat the competition', 'we know what the customer needs', 'we never admit defeat', or 'we always move forward'?
- Strategic Risk 3: Does the strategy address significant market opportunities or is it too marginal to have an impact?

Boards should first assess the strategy and the proposed move by establishing measures or at least perspectives on each subrisk category. They should then assess competitors' moves, customers' needs, and value chain opportunities. Each dimension can thus be assessed to establish a strategic risk evaluation.

The board will then address execution of that strategy, probing how management intends to achieve the goals, what principal moves have been selected, how people across the organisation will engage in the strategy, and what the fallback options are. Execution is of course itself a key risk, while of a different nature to the strategic risk analysed here.

Even smart strategies can fail, perhaps because the environment changes or competitors move unexpectedly, or because they were not well executed. Organisations and their boards may then need to align again, revisiting all previous risks. High-quality boards will recognise this. Remaining open to such moves is part of the awareness provided by solid governance. This brings us finally to governance risk.

The Governance Risk Check

Leaders fail, organisations drift, and environments change. Leaders are human, and although the selection process may be rigorous, good leaders in some circumstances may prove to be bad ones in

In January 2019, the share price of China Traditional Chinese Medicine Holdings (China TCM) plunged after an independent non-executive director resigned, accusing the company of governance shortcomings. In an open letter to China TCM shareholders, Zhou Bajun said he would resign owing to the company's governance problems, in a rare public spat over a board position at a listed Hong Kong company. Zhou alleged that China TCM failed to keep proper records and written minutes of board meetings after its Hong Kong-based external company secretary stopped attending them. Zhou also said the company had yet to convene a meeting involving its strategy committee, of which he was one of five director members, since it was formed five years earlier.

others. Organisational culture changes, corporate conscience deteriorates, integrity gets lost, the context changes. The problem comes when governance is too weak to recognise and address these threats fast enough. This is where governance risk arises.

In order to control for that risk, governance rules need to apply. These should not constrain, but rather make sure that leadership failure, organisational deterioration, and contextual changes, when they happen, do not become too costly to the organisation.

Boards in any organisation can self-check for well-known governance risk factors. In particular, these include:

- a poorly defined role of the board;
- a domineering CEO (or chair);
- an inefficient board: size, independence, personalities, the role of outsiders, and the structure of board committees all matter;
- conflicts of interest at board or senior management level;
- compensation schemes that have strong side effects;
- a board that is not well aligned with its mission (whether supervisory, strategic, connecting or hands-on); and
- a poor governance culture (values, understanding, and dynamics).

Good governance should be maintained even when things go well. In fact, this is the best time to make improvements, because it is usually less hectic than when things are not going well.

When organisations have done their physical and mental risk checks, have smart strategies in place, and the structures to ensure good governance, then they have a sound basis for success even during difficult times. In fact, these become times of re-incubation, when a company's distinctiveness becomes deeper and new opportunities fuel success. This is hard work, but instead of being a bitter pill to swallow, a recession can turn into a true medicine for such an organisation.

Good risk thinking for the board should thus not stop at classical physical risk, such as input costs and product prices. Given increased social, technological, and geopolitical uncertainty, mental biases or psychological risks compound the physical risks. All of these need to be addressed through the right strategies, and thus strategic risk completes them. And as strategy is now more challenged than ever by changes in the environment, keeping governance healthy and spotting the key governance risks is part of good risk thinking too. In this chapter, therefore, we have offered a mapping of high-quality risk thinking for a board.

Yet increasingly, board members must have an awareness and understanding of technical risks that go beyond the checks we have discussed in this chapter. We now turn our attention, therefore, to more advanced risk techniques.

Elements of Advanced Risk Techniques for Board Members: From Quants to Cyber

As guardians of key stakeholder interests, board members need to develop a broad working knowledge of advanced risk-assessment techniques. Only then can they be confident that management is choosing the right path.

Although the current narrow focus on compliance is warranted in the wake of recent corporate scandals, it has distracted the business world from the broader purpose of corporate governance: ensuring a balanced risk/return trade-off for all stakeholders. Boards and managers need to return to a wider view of corporate health and sustainability, including in the risk techniques they use.

Corporate governance generally, and boards specifically, have multidimensional responsibilities in steering top management towards the right risk choices. Boards should:

- systematically monitor the risk situation of the company to identify and evaluate multiple sources of risk;
- understand and influence management's risk appetite;
- take a portfolio view of corporate risks;
- be apprised more specifically of the major risks (or risk combinations) that could significantly alter business perspectives;
- evaluate how management has embedded risk management within the corporation, asking organisational questions such

as 'Do we need a chief risk officer?' and technical questions such as 'Which tools are being used?';

- implement joint decision-making procedures for major deals, such as acquisitions and significant investments.

Well-informed risk thinking, as opposed to pure risk avoidance, has become an essential aspect of good corporate governance. True, boards tend to be conservative on risks. But avoiding risks is a risk by itself, as opportunities usually come with risks attached. Some companies, most notably in the financial and oil and gas industries, have developed sophisticated risk assessment tools. Yet, even at international banks and insurance companies, boards have failed. Risk models can become 'black boxes', hiding the complex reality from board members with limited technical understanding of risk issues.

Boards that want to rise to the challenge of broader risk thinking must therefore have a solid understanding of the latest risk-assessment and risk-management techniques.

The Why and How of Quantitative Risk Assessment for Boards

Risks can never be assessed exactly, so why should boards and organisations make any effort regarding quantitative risk assessment? Yet even when such techniques are not as objective as they look, they still offer four advantages in particular beyond informal risk discussions.

First, quantitative techniques foster risk thinking, and help boards and management identify major risk drivers. Consider the impact of changes in oil prices on a car manufacturer such as Ford. The oil price affects a number of variables in the complex web of today's economy, including secondary energy prices, the cost of inputs for production, and consumer demand for fuel-guzzling cars versus hybrid or electric models. It also affects inflation – and, therefore, the interest rates that drive demand for cars by altering leasing or borrowing costs.

In other words, the impact of oil-price changes on car sales is manifold, especially in an industry where financial services often contribute between 50 and 100% of profits. Resilience to interest-rate changes – as determined by financial leverage, cash flow, protection from exchange-rate volatility, exposure to consumer or supplier default risk, and so on – is vital to the company's competitive position.

Awareness of this web of risks, and how they come together, is essential to understanding management's decisions and, possibly, challenging them. The portfolio view becomes a necessity at board level – and simple numbers help clarify the thinking. What is the company's sensitivity to oil prices in the context of its costs? How do funding costs increase when interest rates go up or down by 1%? And how many sales would the company lose?

Second, quantitative techniques clarify risk issues by creating a common language. They encourage clearer communication between managers and the board, and within the board; allow board members to understand management's risk appetite; and stimulate risk understanding by objectifying subjective viewpoints. For example, I have seen two board members assessing the same project, with one viewing it as very risky and the other as moderately risky, although both agreed that the probability of the project failing was around 10%. Their different assessments reflected their personal levels of risk aversion, rather than any objective risk evaluation.

Third, metrics encourage better risk management by helping board members to focus on major risks. Without a clear scaling of risks, boards and even management can be overwhelmed by their breadth and complexity. As a result, they may tend to focus on classic risks, such as currency risk, rather than analysing those that truly impact the business, such as a dramatic loss of market share.

Finally, well-designed quantitative models can help businesses price risks. For example, Moody's KMV model helped investors, lenders, and corporations adopt tools to measure and manage credit risk. Its EDF™ (Expected Default Frequency) credit measure dramatically changed the way credit risk was priced throughout the world. And its LossCalc™ became the first commercially available predictive model of Loss Given Default (LGD).

Classical Quantitative Techniques

The most basic risk assessment techniques start with a sensitivity analysis showing how one value dimension is sensitive to one risk driver, sometimes done within a so-called 'tornado of sensitivities'. It is surprising how many corporations do not even use this simple method to evaluate risk.

For example, most investment bankers these days present an acquisition analysis with cross-sensitivities to the cost of capital and growth rates. Most of the time, a normal spread on the sensitivity analysis will bring out negative perspectives on the acquisition. Yet many boards have approved such deals without paying attention to these, and without questioning future drivers of growth and costs of capital.

Royal Dutch Shell's acquisition of BG Group in 2016 was driven on the valuation side by strong oil price and growth assumptions. Shell paid $53 billion to transform the company into a more specialised group focused on the rapidly growing liquefied natural gas (LNG) market and deep-water oil production. The acquisition price was highly sensitive to the oil price – the deal seemed to assume that the price for Brent crude would reach $90 a barrel by 2018 from less than $45 in 2016. Yet the average Brent crude price in 2018 was only $71 a barrel. Analysts therefore remain sceptical about the merits of the deal.[1]

However, sensitivity analysis methods are poor (if not altogether inadequate) at jointly evaluating multiple risks. Nor do they allow for the assessment of extreme risks. Scenarios are a good way to encompass multiple and extreme risks. This technique is a step above simple risk identification and basic sensitivities, but remains highly subjective.

The Monte Carlo simulation has brought the world of scenarios to a new, scientific age, by combining hundreds, possibly thousands, of probability-weighted scenarios into one result – potentially giving boards a clear overview of the risk situation. The technique is used frequently in engineering and banks, but is less common elsewhere, although modern software has made it user-friendly. Banks, for example, are switching their Value at Risk (VaR) models, which assess the probability of a certain level of loss or profit, to a Monte Carlo basis. Since banks make money out of risk-taking, being able to evaluate and measure risk is a core competence. Engineering firms and oil and gas companies use this technique with their P10, P50, and P90 probabilities, meaning the probabilities of reaching a defined outcome (at 10%, 50%, or 90%).

Specific tools to address particular situations have also been developed. For example, option pricing, which is used to calculate the theoretical price of an equity option, has been particularly successful at assessing the economic exposure to specific risks – such as those related to currencies, interest rates, the oil price, or credit and corporate default. As a result, corporations can now provide the board with the precise cost (and value) of a hedging programme, or

---

[1] https://www.bloomberg.com/opinion/articles/2019-01-31/royal-dutch-shell-still-isn-t-earning-enough-money.

a more precise default risk for a major supplier or customer. This is all the more important given the current trend for outsourcing. Similarly, the impact of external or strategic changes on funding costs can be assessed much more precisely.

A good board can expect interesting assessments from these tools. For example, when considering a major joint venture, acquisition, or supply agreement, the board can use an assessment of the credit risk of the other party to challenge a deal. Better still, it may want an assessment of how the joint venture would affect the company's own position.

In addition, the derivatives markets are providing a wealth of information besides commodity and stock price movements, through futures, forwards, swaps, and options. Credit default swaps, which allow an investor to buy protection against a corporate or sovereign default, can give an assessment of a country's risk for a company thinking of opening a new plant there. A board could easily compare possible investments in Russia and Brazil, for example, despite the long distances involved and the complexity of the two economies.

Hard-to-quantify risks   Strategic risks are often so complex that even modern tools, such as game theory, are poor at assessing them accurately. Nonetheless, the board needs to assess strategic and other hard-to-quantify risks in order to have a proper overview. In the case of customer demand risk, for example, what is the risk of a major downturn? More importantly perhaps, how does the board and the organisation prepare for that risk? Is the company being run to simply enjoy the good times, or can it handle the hard knocks as well? Better, can it take advantage of a downturn to gain business from competitors? Or is a digital transformation disruptive enough to the industry to warrant the investment?

Integration of Risks

Financial institutions have become highly sophisticated at integrating different market risks into their VaR models. Some corporations use a related model, cash flow at risk (CFaR), which assesses the probability of the firm having a cash flow below a certain level. However, these models do not encompass all risks – how many of them can combine commodity price and credit risk, and operational and strategic risks, with standard financial risks? Dependencies between these risks make them extremely complex, although the latest tools, such as copulas, which assess how risks move together, may bring greater awareness in this regard. For now, however, even the most complex risk models cannot integrate all factors and their interdependencies. Board members need to be aware of that fact.

Unfortunately, as risk models become more complex, they also become black boxes to most board members. And that makes these models a risk in themselves. Often, simpler thinking may then prevail, at least for the less risk-aware board member.

In general, with integrated risk thinking, we are getting to the point where boards will rely more on their business sense and the corporation's processes than on complex risk models. Nonetheless, an awareness of all dimensions of risks, assessed whenever possible with quantitative techniques, will help the best board members to have a more accurate sense of the business.

The Outcome of Risk Assessment

Once a corporation has adequately assessed risks, its board can be more confident that management is doing a good job of taking and managing them. Should an airline take on oil-price risk? Should a German luxury car manufacturer take on the risk of the euro/dollar exchange rate? Although absolute yes/no answers are often given, more sophisticated choices are often the winners and will reveal management's abilities to the board. For example, a company may decide to cap risks that could put it in jeopardy rather than hedge the whole risk. Or it may decide to take on the risks and inform investors accordingly so that these risks are transparent.

In a complex global company, any risk programme should be designed with value creation in mind. Often, a company creates value when it provides customers with added value or strengthens a competitive situation. Structuring risks has become the name of the game for top-quality management.

In the mid-1980s, Disney was heavily criticised for hedging the yen royalties of its Tokyo theme park when the US dollar was at its peak, thus depriving shareholders of valuable foreign-exchange gains when the dollar subsequently weakened. Disney's assessment was that the currency markets were quite far from the Mickey Mouse business, its core competence. It is hard to assess what the value of currency management to Disney shareholders could have been.

On the other hand, Vodafone has chosen to minimise foreign-exchange hedging, saying that its exposures are quite transparent and that shareholders are aware of the risks they take (and can diversify or hedge on their own). Companies have different personalities and policies in this regard. Transparency will help shareholders (and other stakeholders) make the right choices.

Companies must be aware of the risks that will inevitably accompany innovative business models. For example, Schlumberger, a leading oil-services company, now has complex projects in which it shares revenues with clients, instead of going for straight sales. This move has created new opportunities that enhance profitability – but also lead to new and/or higher risks. A good understanding of the risks taken may lead to new risk management programmes, such as hedging for oil-price risk.

Structured deals in acquisitions (such as earn-outs, in which the purchase price is paid from the earnings realised after the acquisition) have become commonplace. Few acquisitions can justify being straight deals anymore. Instead, the price is structured to share the risks more evenly between buyer and seller, for example by having sharing agreements (in which upside is shared) or support agreements (in which downside is shared). Typically, sharing structures are like call options (the option to buy), while support agreements are like put options (the option to sell). Basic option thinking is thus also important for board members' risk assessments. For example, cement producer LafargeHolcim has been building its global presence through joint ventures followed by acquisitions, while its major competitors have grown through outright acquisitions. This is typical risk thinking: in a high-risk environment where delays are not particularly costly, why not get a foot in the door with an option to expand? The option is all the more valuable when the risk is higher (as option traders know well). Boards with that basic understanding can effectively supervise a company's acquisition programme.

Just as a patient is unlikely to accept being operated on with medical technology from the 1960s, so companies today require board members who have a solid grasp of modern risk evaluation and management techniques. Short training courses, coaching, and some reading will take most directors a long way. Rather than acquiring an in-depth understanding of technical subtleties, board members should look to leverage their deep knowledge of business to engage in the competent risk thinking required by modern organisations.

Applying these methods in new areas remains a constant challenge. The current risk area of attention is cyber, at the crossroads of tech, social, and geopolitical risks.

Cyber Risk

Cybersecurity is something that is not just about technology. Innovation, processes, and intellectual property have virtual elements which need to be protected. One key element in the property paradigm shift is that digitalisation changes the definition of ownership. Typically, in the real world, ownership is linked with a physical object. When we go digital, we can first ask ourselves what 'owning data' means.

The question is even more important about owning private data. For example, you might have to communicate your data, such as date of birth. It may be your data, but not just yours. It's also shared. What about data that are aggregated? For example, the aggregated data that are used for cancer treatment. Do you own the data that are extracted from what is partially from you, partially from somebody else, or what? Finally, what does it mean when your data is stolen? Basically, you have secret information. If somebody has stolen it, you still have it, but it's worth less, because somebody else has it.

So, access to data becomes as or more important than ownership.

The concept of ownership for the digital domain needs to be reviewed. It is more about ruling and protecting the way data:

- Is stored (how and for how long)?
- Can be accessed (by whom)?
- Can be used (for what and by whom)?
- Can be aggregated with other's data (for what and by whom)?

In its early days the internet was the I4H (internet for humans). We had two separated worlds: the real world and cyberspace. This has fundamentally changed. The first element is that cyber-attacks can reach the real world, including money. Not only is the technology increasing, but risky behaviours are as well: critical functions of society are internet based, such as payments via the internet. Personal data is digital and communicated via emails and social networks. At the same time, technology is moving fast and offering new hacking capabilities. Our laws have borders and are slow to react, while hackers are fast and borderless, and sometimes state sponsored.

In cyberspace,[2] all countries are neighbours, sometimes even embedded. A service provider, a bank, a financial institution, or any company, may need 24 months of development to launch a new product or solution. Then there may be nine months of integration, six months of testing, and then about five years of operation. A hacking system may be able to exploit any time during the five years of operation. A hacker will attack a seven year-old system with the latest technology. The risk is asymmetrical. Thus, it's important to design evolving solutions fast enough to address the hacking risks. A successful approach against hackers will combine:

1. Secure technology:
   a well-designed secure architecture;
   secure system components (not too many holes);
   excellence in implementation.
2. Active monitoring:
   cyber monitoring;
   operations in the field (identify the person and where the
      attacks are from and see what has happened).
3. Proactive response:
   upgrading the solution;
   cyber countermeasures (basically destroying pirate devices);
      legal actions (not always possible depending on countries).

Most systems have vulnerabilities that are not discovered early but are discovered with time. What is important is constant monitoring and thus culture and conduct become an important element of risk management, which cannot be seen only as technical. Which types of attacks have appeared at your premises and at others? If you have no or little awareness, you probably are not fulfilling your cyber risk responsibilities as a board member. Not only is this a way that the company can anticipate where the hackers are looking and what they are searching for, but more importantly it engages you on awareness of the level of risk and preparedness in your organisation.

Finally, cyber is less and less about instantaneous attacks and more and more about compromised systems and personnel over long time periods. The technical side of cyber matters and boards need to

---

[2] I am grateful for presentations by and discussions with André Kudelski for many of the insights on cyber in this chapter.

gain technological expertise but cannot consider their responsibility limited to this technical knowledge acquisition. They also need to fulfill their responsibility by accomplishing the usual tasks: assess whether the culture is prone to individuals that would compromise the organization's security, support values and systems that enhance security and monitor both efforts and failures of management.

In 2019, the US National Security Agency (NSA) and the United Kingdom National Cyber Security Centre (NCSC) released a joint advisory[3] on advanced persistent threat (APT) group Turla—widely reported to be Russian and also known as Snake, Uroburos, VENEMOUS BEAR, or Waterbug. Turla uses the malicious Neuron, Nautilus, and Snake tools to steal sensitive data and hide behind various foreign states APT infrastructure and resources, thus appearing first as foreign state attacks.

Waterbug's campaigns have involved a range of new tools including custom malware, modified versions of publicly available hacking tools, and legitimate administration tools. The group has also followed the current shift towards "living off the land," making use of PowerShell scripts and PsExec, a Microsoft Sysinternals tool used for executing processes on other systems.

Turla was able to contaminate government offices including ministries, embassies, as well as multinational organisations and corporates across many countries in Europe, South East Asia, Middle East and Latin America. Compromission lasted for years and was supported by staff in some cases.

How boards identify, assess and manage risk is crucial. But as we will see in the next chapter, they often face their ultimate test in a crisis.

---

[3] https://media.defense.gov/2019/Oct/18/2002197242/-1/-1/0/NSA_CSA_TURLA_20191021%20VER%203%20-%20COPY.PDF.

CHAPTER 12

Crisis Management

*J*uly 2008 – *Joanne Marker had recently received an email from a search firm asking if she would be interested in joining the board of RGen, a major engineering and infrastructure firm. One of the first questions she had asked the company's chair, Mauro Wright, was what their crisis management plan was in the event that disaster struck. She clicked open Wright's email:*

'Dear Joanne,

I know that your Virtuous experience may have been a traumatic one. Attached you will find our plan, should anything happen to me or to Roger (the CEO). I hope you will find this satisfactory'.

The attachment was a rather generic crisis management plan.

Joanne frowned, remembering the morning of 12 April 2017. She had awoken at her usual time of 5 a.m. While making coffee in her kitchen, she reviewed the Google alerts on her phone. As she scrolled through, one piece of news gave her pause: there had been a helicopter crash in Brazil. She knew that the Virtuous Ventures executive team had recently held a retreat following a major client meeting in Sao Paulo. With beads of sweat forming on her brow, Joanne opened the article. Her worst fear was realised: it was the Virtuous team on board the fateful helicopter. She phoned Adrian Holmes, the lead director. He agreed to call an extraordinary board meeting for the following morning.

Joanne knew that initial details of the accident might be sketchy and contradictory, and would likely take days to trickle in. But time was not on the Virtuous board's side. To begin with, being physically present near the site of the accident in Brazil was, under the circumstances, the only way to gather reliable information. Furthermore, it was symbolically and morally important that the board not deliberate on a human and organisational tragedy of this scale from thousands of miles away. Among other considerations, someone had to be on the ground to thank personally the first responders who had risked their lives in the aftermath of the helicopter crash.

At the top of the extraordinary board meeting's agenda should be establishing who was in charge. Being a director is not automatically the same as being a crisis controller, and precious time could be wasted if several directors were to jostle for some degree of control, instead of focusing on the crisis at hand. Virtuous's business continuity plan should stand the board in good stead, at least as a departure point for setting up working teams to tackle the crisis, and dividing their responsibilities between gathering information and acting on that information to make decisions. Each team would have a leader and a deputy, and would comprise a mix of board members, staff, and possibly external stakeholders such as regulators and insurers.

Inevitably, in the raw days after a fatal tragedy, time was running against the board and its crisis response, no matter how judiciously and meticulously crafted it was. Because there was so little time to work with, immediacy would often overrule everything. It seemed to take just one hour for social media reactions to the crash to spread. Nevertheless, an hour should be enough time for well-structured teams to clearly identify the issue. And after another hour inside Virtuous's communications war room, initial communications had taken shape, soon followed by a first set of public responses.

The toll that the Brazil disaster had taken on Virtuous's executive team made it even more important for the board to get on the front foot in managing the organisation's response. There were stakeholders to reach out to with carefully crafted, reassuring, and appropriate messages. There was understandable pressure, even duress, applied by shareholders, authorities, and the general public, as well as families affected by the tragedy. And while the human aspect of the disaster unfolded and continued taking its toll, there was a company to be run. For the time being, board members and company officers, led by the chair, would be responsible for day-to-day operations.

The stakeholder outreach included the media, because an air crash with international implications was guaranteed to grab headlines instantly. Arranging a company press conference would not only help to shape the flow and focus of information to the media; it would also project a strong sense of leadership and unity from the Virtuous board in the face of a major setback. This was to be followed by daily briefings on the situation. And despite its best efforts, the company would no doubt also find itself having to respond to criticism about its information and accessibility, and its help for the executives' families.

The Brazil events were not something a director could ever be fully prepared for psychologically and emotionally. But notwithstanding the grief and personal trauma they all shared, the Virtuous board members would quickly have to come to terms with what had happened, and make sure that the executives' families were assisted in coping with their loss. The board would also soon have to consider the event's financial ramifications. Analysts were expecting urgent updates on what financial impact on Virtuous they should expect. Conference calls were set up to assure investors that the company's financials were in good shape, and to inform them that Virtuous may need to nominate its group controller as chief financial officer on an interim basis while the CEO succession unfolded, with the chair taking a temporary executive role.

XYZ, Virtuous's global PR and communications partner, had drafted a guidebook on crisis preparedness. This outlined specific, practical sets of messages and communication channels to prioritise in different circumstances, with a dedicated social media overview including the main actors and influencers. Although these crisis management blueprints would not always be applicable or appropriate to actual, real-life situations, they were invaluable as cues and handles for the Virtuous board to grab on to. In addition, the guidelines were a tremendous time-saver in a situation when having to design a crisis approach from scratch would have been guaranteed to cast the company in a negative light. In particular, the blueprints provided valuable guidance on identifying the best and most appropriate channels of communication between the board and management; between management and shareholders, employees, customers and stakeholders; and with law enforcement authorities and regulators.

In the midst of this frenzied communication, Joanne also understood that no amount of preparation could provide the authenticity of a human touch. This could only come from drawing on one's personal values – as well as, in part, those of the board and the organisation – and allowing them to resonate with the tragedy and drama. This would not always align neatly with the plans and blueprints, but it would give the board's actions the moral centre and human depth that the circumstances called for. She had a thought for those who were close to Amin, the CEO, his family, his collaborators, and the sudden tragedy hitting them. She knew him closely, but it was the same for everyone who was right there with him. She felt like crying.

Joanne was mature enough as a director to see the crisis response as her personal responsibility. It was a role she was not unfamiliar with: 20-plus years of serving on boards of companies and public organisations saw her ride out a number of outsized crises, and remain calm amid great turmoil. She knew well that the task facing the Virtuous board could never be done by one person. What's more, the board would have to move heaven and earth in its response to the tragedy, and would still have the value and quality of its decisions scrutinised. This situation would relentlessly test the mettle of each director. But if the Virtuous board was functioning well before the crisis, a test on this scale should help it to emerge even stronger, with more trust and goodwill to carry it through future crises.

In Chapter 3, we pinpointed judgement and integrity as the main qualities that can make or break the performance and tenure of directors and boards. We also said that these attributes may be severely tested in a time of crisis.

The cautionary tales of boards caught out and paralysed by the scope and velocity of events – be they related to company finances, products or clients, social impact, cyberattacks, or dramatic developments within the board itself – have been widely publicised. A crisis can ensue because of threats to a company's value or reputation, or even to its very existence. These often transcend the operational level and involve shareholders, regulators, and law enforcement agencies. Crises can also revolve directly around board members, for example through controversies in exercising leadership, or nominating and removing senior executives.

Crisis as a Turning Point

Like many words of Greek origin, 'crisis' in its original sense is largely devoid of negative connotations. Ancient physicians including Hippocrates used the term *krisis* to describe a 'turning point' or 'deciding point' in the progression of a patient's disease, after which things could go either way. In today's usage, the meaning of 'crisis' has shifted more toward 'dislocation', but the fundamental if hidden subtext of being subjected to a decision, of making a choice, remains; in many situations, a crisis is what we make of it. It is a time of decisions.

Boards can and should play a critical role during times of crisis, even if only by acting as a safe base for management. In fact, it is *especially* when unforeseen situations shake the organisation's very foundation that it becomes essential for the board to assume its key responsibilities. This is precisely when the board is expected to shine.

Boards can also help to make their organisations more resilient through preventing, managing, and responding to crises. How, then, can boards groom the judgement skills and rational outlook of their members and management? Can a board prepare for dealing with a crisis before it hits?

There is Work to Be Done In Peaceful Times

There is never a better time to start preparing for a crisis than when a company is sailing smoothly. Doing the groundwork required to build resilience is a key weapon in this pre-emptive battle. Boards should begin with risk analysis and management using robust tools and methodologies, as we discussed in Chapters 10 and 11. Extreme risk preparation on an annual basis is also useful.

The current environment, in which 'the only certainty is uncertainty', has popularised a number of techniques that facilitate scenario planning. Among these, 'black swan' simulation is one such 'scenalysis' tool. The term 'black swan' appeared in the aftermath of the 2008 financial crisis to describe random, highly improbable (and therefore unexpected) events which, when they do occur, result in catastrophic consequences.

The dotcom meltdown, 9/11, the subprime housing loan collapse, and the 2019 trade wars were each black swans in their own right, as virtually none of the credible sources of economic and political forecasts saw them coming. Black swan simulation tools allow the user to experiment with various real-time variables in order to anticipate even extreme outcomes, the probability of which can only be estimated rather than measured. A simple simulation of such an event can help boards prepare themselves and be readier (rather than ready) for when it occurs.

Communication Principles

Learning to imagine the unimaginable and simulate our environment around it is an increasingly useful skill and mindset. When crisis does hit, however, taking action – even when this is anticipated, premeditated, and carefully rehearsed – is only part of the challenge. Equally importantly, the organisation – and its board, when necessary and productive – *must be seen and heard taking decisive action*. This includes sharing accurate and up-to-date information, elaborating on the company's decisions and projected outcomes, reassuring internal as well as external stakeholders, and seeking assistance and support from public agencies if necessary.

Richard Cousins, the 58 year-old CEO of catering giant Compass Group Plc, died in a seaplane crash in Australia on New Year's Eve 2017. Dominic Blakemore, the group's chief operating officer since 2015, had been appointed deputy CEO in October 2017 under the company's succession plan. Upon Cousins' death, Blakemore assumed the chief executive role ahead of schedule.

All of these activities seem self-explanatory. Yet without preparation, making them happen 'on the day' will be next to impossible. In the wake of truly cataclysmic events when every minute counts, the public will very likely be in an anxious mood, and hungry for information. Any silence or indecision from the firm in question – and its board – will be deafening. News audiences will speculate the worst, and fundamentally question the organisation's values, leadership, and management competence. Reputation and goodwill that took decades to build may be washed away in one fell swoop.

Preparedness is the key. With sound preparation and planning, one email or call should be enough to set a pre-planned crisis response in motion immediately. Crisis teams will assemble, with each member assuming the specialised task he or she has been trained to handle. Predetermined ad hoc task forces will address stakeholders, call a press conference, engage with the media, issue press releases, track key social media, and react quickly to posts. Guidelines, toolkits, and written scripts will help automate and coordinate the procedural aspects of the response. Initially, details of the event that precipitated the crisis may be trickling in little by little; likewise, finalising the exact wording of the messages to go out may require a bit of time. But that time will be more productive if the question of 'who does what' has already been clearly decided.

Not all of this has to be tackled in house, or by the board itself. An external communication partner can be helpful in putting the necessary processes and channels in place. They will come up with coherent sets of scenarios, outreach roles, and messages targeted to specific audiences. This may go a long way towards bolstering the organisation's resilience in the face of crisis. The external partner (for whom dealing with crises may be their bread and butter) can also lead the effort to design what is essentially a new language for dealing with dramatic, unexpected events unfolding inside or outside the company.

In the days after Malaysia Airlines flight MH370 disappeared in March 2014, the response by the Malaysian authorities, including the Home Ministry, Malaysian Airline System, and Malaysia Airports Berhad, was sometimes improvised. This generated a considerable amount of negative publicity for Malaysia's vital tourism sector, particularly in the previously buoyant Chinese market. (Most of the passengers on the flight were Chinese citizens.)

All this preparation, and the resulting tools and techniques, will stand board members in good stead, and help them to cope with the shock of being thrust into the spotlight by stakeholders and especially media. It is better for boards to stick to the 'one-voice principle' and keep any dramatic discussions behind the scenes.

Another Powerful Weapon: Gathering Information

Having sleek and quickly assembled crisis management teams in place can ensure that a firm doesn't lose the war on day one. But this may not be quite enough. For sure, reading from a script is always better than an information blackout. Yet to be credible and reassuring in a crisis, the firm's leadership, including the board, must be able to contextualise and present often conflicting information. It helps, therefore, if the company and the board have been continually gathering relevant information for the past few years – as we already discussed in Chapter 5. This includes data on the company, its market and operating environment, client needs, competitor trends, and stakeholder motivations, for example. In many scenarios, what is typically referred to as 'external pressures' can be usefully redefined as information. Indeed, weak signals, complaints, and reputation hits become magnified in times of crisis and a board that has paid attention to all these smaller signals has a better chance of going through the crisis easily. For example, a culture that is strongly under financial pressure may well create a crisis linked to small savings with large safety or health impact. A board that spots this early and maps responses and balances the organisation has better chances of getting through the crisis.

In an environment of pervasive uncertainty, directors should also get information from regular conversations with people at all levels of the organisation, including executives, workers on the shop floor, and also customers. These discussions can give directors a real

In early 2016, Swedbank, Sweden's biggest mortgage bank, ousted its CEO, following a series of controversial, allegedly conflict-of-interest deals pursued by several of the bank's top executives. The transactions were judged to have hurt confidence in the bank. Just as damagingly, customer satisfaction surveys showed the bank underperformed industry among both corporate and private clients. In an internal letter issued by the bank's chair indicated that Swedbank needed new leadership 'that can be close to our operations, our customers and our employees'.[1] Just three years later, after the case against the previous CEO was dropped, Swedbank had to fire its latest chief executive for her handling of an alleged money laundering scandal. Some Swedes expressed dismay that she would walk with a 22 million Kr ($2.4 million) payment. During the AGM, the chair apologised for the bank's actions. Some investors called for the chair to be replaced too.[2]

feel for what is happening 'out there', which in turn may help them to foresee and react to a future crisis.

Many of the spectacular boardroom failures we describe in this book share one essential ingredient: the directors' failure to grasp what was going on in the trenches. Ad hoc internal surveys, client feedback, social media scans, and informal testimonials can all be of great value in helping directors build up a nuanced, three-dimensional view of the organisation and the world in which it functions.

In the event of a crisis, having had all-round access to information will help a company's board to make tough decisions and weather the situation through a managed response. Dealing with a crisis in a purely reactive way, and only when compelled to do so by external circumstances, is no longer acceptable. Such an approach undermines confidence in the company's operations, leadership, and integrity – which is hardly surprising. If a stakeholder cannot trust one part of the organisation, such as its publicity engine or the board's handling of a crisis, then why should it trust anything else? Once goodwill and confidence have been undermined, they may be impossible to restore.

By contrast, a focused, dedicated, and energetic board will include directors who see crisis preparedness as a personal responsibility. They will readily assume a public role and take centre stage

---

[1] www.bloomberg.com/news/articles/2016-02-09/swedbank-ceo-michael-wolf-to-be-replaced-after-seven-years.

[2] For more details, see Bloomberg, 28 March 2019 or https://www.bloomberg.com/news/articles/2019-03-28/swedbank-ceo-has-been-fired-amid-mounting-laundering-allegations.

Singapore's reputation for clean government, low levels of corruption, and a virtual absence of corporate malfeasance made the 2005 scandal involving the country's National Kidney Foundation (NKF) particularly noteworthy. Reports of the CEO's lavish spending and first-class travel, amid inflated estimates of the foundation's fundraising efforts and the number of patients it served, eventually led to the dismissal of the entire board.

An independent investigation later revealed that the NKF board had bestowed its authority on the executive committee, which had in turn delegated its authority to the CEO. Meanwhile, only 10 cents out of every dollar raised was actually used for patient treatment.

As is often the case when a sudden crisis is not met with a coherent communication plan, off-the-cuff statements by the foundation's trustees and patrons served to make things worse. For instance, the description by a national politician's spouse of the CEO's SGD 600 000 (roughly US$450 000) annual salary as 'peanuts' sparked outrage in a society where many middle managers struggled to earn a tenth of that amount. This happened despite the moderate nature of the city-state's tabloid press and blogosphere.

when circumstances call for it (which is rare, as the board acts as the safekeeper of organisational integrity and communicator of last resort). Because a crisis will inevitably bring out the best and the worst in board members, they need to prove themselves competent and in charge. A sense of urgency and good timing is also critical. Many recent crises have shown that delayed reaction, lack of reaction, or overreaction may prove to be a magnet for negative press coverage, which ultimately becomes more damaging than the crisis itself.

A Crisis Will Shed Light On Boardroom Fissures

One of the main themes of this book is the intrinsically social nature of the boardroom, and of governance and business in general – something that is often underestimated. Directors do not come to the boardroom just to attend meetings and dispense guidance. As in all social settings and gatherings, they piece together formal and informal narratives, interact and make sense of things, arrive at new meanings, and create stories. Whenever divisions and schisms within the board have been papered over, they are bound to be exposed, sometimes painfully and embarrassingly, once a crisis erupts. Crises often cast board members in unfamiliar roles that are quite distinct from those assumed by management, and any disharmony can become glaring under the media spotlight.

When the same type of aircraft from the same manufacturer, flown by 2 different airlines, crashes twice within 5 months, killing 346 people, big questions arise about the company and the people responsible for running it. Boeing, the manufacturer of the 737 Max aircraft that crashed in October 2018 (Lion Airways) and March 2019 (Ethiopian Airlines), has faced an intense investor backlash since the crashes.

Leading shareholder advisory firms – Institutional Shareholder Services and Glass Lewis – demanded changes to Boeing's governance structure. The dual role of the company's CEO and Chair Dennis Muilenburg has been questioned. ISS advised Boeing that 'Shareholders would benefit from the most robust form of independent oversight to ensure that the company's management is able to regain the confidence of regulators, customers and other key stakeholders.'

Some board members sat together on two other prominent boards, prompting considerations of a network effect of "old boys club" and the chance that the board was in a comfort zone rather than truly challenging the management on risk issues and its ability to deal promptly and effectively with the crisis.

Finally, Boeing's board did not have a risk committee at the time of the crashes. Risk was instead under the purview of the audit committee, prompting Glass Lewis to recommend the removal of Lawrence Kellner, the committee's chair.

'Considering the loss of lives in the accidents, the reputational harm to the company, and the negative impact on future sales of the aircraft, we believe these incidents indicate a potential lapse in the board's oversight of risk management,' Glass Lewis said in a report to clients ahead of Boeing's annual meeting in Chicago on 29 April 2019.

In the past few years, numerous companies and their external advisors have described the many rounds of approvals, comments, and reviews behind their crisis management blueprints – some of which run to hundreds of pages. This is a laudable and encouraging trend, which should greatly reduce the risk of future corporate crises taking on the scale of earlier ones such as the BP oil spill of 2010. These blueprints are even more effective when they take into consideration culturally specific modes of communication, reporting lines, and other intricacies of the board's interaction with the C-suite. On the other hand, placing too much focus on the formal, ritualistic aspects of drafting a plan – as often happens in organisations and bureaucracies – may lead to a false sense of security, and a feeling that 'as long as it is written down, it will work'.

Notwithstanding the limitations of the formal, hard-wired aspects of crisis management, the board's structure can in itself be a good source of resilience in decision-making – especially if it systematically prevents conflicts of interest. The alternative, with personalities in the thick of a crisis outwardly projecting ambiguous and at times conflicted roles – has proven to have far-reaching negative ramifications.

In 2016, as Volkswagen reeled from its emissions cheating scandal, the elevation of the company's chief financial officer to be the head of its supervisory board led to further embarrassment. Critics said this was tantamount to handpicking someone who had been directly complicit in the scandal and giving him the task of diffusing and investigating the situation.

The restructuring of Tesla's board in 2018, which followed seemingly erratic communication from CEO and Chair Elon Musk about possibly taking the company private, was also controversial. As part of a settlement with the US Securities and Exchange Commission, Musk was forced to step down as Tesla's chair. However, the board was still dominated by the famous CEO (who is also the company's largest shareholder). Despite calls for an independent chair who could exert some control over Musk, the board chose an independent director who had not strongly counteracted him before.

Procedure vs. Authenticity

For directors in particular, rising to the occasion during a crisis requires a lot more than following 'what's in the manual'. Whereas an overwhelming series of events may lead management to frame and view problems in narrow – typically technical or legal – terms, the board's challenge will be to reassure shareholders and other groups of stakeholders with measured, appropriate messages. To reassure and resonate with these audiences, such messages must be seen as authentic. They will therefore need to be rooted in directors' personal sense of courage, character, empathy, and breadth of vision, rather than plucked from 'how to' guidelines. In other words, board members must live their own values in addition to those of the organisation.

No single individual can provide this deep alignment with a company's ethics, empathy, and social values. Gaining and maintaining trust, or rebuilding it in the aftermath of cataclysmic events, requires strong and sustained board leadership through values, integrity, and good governance. Empathy, professionalism, and experience are always fundamental to good board work, but become especially valuable during crises. In this respect, a board member with direct experience of previous crises can be a highly useful asset to the organisation.

One of the reasons why many Morgan Stanley employees escaped harm during the 11 September 2001, World Trade Center attacks was that the firm's head of security Rick Rescorla had indeed 'seen it before', albeit on a smaller scale. Rescorla had been appalled at the evacuation effort he witnessed during a previous bombing at the Center in 1993. He therefore made sure that in the years afterwards, employees diligently prepared and practised for another evacuation in the future. His preparedness and the procedures he implemented reportedly saved many lives on 9/11 (although sadly not his own) in the immediate aftermath of the attack on the South Tower.

Communicate Your Way to Rebuilding Trust

Organisations will draw on other less tangible – but equally crucial – assets in times of crisis. These include trust, reputation, and goodwill, and need to be accumulated and cultivated all year round. When a company has failed to establish a sufficiently deep pool of trust with clients, partners, or the general public, there will be a strong propensity to believe news that casts it in a negative light.

How can companies build trust, or recover from a perceived trust deficit? Effective communication goes a long way – if what the organisation says is genuine and compelling. They may choose to communicate their vision, generate a sense of urgency about implementing new initiatives, or simply share stories of their successes and accomplishments ('do well – and also let them know you've done well!').

Importantly, building and rebuilding trust must be a targeted effort, as proposed in Figure 12.1 above. Boards should have a view of the organisation's likely allies and champions. These can include opinion leaders and experts who can bestow credibility on the company's efforts; network leaders (the 'old-timers' or 'movers and shakers') who exert informal influence; and social leaders who can extend support. Benchmarking exercises and satisfaction surveys with different stakeholders can help to send out powerful signals about challenging the status quo. Do we have the right allies, in government, in unions, in customers' associations? Having mapped these out, and coupled with a few quick wins, strong management of the crisis can create a sense of positive momentum. But if a company has not continuously built a sense of reciprocity and goodwill with all partners, any effort aimed at regaining trust may come across as self-serving and calculating. It is healthy to ask for support – provided the organisation has already established a strong foundation of goodwill.

A STRATEGY FOR
REBUILDING TRUST

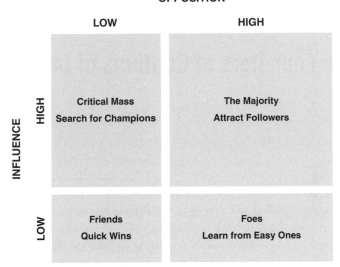

Figure 12.1   Mapping Influencers for Rebuilding Trust

There is a growing expectation that organisations and their boards will not only know what to do in a crisis, but will emerge from it battle-hardened and stronger than before. To handle a crisis in a way that strengthens its reputation, a company needs to draw deeply on existing organisational values and competences. In preparing for, responding to, and recovering from a corporate crisis, the board cannot remain in the comfort zone of an oversight mode. In normal times, crisis preparation should be a regular, yearly exercise for directors, involving the fine-tuning of relevant processes and information.

When emerging from a crisis, organisations may understandably just want to return to normal and regain a feeling of control. In such circumstances, reflection and introspection may not be top of management's list of priorities. But this is precisely where the board can display meaningful leadership by nudging management to draw out the most important lessons from the crisis – including crisis planning, risk management, and how to rebuild trust.

The remainder of Part II focuses on a second major area of board failure: integrity. In the next chapter we look at the responsibility of directors to deal with conflicts of interest, before concluding this section by examining the board's critical role in overseeing fraud risk.

13

The Four Tiers of Conflicts of Interest[1]

Addressing conflicts of interest with integrity is at the heart of the personal responsibilities of a leading board member. Although to some degree ever present, such conflicts can be dealt with efficiently and with awareness. Mapping them, accompanied by a personal (or public) register, can certainly help. We can distinguish four tiers of conflicts of interest (see Figure 13.1).

A **tier-I conflict** is an actual or potential conflict between a board member and the company. The concept is straightforward: a director should not take advantage of his or her position. As the key decision-makers within the organisation, board members should act in the interest of important stakeholders, whether the company's owners or society at large, and not in their own. Major conflicts of interest could include, but are not restricted to, salaries and perks, misappropriation of company assets, self-dealing, appropriating corporate opportunities, insider trading, and neglecting board work. All directors are expected to act ethically at all times, promptly declare any material facts or potential conflicts of interest and take appropriate corrective action.

Tier-II conflicts arise when a board member's duty of loyalty to stakeholders or the company is compromised. This would happen when certain board members exercise influence over the others through compensation, favours, a relationship, or psychological manipulation. Even though some directors describe themselves as

---

[1] This chapter was initially written as an article with Abraham Lu.

FOUR-TIER PYRAMID
CONFLICTS OF INTEREST

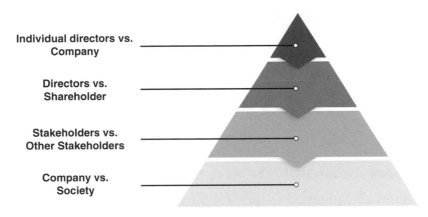

Individual directors vs.
Company

Directors vs.
Shareholder

Stakeholders vs.
Other Stakeholders

Company vs.
Society

Figure 13.1   The Four-Tier Pyramid of Conflicts of Interest

'independent of management, company, or major shareholders', they may find themselves faced with a conflict of interest if they are forced into agreeing with a dominant board member. Under particular circumstances, some independent directors form a distinct stakeholder group and demonstrate loyalty only to the members of that group. They tend to represent their own interest rather than that of the company.

A **tier-III conflict** emerges when the interests of stakeholder groups are not appropriately balanced or harmonised. Shareholders appoint board members, usually outstanding individuals, based on their knowledge and skills and their ability to make good decisions. Once a board has been formed, its members have to face conflicts of interest between stakeholders and the company, between different stakeholder groups, and within the same stakeholder group. When a board's core duty is to care for a particular set of stakeholders, such as shareholders, all rational and high-level decisions are geared to favour that particular group, although the concerns of other stakeholders may still be recognised. Board members have to address any conflicts responsibly and balance the interests of all individuals involved in a contemplative, proactive manner.

Tier-IV conflicts arise when a company acts in its own interests at the expense of society. The doctrine of maximising profitability may be used as justification for deceiving customers, polluting the environment, evading taxes, squeezing suppliers, and treating employees as commodities. Companies that operate in this way are not contributors to society. Instead, they are viewed as value extractors. Conscientious directors are able to distinguish good from bad and are more likely to act as stewards for safeguarding long-term, responsible value creation for the common good of humanity. When a company's purpose is in conflict with the interests of society, board members need to take an ethical stand, exercise care, and make sensible decisions.

Tier-I Conflicts: Individual Directors vs. Company

Directors are supposed to 'possess the highest personal and professional ethics, integrity and values, and be committed to representing the long-term interest of the shareowners'.[2] However, in many cases, shareholders have sued directors for taking advantage of the company. An actual or potential conflict between a board member and a company is called a tier-I conflict.

A company is normally considered as a separate legal entity that is independent from its directors, executives, and shareholders. Powerful directors, such as founders or dominant shareholders, can be accused of misappropriating company assets if they are found stealing from their own company; directors who trade on the basis of material, non-public information can be sued for insider trading; those caught accepting bribes or working for competing companies may be asked to resign; and directors who sign agreements on behalf of the company that mainly contribute to their own enrichment may be charged with self-dealing.

For example, the case of Guth vs. Loft Inc. in the US in 1939 addressed the issue of individuals pursuing business opportunities for self-enrichment. The president of Loft, who was also the owner of Grace Corp., was found to have used Loft's capital, credit, facilities, and employees to acquire and grow Pepsi Cola for himself rather than for Loft.[3] In the language of the court, 'corporate officers and

---

[2] General Electric Company (2016). Governance Principles, p. 1.
[3] Kershaw, D. (2005). Does it matter how the law thinks about corporate opportunities? *Legal Studies* (25)4: 533–538.

directors are not permitted to use their position of trust and confidence to further their private interests'.

When board members fail to dedicate the necessary effort, commitment, and time to their board work, it can result in a conflict between them and the company. Because directors often serve on multiple boards, they may not be able to allocate sufficient time to governing any one firm. According to the Spencer Stuart US Board Index, approximately 25% of S&P 500 boards do not impose a limit on the number of board positions. Stuart Crainer and Des Dearlove have described how directors who were unable to devote enough time to a board 'stuffed the document in their briefcases, all 200 pages or so, and leafed through them in the taxi to the meeting. They extracted, at random, a paper, formulated a trick question and entered the meeting room ready to fire. After all, board work is a power game'.[4] Lack of effort, focus, and dedication are types of conflicts of interest that have not yet received the systematic attention they deserve.

It is well understood that tier-I conflicts arise when directors take advantage of their positions. But when they lack commitment and dedication to their duties, the conflict of interest is somewhat more subtle and much less obvious. Companies need to issue guidelines regarding directors' conflicts of interest and ensure that they follow these rules and act in the interest of the organisations they serve.

Companies can self-assess their exposure to tier-I conflicts by asking the following questions:

- Has the company previously experienced situations in which individual directors have taken advantage of the company through compensation, self-dealing, stealing, insider trading, accepting bribes, or appropriating opportunities for personal benefit?
- How could negligence of, or lack of commitment to, board work present a conflict of interest?

Having clear guidelines, expectations, and standards, including the signing of a code of conduct at the time of a director's appointment, are all helpful.

---

[4] Crainer, S. and D. Dearlove (2008). Boards of deflectors. *Business Strategy Review* 19(1): 59–63.

Tier-II Conflicts: Directors vs. Stakeholders

To whom do board members owe their loyalty? This depends very much on law and tradition, and on the prevailing legal system and social norms or the company's specific situation. For example, directors might declare that they owe their duty of loyalty to shareholders, the company itself, certain stakeholders (customers, employees, or society), or other board members, or a combination thereof.

The Institutional Loyalty of Board Directors

In the US, directors often have a duty of loyalty toward the company's shareholders. The idea of maximising shareholder value has been a strong concept in the past, with the view that executives and directors should focus solely on creating value for shareholders. Others argue that since directors and executives are paid by the company, they are employees and should thus focus on the interests of the firm rather than on those of the shareholders.

According to experts such as the late Lynn Stout, a former professor of corporate and business law at Cornell Law School, shareholder value maximisation is a choice, not a legal requirement. The assumption that shareholders are principals and that directors are their agents is legally incorrect. Corporate law clearly states that shareholders cannot control directors or executives. They have the right to vote on the positions of the directors of the board, and to recover damage compensation from directors and executives if they are found to have stolen from the company, but they have no right to tell executives how to run the business.[5] After all, shareholders are only owners of a financial claim on the assets of the firm, and not the owners of the assets themselves. They rank among other financial claimants in that way.

Being loyal to shareholders is, in any case, easier said than done. Shareholders come and go, and their interest in the company is limited to their shareholding period. Their interests vary depending on their investment horizon, degree of diversification, and investment strategy. Given the many types of shareholders, reaching a consensus for all of them is a daunting task. Individuals and families who invest for their retirement or to fund future expenses are often represented

---

[5] Stout, L. (2012). The problem of corporate purpose. *Issues in Governance Studies Legal Studies* #48: June. Washington, DC: The Brookings Institution.

by institutional investors such as sovereign wealth funds, banks, hedge funds, pension funds, insurance companies, and other financial institutions. These powerful representatives interact with board members frequently and exercise most of the pressure, but when they put their own interest before that of the ultimate shareholders, interests could be misaligned. For example, the representatives may be striving for short-term personal gain or compensation while the ultimate investors may want the same as all other stakeholders: the creation and preservation of the corporation's long-term sustainable wealth.

If maximising shareholder value is a widely accepted norm, then board members would be better positioned if they announced that their loyalty lay with the ultimate shareholders. This would lead them to become stewards of the company, and reduce the risk of their being distracted by proposals that generate immediate stock returns but endanger the long-term prospects of the company.

A 2013 study of directors' duties in all 27 EU member states and Croatia (which has since become a member too) showed that in Europe, directors primarily have a duty of loyalty to their company. This principle is universally accepted and undisputed across the 27 EU countries.[6] All board members, including shareholder representatives, are required to balance the interests of all stakeholders with the long-term prospects of the company. To help ensure this, the composition and independence of the board of directors are often defined in national corporate governance codes.

For example, according to the Swedish Corporate Governance Code, 'boards of Swedish listed companies are composed entirely or predominantly of non-executive directors'. The Code also states that a majority of the members of the board should be independent of the company and its management. Although at least two members must also be independent of the company's major shareholders, it is still possible for these shareholders to appoint a majority of members with whom they have close ties.[7] According to the Code, some directors could also have links with minority shareholders, management, or other stakeholders. These ties with various stakeholder groups potentially create divided loyalties for directors.

---

[6] Gerner-Beuerle, C., P. Paech and E.-P. Schuster (2013). *Study on Directors' Duties and Liability*. London: LSE Enterprise Limited.
[7] Swedish Corporate Governance Board (2015). The Swedish Corporate Governance Code. p. 9.

Table 13.1 Director's Independence Questionnaire

Directors are often requested to answer the following questions to self-assess their independence.

Are you a substantial shareholder or an officer of, or otherwise associated directly with, a substantial shareholder of the company?	Yes/ No
Have you, within the last five years, been employed in an executive capacity by the company or another group member, or been a director after ceasing to hold any such employment?	Yes/ No
Within the last five years, have you been a professional advisor or a consultant to the company or another group member, or an employee materially associated with the service provided?	Yes/ No
Are you affiliated with a material supplier or customer or other related parties of the company or another group member, or an officer of or otherwise associated directly or indirectly with a material supplier or customer or other related parties?	Yes/ No
Do you have any material contractual relationship with the company or another group member other than as a director of the company?	Yes/ No
How many years have you served on the Board and do you believe that this time is such that it could reasonably be perceived to materially interfere with your ability to act in the best interests of the company?	Yes/ No
Do you have any interest or any business or other relationship which could, or could reasonably be perceived to, materially interfere with your ability to act in the best interests of the company?	Yes/ No

The laws of some countries require stakeholder representatives on boards to serve the interests of their respective principals in some situations. For example, bank directors who are appointed to the board when a company is in financial distress must be loyal to their bank, which lent money to the firm in question. While it may be perfectly legal for such interested parties to be members of the board, it can help if each stakeholder group puts their ultimate objectives on the table before starting negotiations. This allows minority shareholders to have their perspectives heard, which in turn may make majority shareholders more inclined to balance their own interests with those of others.

The Influence of Domineering Board Members on Others

Both independent and interested directors can potentially be influenced by powerful CEOs, chairpersons, or other directors. Board members may also forsake their institutional duties out of personal loyalty to the CEO or chair. One way directors can determine whether they have been overly influenced is by asking themselves, 'Have I been influenced or manipulated in order to agree with others?'

Persuasive influence often comes from people holding the combined role of CEO and chairperson, as they can sway other board members' compensation. Even if a board primarily comprises independent directors, it may not be able to remain truly independent from the management. If most of the board members generate a significant total income from board compensation packages, their independence may be at risk if they are not willing to sacrifice their standard of living for the integrity of their decision making.

Personal, family, and professional relationships can also potentially affect an independent director's judgement. The social connections between directors and CEOs or chairpersons cannot always be thoroughly checked. For example, retired CEOs may remain as chairs of their companies' boards, and many of the directors may owe their jobs to them. Or the CEO may invite close friends to join the board as directors. In both cases, the directors in question may be influenced by a sense of loyalty or duty, even if the CEO or chairperson is not acting in the best interests of the company, its shareholders, or other stakeholders. Independent directors may be reluctant to contradict the views of a CEO or chair to whom they felt they owed their loyalty and may instead either comply or step down from their role.

Chanda Kochhar, the former high-profile CEO of India's ICICI Bank, was charged on 24 January 2019 by the country's Central Bureau of Investigation with allegedly defrauding India's third largest lender. It is alleged that Kochhar misused her position to sanction loans, thereby cheating the bank of approximately $242 million.[8]

ICICI Bank found its former chief executive guilty of violating internal bank policies and professional misconduct, following a lengthy investigation. The quid pro quo activities were first uncovered in 2016, when a whistleblower accused Kochhar of nepotism and favouritism. The whistleblower alleged that ICICI had granted loans to the Videocon group and 12 of its subsidiaries, allegedly in violation of the bank's lending policies, in exchange for an investment by the group's owner Venugopal Dhoot in NuPower Renewables – a business owned by Kochhar's husband.

The bank said it would treat Kochhar's resignation as CEO in October 2018 as a termination and would recover all bonuses paid to her between April 2009 and March 2018, estimated at millions of dollars.[9]

---

[8] https://qz.com/india/1532625/icici-banks-kochhar-kamath-booked-by-cbi-in-videocon-fraud-case/.

[9] https://www.bbc.com/news/world-asia-india-47067863.

Boardrooms are dynamic places where heated discussions occur. Those occupying positions of power, such as the CEO and the chair, may manipulate directors into agreeing with their preferred decisions by using psychological tactics. Tone of voice and eye contact, for example, can orient the discussion, rebuff criticism, or intimidate others. This happens even in sophisticated large-cap company boards. In some cases, board members may feel as though they are being victimised or manipulated, while those dominating the discussion may just think they are leading a dynamic interaction. Such unbalanced dynamics, including superiority and inferiority complexes, reduce the effectiveness of board discussions and prevent independent directors from exercising their duty.

Board Directors Organised as a Self-Interested Stakeholder Group

Regulators and researchers have argued that boards should include a greater number of independent directors to ensure that business decisions are not disproportionately influenced by powerful stakeholders. The Spencer Stuart Board Index 2018 survey confirmed that S&P 500 boards elected 428 new independent directors, a 9% increase from the previous year.[10]

The growing tensions between independent directors and management are causing independent directors to form distinct stakeholder groups, which are often recognised by regulators. Such coalitions are growing in power and authority as independent board members increasingly remain loyal to each other in the boardroom, subjugating the interests of the organisations they are supposed to represent to their own. In other words, these stakeholder groups have their own motives and interests, and the strategic decisions they make could benefit themselves rather than the organisations they are paid to serve.

In certain countries, unless otherwise specified, directors decide what their salary, shares, and options will be. If no independent body such as a shareholder committee or a regulator oversees the compensation of directors, this can easily lead to a direct conflict of interest with the company. In the 2015 case of Calma vs. Templeton, the Delaware Chancery Court in the United States allowed a claim that challenged the directors' stock compensation from going forward because it was considered 'excessive'. The compensation

---

[10] Spencer Stuart (2018). Spencer Stuart US Board Index.

plan limited the number of shares to 1 million per year per partici-
pant, which represented a value of US$55 million at the time of the
lawsuit. The court determined that the entire decision process for
compensation was unfair because the awards to the outside directors
were decided by the recipients themselves.[11]

In a *Harvard Business Review* article entitled 'What CEOs really
think of their boards', one CEO was quoted as saying, 'They like
their board seats – it gives them some prestige. They can be reluctant
to consider recapitalization, going private, or merging – "Don't you
know, we might lose our board positions!" I have been shocked by
board members saying, "that would be an interesting thing to do,
but what about us?"' Another CEO was quoted as saying, 'In one
situation, we had a merger not go through because of who was going
to get what number of board seats . . . It is still the most astounding
conversation of my life.'[12] In another case, the chair of a large European bank was invited to sit on the board of a large-cap industrial
while the CEO of that firm came to be on the board of the bank.
Exploring the legitimacy and productivity of such an arrangement is
certainly worthwhile.

High compensation does not always have the intended positive
effect. The more compensation directors receive, the greater is their
personal desire to be re-elected. As a result, they increasingly focus
on remaining on the board, enjoying their status and fame, boosting
their compensation further, and obtaining more directorships on
other boards.

The structure and level of directors' compensation varies internationally. According to the German Corporate Governance Code, the
compensation of supervisory board directors consists of a combination of cash and shares, and is linked to an individual's background
and involvement in board and committee functions. At Deutsche
Bank, 25% of the directors' compensation was converted into shares
of the company based on the average share price during the last 10
trading days of the year.[13]

---

[11] Katy, D. and L. McIntosh (2105). Dealing with director compensation. *New York Law Journal* (21 May 2015).
[12] Sonnenfeld, J., M. Kusin, and E. Walton (1013). What CEOs really think of their boards. *Harvard Business Review* (April 2013).
[13] Deutsche Bank (2014). Annual Report.

In China, not all board members receive compensation from the company they serve. For example, shareholder representatives working full time at the Industrial and Commercial Bank of China (ICBC) receive their compensation from China's sovereign wealth fund – China Investment Corporation (CIC). This means that state owners oversee the compensation of both executive and non-executive directors, which effectively eliminates the possibility of self-dealing. At ICBC, the modest pay still attracts high-quality independent directors, especially those with positive character traits such as conscientiousness, integrity, competence, judgement, focus, and dedication, which cannot be encouraged or discouraged solely with money.[14]

Questions aimed at reflecting on tier-II conflicts of interest could include the following:

- In our legal system, to whom do board members owe their duty of loyalty?
- Can we define whether, in our specific context, loyalty to shareholders or loyalty to the company is paramount? Are there minority shareholders to be concerned about?
- If a director claims to owe his or her duty of loyalty to shareholders, would one be able to specify who the shareholders are? Are they fund managers or activists, large shareholders on the board, minority shareholders not on the board, or the ultimate shareholders?
- If we directors claim allegiance to company stakeholders, do we have a good mapping of our stakeholders?
- Can a director be fully independent when the CEO or chairperson decides on the compensation and succession of board members?
- If a director is independent, can we specify who they are independent from (e.g. management, shareholders, other stakeholders)?
- Are we aware that directors can form coalitions and leverage their full control of the board to benefit one another in an 'I'll scratch your back, you scratch mine' type of relationship?

[14] Cossin D. and H.A. Lu (2012). The ICBC Path to Chinese Governance. IMD Case No. IMD-1-0327.

Tier-III Conflicts: Stakeholders vs. Other Stakeholders

Board members have another duty: exercising due diligence and good judgement when making decisions. In Germany, duty of care is a legal obligation. The law states that 'executive members have to exercise the care of an ordinary and conscientious business leader'. In the UK, ignorance can be deemed criminal for directors of financial institutions. Directors have a fiduciary responsibility to the company from the moment they are recruited, and they are expected to display a high standard of expertise, care, and diligence by gathering as much information as possible and considering all reasonable alternatives in order to make sensible decisions.

The trust placed in directors gives them maximum autonomy in decision-making, and decisions are not questioned unless they are deemed irrational. This business judgement rule protects directors from potential liabilities, as their decisions are not tainted by personal interest. Although directors are not allowed to act in their own interests, they can promote the interests of a particular stakeholder group against the company, or the interests of one group of stakeholders against another, or they can favour one subgroup over another within the same stakeholder group. It is up to directors to make wise decisions when stakeholders are in conflict.

If a board is composed of interested directors who remain loyal to their respective stakeholders while building effective board work, then stakeholder representatives need to cooperate and find the optimal coalition to address common interests. Directors must keep in mind the interests of weak or distant stakeholders to ensure their interests are not overlooked.

Conflicts of Interest Between Stakeholders and the Company

A company can be seen as an aggregation of stakeholders bound together by economic interest. All stakeholders expect to receive a sizable slice of the pie in exchange for their input. Each group of stakeholders has a different contractual arrangement with the company and distinct motives, which means they will be more likely to push for decisions that benefit themselves first and foremost. For example, creditors, such as banks, will prefer the company to play it safe in order to maximise the chances that it will pay off its debt, but this low level of risk-taking could hurt the company's long-term growth potential. At the other end of the spectrum, shareholders can benefit from the successful outcome of a risky project while their losses are limited to the amount of their investment, so they are more likely to encourage risk-taking, even if it means putting the company's survival at risk.

Employees receive cash compensation plus benefits. By negotiating above-average compensation for workers, unions put the profitability of the company at risk. Companies have gone bankrupt as a result of out-of-control labour costs. In 2008, for instance, workers at GM, Ford, and Chrysler were among the most highly paid in the US with over US$70 an hour in wages and benefits once retirement benefits were included in the calculation. This was considerably higher than the average hourly labour cost of US$25.36 for all private-sector workers, and the three car manufacturers were paying about US$30 per hour more than their Asian rivals operating in the US.[15] GM and Chrysler declared bankruptcy, whereas Ford managed to survive without bailout funds. Eventually, all three recovered by adjusting labour costs to be more or less in line with those of their competitors, which they did by creating private trusts to finance the benefits of future retirees.

As a result of the financial difficulties that many companies encountered during the 1980s and early 1990s, some US firms allowed labour unions to designate one or more members of the board of directors, a practice well developed in some European countries. The first major US company to elect a union leader to its board was Chrysler in 1980. Board members representing unions have a delicate balancing act to play, and they need to be aware of the potential conflicts of interest inherent in their role. On the one hand, if they push for high wage increases, they could lead the company into difficulties and negatively affect all stakeholders in the long run. On the other hand, if they agree to substantial wage reductions, they would hurt the workers they are supposed to defend and represent.

Consumers and customers depend on companies for the reliable supply of products and services. When a firm changes its pricing strategy, this can potentially have serious repercussions for consumers. In September 2015, Turing Pharmaceuticals raised the price of

---

[15] Sherk, J. (2008). UAW workers actually cost the big three automakers $70 an hour. *Heritage* (December 2008).

Daraprim – a 62 year-old drug for the treatment of a life-threatening parasite infection – from US$13.50 to US$750 per tablet. For some patients, treatment became unbearably expensive, and hospitals were forced to use less-effective alternatives to limit costs. Martin Shkreli, the 32 year-old founder and chief executive of Turing, said, 'This is still one of the smallest pharmaceutical products in the world . . . It really doesn't make sense to get any criticism for this'.[16] But in December 2015, Shkreli was arrested for 'repeatedly losing money for investors and lying to them about it, illegally taking assets from one of his companies to pay off debtors in another'.[17]

It is challenging for directors to decide which stakeholder group to prioritise when it comes to value distribution and slicing the pie. Only integrity and good judgement skills can help in the many ambiguous situations that boards face. In conflicts, customers can hurt companies, and companies can harm the interests of customers. Closely involved stakeholders, such as creditors, employees, top management, and shareholders, all have motives to push for decisions that benefit themselves but may potentially hurt the company's interests in the long run.

Conflicts of Interest Between Different Classes of Stakeholders

Conflicts can arise between different groups of stakeholders, such as shareholders and creditors. Creditors, such as banks, play an important role in corporate governance systems. In some countries, they not only lend to firms but also hold equity so that they can have board representation. In the US, regulations prevent banks from dealing with debt–equity conflicts through equity ownership as they are not allowed to hold stakes in a firm to which they lend (note that this can get confused with modern asset management). With the Federal Reserve's quantitative-easing programme, share buybacks became the preferred way for companies to boost their stock prices for the benefit of shareholders. In 2015, S&P 500 index companies returned more money to shareholders through share buybacks and dividend payments than they earned. Some of them even borrowed money to pay dividends. This represents a direct transfer of value

---

[16] Pollack, A. (2015). Drug goes from $13.50 a tablet to $750, overnight. *The New York Times* (20 September 2015).
[17] Smythe, C. and K. Geiger (2015). Shkreli, drug price gouger, denies fraud and posts bail. *Bloomberg Business* (17 December 2015).

from creditors to shareholders, since a higher level of debt increases the probability of default and reduces the value of the creditor's claim on the assets of the firm.

Executives may sometimes act controversially in the name of shareholders' interests. Lou Gerstner had a record of fixing ailing companies and was credited with rescuing IBM through tough decisions, including massive layoffs. One major change took place in 1999, when IBM under Gerstner shocked long-term employees by overhauling its pension plan to help cut costs. In 2002, Gerstner ended his tenure with an annual salary of over US$1.5 million, an annual pension of over US$1.1 million, and over US$288,000 in deferred compensation in 2001 alone.[18] IBM employees later filed a class-action lawsuit over the pension changes, and in 2004 the company agreed to pay US$320 million to current and former employees in a settlement.[19] If an executive's compensation is linked to cost savings on the back of employees, the two groups are considered to be in a conflict of interest.

Even when executives proclaim that they are dedicated to shareholders' interests, the fact that they try hard to minimise shareholder involvement in corporate governance shows there is a conflict of interest between the two groups. In a 2013 referendum, Swiss voters passed a popular measure 'against corporate rip-offs', which allowed shareholders to control the transparency and format of top executives' income and called for jail time for non-executive directors who would not comply. The reform, which was approved by 67.9% of voters, stipulated that the shareholders of all publicly listed Swiss companies must elect all the members of the firm's remuneration committee, and that all board directors are subject to annual re-election. Supporters spent CHF 200 000 to promote the initiative, while opponents spent CHF 8 million trying to block it. The initiative made it compulsory for shareholders to vote their shares. This Swiss referendum was a strong social response to the conflict of interest between executives and shareholders, and between executives and society at large.

The initiative was launched by businessman Thomas Minder, whose own story illustrated how entrenched executives could

---

[18] 'IBM in the Gerstner Years: An Employees' Perspective,' IBMEmployee.com (April 2002).
[19] Johnston, D.C. (2004). IBM employees get $320million in pension suit. *The New York Times* (30 September 2004).

damage all other parties to benefit themselves. Minder's company, Trybol, supplied cosmetics to Swissair, and suffered significant losses when the airline went bankrupt in 2001 due to a failed expansion strategy. Before the bankruptcy, it was made public that Swissair's top executive was to receive a golden parachute totalling CHF 12.5 million. Minder was so angry that he started the 'anti-rip-off' initiative.[20]

Could certain stakeholder groups, such as management, creditors, or shareholders, benefit specifically from corporate decisions that could potentially hurt other stakeholders? The answer is yes when the value increase for one class of stakeholder is directly linked to the value reduction of another.

Conflicts of Interest within a Group of Stakeholders

In closely held companies, large shareholders can use their control power to exploit minority shareholders. More often, directors are influenced by the controlling shareholder sitting on the board. Using their representation on the board, these shareholders influence capital structure, dividend policy, and investment strategy, or their position with regard to mergers and acquisitions, and might well be in conflict with other shareholders.

In May 2015, Volkswagen AG's 20-member supervisory board included only one independent director. The founding Piëch and Porsche families dominated the board in alliance with labour unions and the state of Lower Saxony. As we saw in Chapter 2, Volkswagen Chair Ferdinand Karl Piëch made the following comment to the media without the board's knowledge: 'I am distancing myself from [Volkswagen CEO Martin] Winterkorn'.[21] These words further inflamed a decades-long battle between the two shareholding families behind Volkswagen and Porsche. Piëch probably instigated this controversy with the intention of extending his influence as a controlling shareholder. But during the shareholder showdown, Winterkorn won the support of some of the other members of the Porsche family, labour leaders and the state of Lower Saxony. After losing

---

[20] Schneider, M. and E. Wolff (2013). Swiss referendum against rip-offs. wsws.org (2 March 2013).
[21] Hawranek, D. and D. Kurbjuweit (2015). Blood feud: behind the scenes of Volkswagen's dynastic battle. *Spiegel Online International* (6 May 2015).

the battle, Piëch resigned as chair. However, just a few months later, Winterkorn himself had to resign as CEO amid the Volkswagen emissions scandal.

The Volkswagen case shows that it is difficult even for the board of a sophisticated, large-scale enterprise (with 600 000 employees and EUR200 billion in revenue) to optimise the interests of shareholders when these conflict. In practice, when most directors on a board are shareholders or stakeholder representatives, infighting becomes a common issue. Minority shareholders are vulnerable when the controlling owner attempts to squeeze out the other shareholders and gain control of more corporate resources, for example by buying, selling, or leasing assets at non-market prices.

Conflicts within groups of stakeholders are not limited to shareholders. Creditors on boards could have an unfair advantage over other creditors if they use insider information to shield themselves from potential trouble and hurt other classes of debt holders, especially when the firm is in financial distress. Employees can be in conflict with customers' interests. Even customers can be in conflict with society's interests.

The following questions can help directors reflect on tier-III conflicts of interest:

- Is a key stakeholder group pushing for decisions that may benefit them but potentially hurt the interests of the company in the long run?
- How aligned or misaligned are our shareholders, and on which matters?
- How can the pie be divided when there are conflicts of interest between different classes of stakeholders, such as shareholders vs. customers, executives vs. employees, or executives vs. shareholders?
- How can conflicts of interest between subgroups of one particular stakeholder group be dealt with?
- How can I as a director make a wise decision when stakeholders have conflicting incentives and goals?

Tier-IV Conflicts: Company vs. Society

How a company views its purpose will affect its notions of responsibility, accountability, and how it creates value. Business ethics have been discussed since the market economy emerged more than

750 years ago.[22] In general, companies and society are not in conflict. Corporations contribute to society by inventing new technologies, fulfilling consumers' demands for goods and services, and creating jobs; society creates the conditions that allow companies to harness their potential for the common good of humanity.

In 1981, the Business Roundtable, an association of chief executive officers of leading US companies working to promote sound public policy, stated that 'Corporations have a responsibility, first of all, to make available to the public quality goods and services at fair prices, thereby earning a profit that attracts investment to continue and enhance the enterprise, provide jobs, and build the economy', and that 'the long-term viability of the corporation depends upon its responsibility to the society of which it is a part. The well-being of society also depends upon profitable and responsible business enterprises'.[23]

Executives initially accepted this definition of the responsibilities of companies. However, their stance changed dramatically in 1997, when the Business Roundtable redefined the purpose of a corporation in society as being 'to generate economic returns to its owners', adding that if 'the CEO and the directors are not focused on shareholder value, it may be less likely the corporation will realise that value'.[24] Board members soon came under pressure to admit that the sole purpose of corporations was to maximise shareholder value.

If not managed properly, maximising returns for shareholders can strip value generation from other stakeholders – for example, by deceiving customers, defaulting on payments to creditors, squeezing suppliers and employees, and evading taxes. Indirect harmful effects on society include shaping the rules of the game (such as through lobbying to change a law, tax and accounting rules, monopolisation, and subsidies), pollution, market manipulation through collusion, and limiting the opportunities for future generations to improve their lives. Such behaviour may well increase payoffs to shareholders in the short term but will lead to the eventual demise of the corporation and the total destruction of long-term shareholder value. Extracting value from society is no recipe for long-term success.

---

[22] Vogel, D. (1991). Business ethics: new perspectives on old problems. *California Management Review* 33(4): 101–117.

[23] Yang, J.L. (2013). Maximising shareholder value: the goal that changed corporate America. *The Washington Post* (26 August 2013).

[24] Montier, J. (2014). The World's Dumbest Idea. GMO White Paper, December 2014.

The only class of stakeholders that benefits from this short-term value maximisation are chief executives enjoying high compensation, severance packages, and golden parachutes. According to *Equilar*, the median tenure of CEOs of the 500 largest companies in the US (S&P 500) was five years as of 2017.[25] When a CEO believes they could be dismissed at any time, they may be more inclined to take decisions that maximise their own income in the short term in the name of maximising shareholder value. If all CEOs behave in this manner and boards allow it, companies will end up doing more harm than good to society.

In a study for an earlier book on stewardship that I co-authored, companies potentially ranking highly on this dimension used a broad vocabulary in their annual 10-K reports to the US Securities and Exchange Commission to describe their relationships with other stakeholders. They used words including *air, carbon, child, children, climate, collaboration, communities, cooperation, CSR, culture, dialog, dialogue, ecological, economical, environment, families, science, stakeholder, transparency, and well-being.* This mirrored their long-term approach to building rapport with local communities and broader society.

By comparison, companies potentially ranking low in terms of stewardship used words like *appeal, arbitration, attorney, attorneys, claims, court, criticised, defendant, defendants, delinquencies, delinquency, denied, discharged, enforceability, jurisdiction, lawsuit, lawsuits, legislative, litigation, petition, petitions, plaintiff, punitive, rulings, settlement, settlements, and suit.* This indicates that companies rarely benefit from bad actions in the long run, as costs will come back to them in the form of litigation, sanctions, fines or public humiliation.[26]

The aftermath of the 2008 financial crisis demonstrated that greed does not pay. From 2008 to 2015, 20 of the world's biggest banks paid more than US$235 billion in fines for having manipulated currency and interest rates and deceived customers. For example, Bank of America alone paid approximately US$80 billion while JP Morgan Chase paid up to US$20 billion. These fines were intended to deter further wrongdoing and to change corporate culture.[27]

Society and various stakeholders place their trust in boards to run companies, and they hold them accountable for doing so. Directors

---

[25] Marcec, D. (2018). Equilar, Inc. (February 2018).

[26] Cossin, D. and O.B. Hwee (2016). *Inspiring Stewardship.* John Wiley and Sons.

[27] Dzimwasha, T. (2015). 20 global banks have paid $235bn in fines since the 2008 financial crisis. *International Business Times* (24 May 2015).

need to understand that a company cannot prosper if it is in conflict with society, even if some stakeholders may maximise their short-term profits. Furthermore, because board members have the power and authority to recruit, monitor, and support management, they are on the front line when it comes to changing the company's culture. In particular, this can include moving away from a short-term focus to considering the long term when resolving potential conflicts between the company and society.

Self-assessment questions to ponder with regard to this last dimension include:

- Why does our organisation exist?
- How does it create value?
- Is our company a contributor or a value-extractor in society? Where does it extract value? Where does it contribute?
- Do we have the courage to take an ethical stand when our company is in conflict with society?

A company is the nexus that links the interests of each stakeholder group within its ecosystem. The board is the decision-making body, and its successes and failures depend on the ability of directors to understand and manage the interests of key stakeholder groups. Decisions at the board level should be ethical and reasonably balanced.

Boards need to have a specific policy in place for dealing with **tier-I** conflicts of interest between individual directors and the company. This policy needs to specify processes for dealing in an open and transparent way with major actual and potential conflicts, such as misappropriation of assets; insufficient effort, focus and dedication to board work; self-dealing and related transactions; insider trading; and taking advantage of corporate opportunities. If possible, the policy should be signed by all directors and updated regularly, and conflicts of interest should be declared at each board meeting. A register of potential conflicts is also helpful.

To deal with **tier-II** conflicts, directors need to disclose their relationships with stakeholders. This gives them an opportunity to declare in advance who they represent. Even if the law requires all directors to represent the interests of the company, identifying their connections with specific stakeholder groups improves transparency and avoids the risk of conflicts of interest. It is also crucial to specify who nominates new directors, who decides on their compensation, how the pay structure and level are determined, and how pay is linked to performance and function. In performing their duties, all directors need to put aside their ego, follow rules in discussions, respect others, and avoid toxic behaviours in the boardroom. Coalitions can be beneficial when they aim to act in the best interest of the company, but can be harmful when they are formed with the aim of dominating the board or benefitting a particular stakeholder group.

Tier-III conflicts of interest can be minimised when directors and boards 'slice the company pie' properly in an effort to support cooperation and avoid retaliation, fines, infighting, or legal actions. Wise decision-making requires understanding deep-rooted conflicts between stakeholders and the company, between different stakeholder groups, and within a stakeholder group. No company can truly prosper without the input of each stakeholder group: responsible shareholders, understanding debt holders, innovative employees, satisfied customers, happy suppliers, great products and services, friendly communities, and effective and efficient government.

Tier-IV conflicts between the company and society are not only philosophical but can also have real impact. Solving them requires directors to act as moral agents who are able to distinguish 'good' from 'bad'. Do companies compensate stakeholders because they are useful or protected by law, or because they contributed to the success of the company? Should firms consider the interests of future generations who have not directly contributed to profitability and who are not represented on the board? Should companies make corporate sustainability investments because they are popular, because they portray the business favourably and increase profitability in the long run, or because they are a way to show true gratitude to all?

Good governance starts with the integrity and ethics of every director on every board. Directors have a moral obligation not to take advantage of the company, but rather to be loyal to it, make wise decisions, neutralise conflicts among stakeholders, and act in a socially responsible way. An ethical board sets the purpose of the company, which in turn influences all its dealings with stakeholders. The four-tier pyramid summarising the different levels of conflict of interest can help board members anticipate and identify potential conflicts, deal with these, and make sensible decisions to chart the company's future course.

In the concluding chapter of Part II, we will stay with the theme of integrity and assess the board's role in preventing high-level fraud.

CHAPTER 14

High-Level Fraud and Active Board Oversight

In September 2016, Wells Fargo reached a settlement with US regulators over alleged sales abuses at the bank, agreeing to pay $185 million in fines and $5 million to customers. In a fraud that extended over five years, Wells Fargo employees opened 1.5 million bank accounts and applied for 565 000 credit cards in their customers' names without the latter's knowledge. The objective was to meet sales targets for employees and generate fees for the bank. Democratic presidential candidate Hillary Clinton called the account openings 'outrageous behavior'. During a Senate Banking Committee hearing, Senator Elizabeth Warren drilled Wells Fargo Chair John Stumpf pointedly on ethics and accountability in what has become a reference questioning,[1] and concluded:

---

[1] At the September 2016 Senate Banking Committee hearing, Senator Elizabeth Warren questioned John Stumpf, chair and CEO of Wells Fargo, about the unauthorised opening of customer accounts. This refers to accountability and responsibility and the questions that can be asked in a powerful interrogation.

Warren: Mr. Stumpf, Wells Fargo's vision and values statement, which you frequently cite says: 'We believe in values lived not phrases memorized. If you want to find out how strong a company's ethics are, don't listen to what its people say, watch what they do'. So, let's do that. Since this massive years-long scam came to light, you have said repeatedly: 'I am accountable'. But what have you actually done to hold yourself accountable? Have you resigned as CEO or chair of Wells Fargo?

You should give back the money that you took while this scam was going on and you should be criminally investigated by both the Department of Justice and the Securities and Exchange Commission. This just isn't right.[2]

Fraud happens. According to Kroll's 2017/2018 Global Fraud Survey of 768 senior executives worldwide, 84% of companies reported that they had fallen victim to a fraud incident, a significant increase from 61% in 2012.[3] And according to the 2016 Global Fraud Study by the Association of Certified Fraud Examiners (ACFE), the median estimate of fraud loss was 5% of revenues. Applying this percentage to the 2014 Gross World Product of $74.16 trillion gives a projected potential total fraud loss of up to $3.7 trillion worldwide.[4] Fraud is a significant threat to organisations – large frauds have driven companies into bankruptcy, wiped out billions for investors, and cost numerous employees their jobs.

Stumpf: The board, I serve – **Warren:** Have you resigned? **Stumpf:** No, I have not. **Warren:** Alright. Have you returned one nickel of the millions of dollars that you were paid while this scam was going on? **Stumpf:** Well, first of all, this was by 1 percent of our people. **Warren:** That's not my question. This is about responsibility. Have you returned one nickel of the millions of dollars that you were paid while this scam was going on? **Stumpf:** The board will take care of that. **Warren:** Have you returned one nickel of the money you earned while this scam was going on? **Stumpf:** And the board will do – **Warren:** I will take that as a no, then. Have you fired a single senior executive? And by that, I don't mean regional manager or branch manager. I'm asking about the people who actually led your community banking division or your compliance division. **Stumpf:** We've made a change in our regional, to lead our regional banks – **Warren:** I just said I'm not asking regional managers. I'm not asking about branch managers. I'm asking if you have fired senior management, the people who actually led community banking division, who oversaw this fraud or the compliance division that was in charge of making sure that the bank complied with the law. **Stumpf:** Carrie Tolsted – **Warren:** Did you fire any of those people? **Stumpf:** No. **Warren:** No. OK, so you haven't resigned, you haven't returned a single nickel of your personal earnings, you haven't fired a single senior executive. Instead, evidently your definition of 'accountable' is to push the blame to your low-level employees who don't have the money for a fancy PR firm to defend themselves.
[2] Full transcript widely available, for example on https://www.entrepreneur.com/article/282737.
[3] Kroll (2016). Global Fraud Report Annual Edition 2015/16.
[4] Association of Certified Fraud Examiners (2016). Report to the Nations on Occupational Fraud and Abuse.

Who is responsible for the governance oversight of fraud control – the board, management, internal and external auditors, or everyone in the organisation? In the case of Wells Fargo, the chair and management blamed employees rather than the organisation's culture – the bank fired 5300 people in connection with the improper account openings. Investors in Wells Fargo had previously questioned the bank's governance practices and called for it to split the roles of chair and CEO. The bank answered that its governance structure already provided effective independent oversight of management. 'How can they argue against my proposal now? Where is the board? Where is the audit committee of the board? It appears they go to the meetings, they pick up their cheques and they go home', said Gerald Armstrong, an activist investor.[5]

Regulatory changes have made boards and management increasingly responsible for fraud control. An active board will not shy away from its responsibility to oversee fraud risk. In fact, the board has a critical role in dealing with organisational frauds committed by senior executives or directors, setting the tone at the top, and ensuring a strong ethical culture within the organisation. This chapter provides directors and boards with an oversight framework for predicting, preventing, detecting, and remedying fraud risk, as well as some questions aimed at encouraging senior executives to work on fraud control effectively.

Why Does High-Level Fraud Happen?

In the study of the psychology of criminal behaviour, the differential association theory developed by Edwin H. Sutherland is instrumental in explaining what drives a person to commit crime. People used to believe that criminal behaviour was inherited. Sutherland, however, proposed that such behaviour is learned via interaction with others – individuals learn the techniques, drivers, motives, attitudes, and rationalisations for criminal behaviour. In this view, an individual could commit crime if the perceived rewards for being law-abiding are exceeded by the perceived rewards for law-breaking. As a criminal and immoral activity, fraud is an inevitable part of society.

The ACFE has developed the Occupational Fraud and Abuse Classification System, also known as the Fraud Tree. The three major

---

[5] https://www.ft.com/content/07f4bae0-7a88-11e6-ae24-f193b105145e.

categories of occupational fraud are asset misappropriation, corruption, and financial statement fraud. Asset misappropriation includes skimming, theft, asset misuse, and larceny. Corruption includes conflicts of interest, bribery (kickbacks and bid rigging), illegal gifts, and economic extortion. And financial statement fraud includes over- or understating assets or income, and non-financial components such as inventories. In the ACFE's 2016 report, asset misappropriation occurred in more than 83% of all cases reported, but with the lowest losses among the three categories. Financial statement fraud, meanwhile, was involved in less than 10% of the cases, but caused a median loss of $975 000. Corruption fell in the middle in terms of both frequency and losses.

For ease of discussion, we can divide fraud into two categories: occupational and organisational. *Occupational* fraud happens when someone takes advantage of their position to break the rules for personal gain. For example, an employee might steal money from the cash register, a head of purchasing could take bribes or kickbacks to favour a particular supplier, one professional might send bills for hours not worked, and another could falsify documents or receipts for their own financial gain.

While studying embezzlement, Donald Cressey identified three elements of fraud motivation: opportunity, motivation, and rationalisation. Together, these form a 'fraud triangle' (see Figure 14.1).[6]

Cressey proposed that a potential fraudster would not commit fraud unless there is an opportunity – in the form of weak internal controls and the technical capabilities required to commit the fraud. The second element of the fraud triangle is the feeling of pressure, which can be real or imagined and drives the actual motivation to act. Examples include supporting a struggling family on low pay, high amounts of personal debt, unexpected medical expenses, family issues such as divorce, extramarital affairs or problems with children, as well as compulsive behaviour such as gambling, and alcohol or drug abuse. The final element – rationalisation – refers to how a potential fraudster justifies their actions before committing the fraud. Examples include 'I will pay back', 'They owe me', 'I earned it', 'I need it more than they do', 'It's only fair', and 'God will forgive me'. The fraud triangle became the most widely known theory of

---

[6] Cressey, D. (1953). *Other People's Money: A Study in the Social Psychology of Embezzlement.* Glencoe, IL: The Free Press.

FRAUD TRIANGLE

Figure 14.1   The Fraud Triangle.
Source: Based on data from 'Criminology,' by Edwin Hardin Sutherland and Donald Ray Cressey, Lippincott, 1978.

occupational fraud, in which all the elements – opportunity, pressure, and rationalisation – must be present for a fraud to happen.

Organisational fraud happens when senior management, board directors, or chairs commit fraud using the company itself. At Enron, WorldCom, and Tyco, for example, people at the highest levels of the organisation bent the rules or covered up sophisticated frauds. Organisational fraud destroys a company's reputation and shatters trust with stakeholders, including investors and employees, who are left to suffer when a fraud leads to bankruptcy. In the ACFE's 2016 study, only 19% of frauds were committed by owners or executives, but the median loss was $703 000. Employees and managers were more likely to commit fraud, but the losses were lower – $65 000 in the case of employee fraud, and $173 000 for managers. In one business school study, 56% of CFOs reported that the CEO had pressured them to misrepresent accounting.[7] And almost 70% of US SEC enforcement actions involving fraud reveal CEO participation.[8]

---

[7] Feng, M., W. Ge, S. Luo, and T.J. Shevlin (2010). Why do CFOs Become Involved in Material Accounting Manipulations? (12 May 2010). AAA 2009 Financial Accounting and Reporting Section (FARS) Paper.
[8] Annual report, Division of Enforcement, SEC, 2018.

In February 2018, the CEO of Switzerland's third largest bank – Raiffeisen Bank – Pierin Vincenz was accused of illegally enriching himself by making personal investments in two Raiffesisen subsidiaries, Aduno and Investnet. Raiffeisen Bank also joined the criminal probe as a complainant. Vincenz, who headed Raiffeisen from 1999 to 2015 during a period of expansion, was forced to step down from various other business roles as the investigation began. He resigned as chair of Swiss insurance group Helvetica and relinquished a similar position at power group Repower. He was also chair at Aduno during the period under investigation. Zurich's attorney general investigated the former Raiffeisen boss for potentially improper business management – including cashing in on company takeovers of the credit card company Aduno and the investment company Investnet. Vincenz's successor resigned in the aftermath of the scandal, stressing the impact of misbehaviours in an organisation.

Boards need to be aware that although executives and owners commit less than 20% of frauds, these tend to be more costly. This is because high-level fraudsters have greater access to assets and more authority to evade or override anti-fraud controls. In addition, their schemes are generally harder to detect and last longer. This chapter proposes a predictive model to help directors understand the four pre-conditions of organisational fraud: injustice, lax oversight, a problematic culture, and financial illiteracy.

FRAUD RISK

Figure 14.2   Fraud Risk at Board Level

Injustice

Unbalanced value distribution favouring a particular stakeholder group often leads to value extraction and organisational fraud. In the US, in an attempt to enforce the alignment of executive and shareholder interests, corporate boards often reward executives with shares and options. Not surprisingly, maximising shareholder value then directly translates into maximising profitability and share prices for personal financial gains. In many cases, incentivised executives become financial engineers and employ deceptive accounting techniques to boost stock prices. Former Enron CEO Jeffrey Skilling, for example, controlled the company's accounting procedures to 'massage' earnings and meet analysts' expectations.

Other corporate scandals involved more than accounting tricks. Mark Whitacre and other executives at Archer Daniels Midland Co. conspired with other companies to fix the global price of some chemicals. 'With my base salary and stock options combined, my total compensation was in the seven figures', Whitacre said. 'Much of my compensation was in stock options, where there was much incentive to increase company earnings to drive the stock price upward as fast as possible'.[9]

Should boards and executives maximise shareholder value? Many people would answer yes, because shareholders are often considered the owners of the company. But others disagree. Martin Lipton, founding partner at Wachtell, Lipton, Rosen & Katz, has argued with William Savitt that 'Shareholders do not "own" corporations. They own securities – shares of stock – which entitle them to very limited electoral rights and the right to share in the financial returns produced by the corporation's business operations [. . .] Shareholders possess none of the incidents of ownership of a corporation – neither the right of possession, nor the right of control, nor the right of exclusion – and thus "have no more claim to intrinsic ownership and control of the corporation's assets than do other stakeholders"'.[10]

Directors do not have a legal responsibility to maximise shareholder value first and foremost. Instead, the role of the board is to seek what is best for the company itself, which requires balancing the interests of all stakeholders. If not managed properly, maximising

---

[9] Connor, J. (2010). Archer Daniels Midland: price-fixer to the world. Purdue University Working Paper.
[10] Lipton, M. and W. Savitt (2007). The many myths of Lucian Bebchuk. *Virginia Law Review*, 93: 733–758.

returns for shareholders – for example, by manipulating accounting, deceiving customers, defaulting on payments to creditors, squeezing suppliers and employees, and evading taxes – can strip value generation from other stakeholders. Injustice in value distribution among stakeholders is thus a rich source of organisational fraud.

Lax Oversight

In theory, the board is elected by shareholders and is the highest authority in the company under the AGM. The board appoints, directs, supports, challenges, and removes the CEO, and serves as a check on the chief executive in order to protect the interest of the company. However, the board's oversight could be compromised in many situations.

Sometimes, directors fail to exercise oversight even when the CEO or chairperson is not acting in the best interests of the company, its shareholders, or other stakeholders. 'At Tyco, for example, some of the "independent" directors depended directly on the company for the bulk of their income, while at WorldCom many of the directors owed their wealth to Bernie Ebbers, the now disgraced and jailed CEO. At Parmalat, the board was comprised mainly of family or friends. Such boards are unlikely to be effective'.[11] Directors who contradict the views of such a CEO or chairperson may end up either complying or stepping down from their role.

In recent decades, some corporate CEOs have achieved celebrity status and become superstars with the aid of the media. They are often self-promoters with many followers. In a *Harvard Business Review* article, Rakesh Khurana highlighted the risk of relying on charismatic leaders. 'Enron's board of directors also bent to the will of its charismatic leader when it agreed to suspend its code of ethics to allow top executives to participate in the off-balance-sheet partnerships', he wrote. 'As Skilling's example illustrates, charismatic leaders reject limits to their scope and authority. They rebel against all checks on their power and dismiss the rules and norms that apply to others'.[12] Charmed into a false sense of security by the CEO's

---

[11] Hamilton, S. (2008). Who controls the CEO? IMD Tomorrow's Challenge (June 2008).

[12] https://hbr.org/2002/09/the-curse-of-the-superstar-ceo.

charisma and drive, the board does not challenge him or her on major decisions and becomes passive.

Independent directors without ties to the company may take a hands-off approach to overseeing the CEO, allowing him or her to make major decisions. Boards in the US typically include a high percentage of independent directors. Although prominent in other fields, they may lack detailed operational knowledge about the company. They have to rely for information on the CEO, who may bury key facts in huge board packages. Such a board may not be able to exercise proper fraud oversight, especially if the CEO is also the chair.

Problematic Culture

A fish rots from the head down, as the old saying goes. Likewise, when a company fails, poor leadership is usually the root cause.

In 2002, a *BusinessWeek* article described Tyco's then CEO Dennis Kozlowski as a 'corporate tough guy, respected and feared in roughly equal measure'.[13] Kozlowski was equally tough in fighting his way to the top of the company. After his aggressive acquisition strategy clashed with the more conservative instincts of former CEO John Fort, he persuaded Tyco's board of directors to side with him. Fort had to resign as CEO and chair, and Kozlowski took over. But Kozlowski and Tyco subsequently became household names after he was sued for misappropriating over $100 million of company funds for himself. This included more than $1 million for a lavish celebration of his wife's birthday, as well as having Tyco pay for his $30 million New York City apartment, equipped with $6000 shower curtains and $15 000 'dog umbrella stands'.

The 'tone at the top' determines the ethical standards for the whole organisation, not least because boards and executives tend to hire people similar to themselves. If the company's leaders set a ruthless tone, its employees will be more inclined to have the same values. This will very often result in office bullying and a culture of corporate fraud.

'When I worked at Wells Fargo, I faced the threat of being fired if I didn't meet the unreasonable sales quotas every day, and it's high time that Wells Fargo pays for preying on consumers' financial

---

[13] The rise and fall of Dennis Kozlowski. Bloomberg Business Week (December 2002).

livelihoods', said Khalid Taha, a former employee.[14] When Wells Fargo executives put pressure on their employees to meet unrealistic goals for cross-selling products, they bore a deep responsibility for how these employees pursued their targets – including through improper practices.

Pressure plays a major role in increasing the risk of fraud. Many regarded the autocratic management style of former Volkswagen CEO Martin Winterkorn as one of the factors that led to the emissions scandal that has cost the company some €28 billion to date. Winterkorn did not like failure, and the pressure on managers was unusually high. Several former VW executives have said that Winterkorn's style fostered a climate of fear. 'There was always a distance, a fear and a respect . . . If you presented bad news, those were the moments that it could become quite unpleasant and loud and quite demeaning', said one employee.[15]

Supremely selfish top executives are not too difficult to identify. These individuals are often greedy and demand money, titles, status, authority, perks, position, power, or services; they are arrogant and rude, at least to some; and they feel entitled.

Some boards believe that strong leaders need to have extreme traits, such as being overconfident, egocentric, ruthless, bold, tough, or selfish. But this is a stereotype. There is also a kind of leadership that speaks softly and gets things done cleanly and firmly. These leaders know where they are going, carefully think through how to get there, and execute precisely. Colman Mockler, the CEO of Gillette from 1975 to 1991, transformed the company, generating strong growth and returns for shareholders. Mockler was quiet, humble, gracious, and shy of publicity, and declined most requests to be interviewed and photographed. Yet no one could mistake his modesty for weakness.

It is crucial for boards to set an ethical example by reining in egocentric executives and balancing the character weaknesses that most CEOs have. Getting the right people on board can create a healthy corporate culture based on trust and discipline. The wrong people, however, can instil a toxic culture based on fear and greed.

---

[14] https://www.bloomberg.com/opinion/articles/2016-09-09/wells-fargo-opened-a-couple-million-fake-accounts.

[15] https://www.reuters.com/article/uk-volkswagen-emissions-culture/fear-and-respect-vws-culture-under-winterkorn-idUKKCN0S40MN20151010.

Financial Illiteracy

Directors often see themselves as generalists. They pay significant attention to important board topics such as leadership, strategy, innovation, or relations with the CEO, but tend to regard accounting and finance as a 'technical' subject for specialists. As a result, financial illiteracy is rampant on corporate boards. (In the hope of changing this state of affairs, Chapter 16 provides a primer on finance essentials for directors.)

Running a business without understanding basic financial and accounting concepts is dangerous, because it creates opportunities for executives to manipulate financial results and commit fraud. Boards lacking specialised knowledge cannot prevent, detect, or intervene in fraudulent activities effectively.

Financial illiteracy at board level is a lesson learned hard. After the Enron scandal, the SEC and other US regulators tightened the criteria for membership of boards and audit committees of public companies. Audit committees are now required to consist of independent directors, with at least one member being a 'financial expert'. This is defined as a person with fluent knowledge of US Generally Accepted Accounting Principles (GAAP), who has experience preparing, auditing, analysing, or evaluating complex financial statements in depth, and understands internal controls, financial reporting procedures, and audit committee functions. Every public-listed company board should have sufficient accounting and auditing expertise to provide effective fraud oversight.

However, independent directors who are financial experts may lack the specific industry knowledge to check intricate and carefully concealed insider misconduct. And although boards and audit committees may comply with the financial expert requirements, effective fraud oversight lies in the nuances of structures and processes. If internal control mechanisms and external auditors report functionally and administratively to management, rather than to the board or audit committee, this weakens the independent check on executives. The same is true if independent expert directors cannot freely meet employees, customers, and suppliers and have to rely on information from management.

By comparison, privately held companies generally have fewer or less comprehensive reporting requirements and transparency obligations. Financial literacy on boards and audit committees is not a legal requirement for private firms, which may lead to similarly large scandals.

Theranos, a privately held Silicon Valley start-up, was valued at $9 billion in 2015 because of its 'breakthrough advancements' in blood-testing technologies. The company claimed that its technology would enable laboratories to run medical tests with a finger-prick of blood. Theranos' original board consisted of retired government officials with no medical or technology experience, and no accounting or auditing expertise. Theranos' former CFO Henry Mosley had been fired in November 2006 after questioning the company's honesty and the reliability of its technology, and since then Theranos had only had a corporate controller. The company failed to prove its scientific claims, and its technology was seen as a fraud following civil and criminal investigations by US authorities in 2018.

How to Create an Effective Oversight Environment

The importance of boards actively managing the risk of high-level fraud cannot be overstated. Board members' proactive insights on the roots of corporate conflict help to shape a fair system, and the tone from the board sets the foundation for an ethical culture. Moreover, by strengthening oversight capabilities and frameworks, the board can act as a strong deterrent to high-level fraud. Potential fraudsters will be less likely to misbehave if they realise that they will be caught sooner or later.

With high-level fraud, prevention is always better than a cure. This is why boards must deal effectively with injustice, lax oversight, culture, and financial illiteracy. An active board therefore takes responsibility for broadening the notion of conflict of interest, building an appropriate oversight framework, creating a great corporate culture, and strengthening its own oversight expertise (see Figure 14.3). These steps are crucial for preventing potential high-level fraud, mitigating fraud risk, and guarding against any potential fraud losses.

Preventing Injustice: Broaden the Notion of Conflict of Interest

The notion of conflict of interest should be widened to include situations when a board member's duty of loyalty to stakeholders or the company is compromised. As we saw in Chapter 13, this can happen when some directors exercise influence over others through compensation, favours, a relationship, or psychological manipulation.

EFFECTIVE CONTROL ENVIRONMENT

Figure 14.3   Creating an Effective Control Environment

Even directors who describe themselves as independent may face a conflict of interest if they are forced into agreeing with a dominant board member. And sometimes, independent directors may form a distinct group and represent their own interests rather than those of the company. Situations such as these increase the risk of fraud.

Broadening the concept of conflict of interest helps board members to uncover potential injustice. Directors must deal with injustice when the interests of stakeholder groups are not appropriately balanced or harmonised. Conflict of interest and resulting injustices are a major source of high-level fraud. Board members must therefore address any conflicts responsibly and balance the interests of all individuals involved. When a company's purpose is in conflict with the interests of society, directors need to take an ethical stand, exercise care, and make sensible decisions.

Preventing Lax Oversight: Build Appropriate Frameworks

Boards fail when they do not have a formal and well-executed oversight process. Directors should begin by asking themselves what the ideal oversight mechanism should look like. For example, if an audit committee is not truly independent from management, its evaluation of high-level fraud risk cannot be effective. Direct reporting to the audit committee is thus important.

To ensure adequate controls on high-level fraud, a board needs to give special attention to the accountability matrices, reporting design, and oversight effectiveness of the audit committee. This should include discussions about the internal audit reporting line. Although there is no universal rule, it is not uncommon for a company's internal audit team to report both functionally and administratively to the CFO. But that raises questions regarding the credibility of the internal audit process.

In most cases, internal audit reports functionally to the audit committee but administratively to a C-suite executive. According to a 2013 Institute of International Auditors (IIA) survey, 70% of chief audit executives (CAEs) – and 75% of Fortune 500 CAEs – said they reported administratively to the CEO or the CFO, with an increasing shift toward the CEO. Functionally, the majority of CAEs reported to the full board or its audit committee.[16] IIA President and CEO Richard Chambers said, 'The higher up in the organization a CAE reports, the more objective that individual can be in overseeing audits of tough areas of responsibility and the more independent the internal audit function becomes in the eyes of stakeholders. It enhances the credibility of the CAE and the internal audit function across the rest of the organization'.

Although reporting to the CEO rather than the CFO represents a step up, it may not shield the company from CEO or board-level fraud. Directors must have a process for identifying and assessing such high-level fraud.

Here, it may help to borrow from Eastern supervision practices, and in particular the more complex process in China, where a board of supervisors works alongside the board of directors. The board of supervisors is normally composed of five to seven stakeholder professionals, some of whom are full-time onsite supervisors. By attending board of directors meetings as non-voting delegates, supervisors can monitor the performance of directors and senior management, the overall activities of the company, and decisions that affect the firm in the short and long term. Monitoring is based on criteria such as work attitude, behaviour, capacity to fulfil one's duties, and overall contribution, as well as any activities related to fraud. In addition, retiring and departing directors, and members of senior management, have

---

[16] The Institute of Internal Auditors. (2013). 2013: Time to Seize the Opportunity North American Report – March 2013.

ICBC organisational and supervisory structure

Figure 14.4   Corporate Governance Framework of Industrial and Commercial Bank of China (ICBC)

Source: Based on data from ICBC annual report 2016.

to undergo an auditing process led by the board of supervisors. By periodically and systematically evaluating senior management and board directors, the board of supervisors creates appropriate checks and balances at the very top of the organisation.

In Chinese state companies, the board of supervisors is integrally involved in identifying high-level fraud, determining the company's fraud risk process, and ensuring that the actions of directors and senior management are aligned with the company's interest and strategy. As shown in Figure 14.4 above, internal auditors report primarily to the audit committee, with a secondary reporting line to senior management and the board of supervisors. Active oversight by the audit committee and the board of supervisors serves as a deterrent to high-level executives and directors engaging in fraudulent activity. Given the devastating consequences of high-level fraud, a Chinese-style board of supervisors charged with governance in this area might be an alternative to Western practices.

Organisational design and reporting structures are the fundamental elements of an anti-fraud oversight mechanism. It is crucial to define clearly who is responsible for which level of fraud management, and then to establish control mechanisms that fit with their respective responsibilities. The message must be that no one, including board directors and CEOs, has the authority to commit fraud. Fraud risk management activities and control mechanisms might include, but are not limited to:

- an anti-fraud policy that defines the specific responsibilities for fraud management within the organisation;
- the ownership of fraud risks at different levels;
- the reporting lines of crucial functions such as internal audit, fraud examination, risk, legal, compliance, human resources, and security;
- the fraud detection methods and controls for all employees, including high-level executives and directors;
- the levels of access to fraud-related information;
- an ongoing monitoring process that is revisited regularly;
- the current development of fraud detection technologies;
- the establishment of a confidential hotline, online form, or email system to receive tips from all stakeholders;
- the overall protocols to deal with fraud-related issues in a timely way;
- an environment of safety for employees to report misconduct;
- rewards and protections for whistleblowers;
- the disciplinary measures for ethical violations.

Preventing Toxic Behaviours: Create a Positive Culture

Tight control mechanisms alone are not enough to make a company fraud resistant. In addition, the board of directors must create an atmosphere of zero tolerance for fraud, and actively foster a culture of 'doing the right thing'. These days, the corporate world is moving away from the narrow rules-based compliance of checking 'dos and don'ts', towards a values-based approach focused on integrity (see Figure 14.5 below, which was provided by Diane de St Victor, a key executive involved in tackling such issues). This requires judgement, and not only rules, to define the right culture. Board

From Compliance to Conduct

Compliance	Conduct / Integrity
Following the rules so we don't get in trouble	Following our framework because it's the right thing to do
Enforcing policies as a measured target	Rules are internalised and turned into standards of conduct
Telling people what they should not do	Fostering an environment where people identify what they should do
Controlled by sanctions	Supported by personal and company character / values
Success measured by how well we follow the rules	Success measured by how well we integrate integrity into our business, leading to acceptable conduct
Can be delegated	Taking personal responsibility
Knowing what is right	Doing what is right even if no one is looking

Figure 14.5   The Evolution from Compliance to Conduct and Integrity.
Source: Based on data from Diane de St Victor, ABB presentation. Corporate conduct and corporate reputation, 15 May 2015.

members should ask whether a corporate action passes their own personal integrity test.

The tone at the top is the ethical atmosphere created by the company's board and senior management and has a trickle-down effect through the organisation. The board has the responsibility to encourage ethical behaviour, and to empower internal and external stakeholders to meet these standards all the time.

Yet this is only a starting point. It is not enough for boards or executives simply to hand out a written code of ethics for others to comply with. They have to 'walk the talk' and demonstrate their commitment to ethical behaviour through their words and actions. They have to communicate what is expected of employees, make clear their intolerance for dishonest and unethical behaviour, and lead by example. To make this work, boards need to monitor and assess the actual tone that senior executives use when motivating employees or communicating with external stakeholders.

For a board to lead by example in this regard, it should be a high performance board across all four pillars of effectiveness – dedicated people, effective information architecture, efficient structures and processes, and positive group dynamics. This usually starts with the selection of board members, and the hiring and firing of the CEO. Fraud at the hiring stage is not uncommon if the process is hastily conducted: Yahoo CEO Scott Thompson was fired after only four months due to resumé fraud, for example. Fraudsters often display character traits and styles that could indicate their intention to commit fraud – such as being extremely tough, political, ruthless, selfish, and greedy. It is crucial, therefore, that boards observe and listen to candidates for the C-suite and boardroom (and to their former employers) to determine if they are morally sound. Board members should be able to read human nature well and weed out those whose characters might lead them to commit fraud.

In addition to hiring morally sound senior executives and directors, companies should set realistic performance goals. These are targets that can be met without unethical behaviour such as linking flawed compensation schemes to aggressive sales goals, as described above in the Wells Fargo case.

A company can cultivate a positive culture by rewarding employees for other things than just meeting financial goals. In particular, an organisation could reward an employee who has underperformed targets for the right reasons. Meeting the target would then not be the sole measure of success. Ethical behaviour and integrity should be rewarded and formalised into incentive programmes, while unethical actions should be punished and not tolerated. This will reinforce a strongly positive, anti-fraud culture.

Companies are more likely to maintain such a culture if all employees are aware of different types of fraud and their consequences. Anti-fraud training can raise awareness of this risk throughout the company. Good employees will be aware of possible signs, acts, and omissions of fraud, and know their responsibility to report questionable activity. Bad employees who plan to commit fraud would know that they were being watched, with a high chance of being caught should they transgress. A positive culture will reduce the opportunity for fraud, and make it more likely that such activity will be either deterred or detected early.

A positive work environment is part of a healthy corporate culture. An open-door policy, candid conversations, and easy access to high-level management all help to prevent fraud by making communication easier. Fraud occurs less frequently when employees have positive feelings about an organisation than when they feel unequal, exploited, ignored, abused, unrecognised, or threatened. Excessive pressure and expectations, ruthlessness, and office bullying do not make for a positive work environment and should be avoided at all cost. These are toxic behaviours that spread quickly and create room for fraud.

Strengthen Board Oversight Expertise with Special Focus on Legal, Compliance, Risk, Fraud, and Financial Reporting

Boardroom failures and scandals involving fraud often lead to the conclusion that the directors did not have the expertise to oversee the complexities of the business. The quick solution is to hire experts to sit on the board. Certified Public Accountants (CPAs), CPAs certified in Financial Forensics (CFFs), Certified Fraud Examiners (CFEs), and Certified Internal Auditors (CIAs) can all add oversight expertise as directors. These professionals can oversee and consult on internal control audits, risk management, compliance, and forensic analysis.

Another critical step is to increase fraud awareness at board level. Directors must have a solid understanding of fraud risk in general, fraud risks facing the company and their underlying drivers, and anti-fraud strategies. This includes being aware of the four factors contributing to fraud that we have discussed in this chapter. During board discussions on fraud risk, directors should consider the presence and weight of these factors and act accordingly to prevent fraud.

Board members also need to gain insights on regulatory and governance requirements regarding fraud, compliance, and other

In April 2019, Nissan Motor Co. severed its two-decade connection with former saviour Carlos Ghosn. Shareholders removed the former chair and CEO from the company's board following his arrest for numerous alleged financial crimes. In the spring of 2019, the company had received a report from an external panel that said Ghosn's long tenure at Nissan led to power being 'concentrated in his hands'. The report also called for measures to improve the carmaker's governance. Nissan's new CEO Hiroto Saikawa, Ghosn's protege-turned-accuser, said the company may claim damages against its former chair. 'Today is a key turning point for Nissan', Saikawa said on 8 April 2019 on NHK, Japan's broadcaster. Ghosn denied the legitimacy of the charges.

issues. For global companies, boards need greater expertise on national laws, global stock market regulations, international law enforcement, institutional investors, NGOs, and communication.

Tools For Anti-Fraud Activities: Assessment, Prevention, Detection, and Investigation

In today's fast-changing environment, fraud is increasingly complex and sophisticated. What's more, a company might be judged by public opinion long before any fraud case comes to court. Directors must therefore move with the times and adjust their attitude and mentality regarding anti-fraud activities, as Figure 14.6 provided by Diane de St Victor, outlines.

Yesterday vs Today: Compliance and Integrity

Yesterday	Today
Is this something we can do legally?	Is this something we can live with?
Is it permitted?	Is it acceptable?
Compliance	Integrity / conduct
No one will know	It will come up
Don't get caught	You will be caught
Being judged based on standards of conduct applicable at the time	Yesterday's conduct being judged on today's standards
Local impact	Global impact
Slow impact	Immediate impact
You knew	You should have known
One thing at a time	It's all commingled

Figure 14.6   Compliance and Integrity – Yesterday and Today.

Source: Based on data from Diane de St Victor, ABB presentation. Running your business with high integrity standards, 16 September 2015.

Effective anti-fraud activities should concentrate on assessment, prevention, detection, and investigation.

Assessment

The board of directors or the board of supervisors should regularly assess the organisation's fraud risk. This includes reviewing the current status of the four main factors that might lead to high-level fraud (Figure 14.7). Boards should assess the likelihood and significance of fraud along each dimension, and the effectiveness of the organisation's anti-fraud controls. Such a process will allow the company to build on its strengths and address areas of weakness on a continuous basis.

Prevention

The board of directors or supervisors should focus on prevention to reduce fraud opportunities in the organisation. Figure 14.8 below identifies some priority actions for directors in this regard.

Detection

A board member must have a healthy level of scepticism and ask lots of questions. The educated director should think like an investigator,

FRAUD FACTOR ASSESSMENT

	INJUSTICE	LAX OVERSIGHT	FINANCIAL ILLITERACY	PROBLEMATIC CULTURE
LIKELIHOOD				
SIGNIFICANCE				
PREVENTIVE ACTIVITY				
DETECTIVE ACTIVITY				
INVESTIGATIVE ACTIVITY				

Figure 14.7   Fraud Factor Assessment

PREVENTIVE ACTIVITY

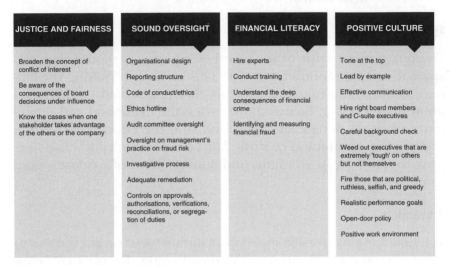

JUSTICE AND FAIRNESS	SOUND OVERSIGHT	FINANCIAL LITERACY	POSITIVE CULTURE
Broaden the concept of conflict of interest	Organisational design	Hire experts	Tone at the top
	Reporting structure	Conduct training	Lead by example
Be aware of the consequences of board decisions under influence	Code of conduct/ethics	Understand the deep consequences of financial crime	Effective communication
	Ethics hotline		Hire right board members and C-suite executives
Know the cases when one stakeholder takes advantage of the others or the company	Audit committee oversight	Identifying and measuring financial fraud	Careful background check
	Oversight on management's practice on fraud risk		Weed out executives that are extremely 'tough' on others but not themselves
	Investigative process		Fire those that are political, ruthless, selfish, and greedy
	Adequate remediation		Realistic performance goals
	Controls on approvals, authorisations, verifications, reconciliations, or segregation of duties		Open-door policy
			Positive work environment

Figure 14.8   Preventive Activity

understand what management is doing, and identify red flags at an early stage (Figure 14.9).

Investigation

It is the board's job to assess, prevent, and detect high-level fraudulent activity. When bad things happen, boards need to get actively involved in the investigation and ensure that the process is thorough and effective. This should include appointing a competent, independent internal or external legal counsel charged with carrying out the investigation, access to confidential information, timelines for regular reports, process of resolution, communication, disclosure, and protocols to follow legal and regulatory requirements.

When things start 'going south' as unethical behaviour or financial crime are discovered, the company's reputation will most probably be severely damaged. Boards need to face reality, act swiftly, take responsibility, and mitigate fraud risk to reintegrate integrity, and reduce exposure and further damage. Mitigation strategies need to take into account whether this was a systemic issue.

HIGH-LEVEL FRAUD DETECTION

	BOARD	BOARD COMMITTEES	C-SUITE	OTHER SENIOR MGT	LOWER MGT
ATTITUDES					
INCENTIVES					
PRESSURE					
OPPORTUNITY					
INVESTIGATIVE ACTIVITY					
POTENTIAL SCHEME					
FINANCIAL REPORTING FRAUD					
MISAPPROPRIATION OF ASSETS					
EXPENDITURE & LIABILITIES MANIPULATION					
FRAUDULENT REVENUE AND ASSETS RECOGNITION					
OTHER MISCONDUCT					

Figure 14.9   High-Level Fraud Detection

The case of Wells Fargo serves as a reminder that fraud happens frequently and can occur in any organisation, country, or industry. High-level fraud is especially damaging as it can result in huge financial losses for the company and its stakeholders, legal costs, and ruined reputations that can ultimately lead to the organisation's demise. If the board turns a blind eye to such fraud, directors may themselves face litigation by shareholders.

Directors have a legal and moral responsibility to implement a proactive oversight framework, lead by example, communicate constantly, and follow through on anti-fraud policies. The costs of preventing fraud are far lower than the potential losses when it happens. By taking the lead on this issue, boards can help to provide essential safeguards and secure an ethically and financially sound future for their organisation.

Throughout Part II, we have seen how boards are constantly challenged and sometimes fail. In Part III, we examine board best practices with the aim of providing guidance and inspiration for directors around the world.

PART III
Board Best Practices

CHAPTER 15

The Board as a Strategic Asset[1]

Boards are responsible for the long-term success of their organisations. This means that strategy must be one of the central elements of board work. Unfortunately, directors are often highly confused as to what they should and shouldn't do regarding strategy. Boards commonly place strategic responsibility on the shoulders of the organisation's executives, believing that strategic thinking is what CEOs and their teams should do. But a board taking this view often ends up acting as a mere rubber stamp of the CEO. And other boards that try to get substantively involved in strategic decision-making often find themselves clashing with the executive team. Neither approach makes sense or allows a board to add real value.

This chapter aims to clarify how boards can better assess their strategic responsibilities in order to make a truly effective and value-adding contribution to the organisation. Although national differences do matter, all boards today have some aspiration to be more engaged in strategy. The real question is how they can use their skills to do that effectively while keeping the executive team fully engaged.

---

[1]This work stems from my work with Estelle Metayer. For more on this topic, see Cossin, D. and E. Metayer (2014). The board and strategy. MIT Sloan Management Review, 2014.

A board's strategic responsibilities cannot be defined in a one-size-fits-all manner. Instead, three dimensions help to determine its impact on strategy. These are:

- **The meaning of strategy** – Strategy can be defined in different ways and have different time frames, and board members must reach a common view on these.
- **The role of the board** – A board can play a supervisory and monitoring role, support management in engaging with external and internal stakeholders, or take on a meaningful co-creation role. Each represents a different way for boards to participate in the strategy process.
- **The context of the firm** – The board's involvement in strategy will also depend on the context in which the company operates. In a chaotic context, a board may need to have a hands-on approach to strategy development that would clearly be unproductive in a simple context.

Five Definitions of Strategy

There is not enough debate about what strategy really means for boards and top executives, and what it can achieve when done well. Boards first need to discuss the timeframe for their strategic reflection. Whereas executives typically look at a three- to five-year horizon in considering strategy, boards may take a longer view over five to ten years. Anchor shareholders of quality, such as families or states, may look even further ahead, perhaps 25 years (to the next generation) or even a transgenerational 50-year view. I tend to see an evolution toward longer timeframes, despite the incredible uncertainty of today's world. This produces a clear division of tasks that helps the relationship between the board and management.

Having clarified the timeframe, the board should address what individual directors understand strategy to be. The lack of a universally accepted, up-to-date definition of strategy often results in boards and management sticking to the most traditional concepts – vision, mission, and actions – rather than reflecting on what they might be able to achieve if they took time to explore what strategic thinking means to them.

Here, boards might consider at least five definitions to refine their notion of strategy:

Strategy as planning. From this perspective, strategy serves to establish the organisation's vision, mission, values, and purpose. It helps to define the firm's long-term objectives, programme of action, and resource-allocation priorities. This is what most of us know as the traditional approach to strategy. It is defined by a structured, step-by-step process that Jack Welch of GE championed in the 1980s to implement total quality management and improve productivity, efficiency, and profit. This view of strategy gave rise to the notion of 'strategic planning', which has become a cherished practice in most corporations, although it has been heavily criticised by management thought leaders such as Henry Mintzberg.[2]

Strategy as redefining one's competitive domain. Here, an organisation uses strategy to address its industry boundaries, the key players, where the company stands, and how the industry might be changing. Amazon, for example, is now entering the health care sector following its acquisitions of PillPack and Whole Foods, and its joint venture with Berkshire Hathaway and JPMorgan in this area. Samsung redefined its industry from electronics to 'lifeware', producing a wide range of stylishly designed digital products including cell phones, televisions, and cameras to rival those of Apple, Sony, and Motorola. And Fujifilm – unlike Kodak – survived and thrived during the transition from film to digital because the company took numerous steps to alter its strategic view of the competitive domain. For instance, Fujifilm jumped out of its traditional industry by using its knowledge of chemicals to diversify into a new line of antioxidant cosmetics and make optical films for LCD flat-panel televisions.

Strategy as a focused response to overcome a key challenge. On this view, well-illustrated by Richard Rumelt in his book *Good Strategy, Bad Strategy*,[3] strategy consists of diagnosing the nature of the key challenges, developing an overall approach to overcome obstacles, and designing a set of coordinated actions to accomplish this. A company's main challenge may

---

[2] Mintzberg, H. (1994). *The Rise and Fall of Strategic Planning*. New York: The Free Press.
[3] Rumelt, R. (2011). *Good Strategy Bad Strategy: The Difference and Why It Matters*. New York: Crown Business.

come from risks and opportunities in the economic and business environment (such as fluctuating oil prices), or from the competitive landscape in the form of a rival with a new business model. It can even stem from internal issues, such as an organisational structure that does not allow for full value creation. Corporations that are often exposed to large risks, such as natural resource or commodity firms, are used to operating with a close eye on risks and opportunities and thus implicitly use this type of strategic thinking. They are well aware of break-even prices and the dynamics of capital expenditures amid market upswings and downswings, and tailor their strategies accordingly. Another example is the automotive industry: in early 2019, BMW and Daimler announced a new €1 billion joint venture aimed at countering the disruption caused by 'Uberisation' and autonomous cars.

Strategy as identifying and reinforcing core competencies. In this case, strategy is a vehicle for achieving long-term, sustainable competitive advantage and profitability. IBM's Research Division, for example, repeatedly reinvented itself successfully, each time reconfiguring its core strategy to find and transform research ideas into businesses with new products. From the 1940s to the 1970s, the division relied mostly on corporate funding to produce long-term research. In the 1970s and 1980s, it emphasised collaborative teams and shorter-term projects funded by the business units. By the 1990s, the research division was looking to its customers and their research arms to jointly develop innovative new projects. More recently, it has been imitating a venture-capital model to fund promising new ventures.

Strategy as optimising value contribution to key stakeholders. This definition of strategy sees the primary role of business as serving customers, or supporting employees and contributing to society in general. Monitoring and optimising how the company maximises benefits for its major stakeholders lies at the heart of such a strategy. In early 2019, for example, outdoor clothing company Patagonia announced that it would donate the $10 million it had saved as a result of US President Donald Trump's corporate-tax cuts to environmental-protection groups.

Given these different meanings, board members should align themselves before addressing executives in strategy sessions. Most management teams are less sensitive to the five definitions than directors are; for executives, strategy is whatever the CEO considers it to be. Boards, on the other hand, need to clarify what they see as primary to the organisation and thus which of the five possible interpretations of strategy they want to focus on – or, if several matter, then which one should dominate. This is not a static decision: one view of strategy may be more essential in the medium term and another in the long term.

Boards are fully justified in doing this: in today's complex environment, such strategic thinking, along with a debate on the appropriate time horizon, can lead to deep shifts in an organisation's orientation. Directors can assess the strategic timeframe and decide which of the five options matters most to them, versus where they see their executive teams focusing. For example, board members can individually assign points to each of the five definitions of strategy, and then tally the results in order to have productive discussions on differences of views among themselves and, later, with management.

By bringing clarity on these issues before engaging with executives, boards can alleviate much of the tension in strategy discussions and retreats, for example. This in turn leads to deeper, richer interactions with management – including in executives' own work on strategy through more classical lenses such as competitive analysis, threats, and opportunities.

Clarifying the Board's Role

Nonetheless, some argue that strategy is a CEO-only role. They say the best strategy resides in a synthetic, actionable view that can only be developed by a hands-on individual with deep knowledge of the company – in other words, the chief executive. But this view nonetheless recognises that the board selects the CEO and can challenge his or her strategic thinking, even if only to convince itself of the chief executive's ability. So even the most remote boards still have a role to fulfil in choosing the right CEO to match the board's view of the organisation's future (and thus its strategy).

Boards also have to balance the different possible roles they might play, which affects how they will engage their strategic muscle. A board's culture, rules, and practices will of course help to determine which roles dominate. A German board, for example, will most likely favour a supervisory perspective, while a Canadian board may see direct involvement as more essential. Three roles in particular tend to dominate board work on strategy:

Supervision and monitoring. A board with a supervisory role focuses on monitoring corporate performance and executive team behaviour against the key performance indicators (KPIs) of the defined strategy. The board is there to ensure the performance of the organisation and its executives in selecting and implementing a course of action. This supervision therefore covers everything: strategy development, design, and implementation. But this role requires the board to have specific supervisory skills including a systematic view, attention to detail, and an understanding of consistency and control. All of these can be adapted to supervising strategy as well as results. The board must engage in a process of probing and sensing using appropriate hard and soft metrics, while paying attention to risks, strategic inconsistencies, and flaws that could threaten the business. Developing these processes and skills is thus a prerequisite for board supervision of strategy.

Co-creation. Board members typically have vast experience to complement that of the organisation's management. Directors' networks with key stakeholders – regulators, governments, customers, and even employees – can give them an edge in understanding key signals within and outside the organisation and thus help them to co-create strategy with management. Co-creative boards can help to open executives' minds to previously unseen realities and steer the strategy debate beyond any blind spots management may have. Blind spots typically arise because of executive myopia. True co-creation most probably requires regular, highly structured strategic board sessions (perhaps at every other board meeting), complemented by a one- or two-day retreat with management. Successful co-creation will typically leverage both management's internal information and the board's external intelligence and experience to produce a long-term strategic perspective with more options and flexibility than executives' views alone would normally offer.

Support. In this role, the board helps management by coaching and advising executives, and by engaging external stakeholders, including key customers, to ensure the success of the management's strategy. The board thus lends management credibility and authority. In times of crisis, a supportive board can be the key to success, while too much distance can be a recipe for disaster.

In May 2018, the Australian Prudential Regulation Authority (APRA) issued the final report of its inquiry into problems at the Commonwealth Bank of Australia (CBA). The authority highlighted 'inadequate oversight and challenge by the board and its gatekeeper committees of emerging non-financial risks; an over-confidence in the operation of the board and its committees, and a lack of benchmarking to assess effectiveness; unclear accountabilities starting with a lack of ownership of key risks at the Executive Committee level'.[4] In 2013, 2015, and 2016, CBA audit committee reports suggested that the bank was having repeated issues in its compliance with anti-money laundering regulations. But the APRA report said members of the board audit committee were not routinely given, and did not ask for, copies of these audit reports, instead relying on summaries.

Another seeming example of a board failing to provide adequate support was at BP after the Macondo field blowout crisis in 2010. Given that BP had a prior catastrophe in 2005 in Texas, which killed 15 workers, some doubt whether the board did all it should have done to monitor the company's safety management procedures and its overall safety culture. Many also viewed CEO Tony Hayward as being quite isolated during these difficult times, and questioned whether deeper involvement from the board and its chair might have helped BP better manage the situation. Although the board removed Hayward as CEO, its own failings to lead the organisation's culture were arguably equally at fault in the catastrophe. Having a board more focused on a supervisory role may have been fine during the simpler context of normal BP operations. But a quicker switch to strong support during the chaotic aftermath of the explosion might have enhanced the firm's reputation and long-term prospects.

---

[4] https://www.apra.gov.au/sites/default/files/CBA-Prudential-Inquiry_Final-Report_30042018.pdf.

A strong board can thus weigh and map the roles it seeks to play – whether supervisory, co-creative, or supportive, or a combination of these. This will provide greater clarity about directors' involvement in the organisation's strategy debate, so that they can truly add value. What's more, executives will have useful and reassuring clarity regarding the separation of strategic roles, especially when the board might be perceived as micromanaging. The quality of board work improves too. A board that may lack the necessary skills to take on a co-creative role, for example, could design a board education and workshop process to address areas of weakness. What counts is that the board understands its role and how that impacts its involvement in strategy. Once it has clarity on this, the board can better address execution of its strategic responsibilities.

Taking Context into the Mapping Process

When a board maps the five meanings of strategy and its potential roles, directors should take into account the context in which they believe the organisation operates. Boards should ask themselves if that context is stable, or whether it might change sometime in the future. In today's fast-moving world, context can quickly shift from simple to complicated, and from complicated to complex – or even all the way to chaotic.

In general, boards spend far too much time on issues that can be considered simple or at most complicated, such as financials and operations. My view is that boards can add most value in complex or chaotic contexts, where executive teams are typically overwhelmed and lack the diversity of views to fully understand the situation and make optimal strategic decisions. When the dominant context becomes complex or chaotic, boards become essential to the long-term success of the business. Organisational resilience and survival require early detection of threats, along with the ability to interpret these and engage confidently, and then to recover and exploit opportunities quickly. It is a time when experience, judgement, and a willingness to make a strong shift – such as removing rather than steering a CEO – become key to organisational success.

All boards must be prepared to adapt swiftly to changes in context. They must be ready and able to quickly alter their interpretation of the meaning of strategy and adjust their role. Focusing on customers in a stable environment cannot remain a board's priority when a context change puts employee safety or the organisation's entire reputation at stake (as illustrated by Tesla's confrontation with US regulatory authorities in 2018, for example). It may become essential to rebalance not only strategic priorities but also what strategy itself entails. As a result, the board may need to change its role quickly.

The Impact of Context on Strategic Views and Roles of the Board

Figure 15.1 below summarises boards' strategies, roles, and views in different contexts, mapped from simple to chaotic following Snowden and Boone's methodology.[5] The context mapping depends on the number of dimensions to consider (more factors make the context more complicated), and the level of uncertainty or risks within each. For example, Swiss watch manufacturing could be considered complicated, with many dimensions and much sophistication, but less risky than oil drilling. Refineries, meanwhile, could be seen in a chaotic context, because the uncertainty of oil prices and climate change combine with many dimensions and processes.

HIGH-LEVEL FRAUD DETECTION

Figure 15.1   The role of the board in strategy is affected by context

---

[5] D.J. Snowden and M.E. Boone elaborate on this framework. See Snowden, D.J. and M.E. Boone (2007). A leader's framework for decision making. *Harvard Business Review* 85(11): 68–76.

The Board's Ultimate Strategic Significance

Organisational leaders are confronted with an incredible rise in complexity: from society, technology, governments, alternative business models, global changes, and environmental factors, as well as shifting economic conditions. Even the most experienced and fine-tuned leaders cannot be expected to respond consistently well to all these challenges, especially in a chaotic environment.

Boards are now essential to strategic success. Unfortunately, however, most are failing to add strategic value. Past crises have increasingly strengthened boards' fiduciary role toward the company, sometimes at the expense of the strategic value they can add.

More than ever, organisations need strong boards of high-quality individuals who are focused and dedicated. In addition, directors must have access to accurate and well-designed information, be able to establish meaningful structures and processes, and implement board dynamics that foster effective debates and result in good decisions and actions. But even high-quality boards of this type can fail if they do not address the spectrum of responsibilities they have on strategy. Following the mapping process in this chapter can help boards greatly improve their strategic performance and transform themselves into a life-saving, competition-beating, opportunity-enhancing asset for their organisation.

In helping to shape an organisation's strategic direction, boards increasingly need to have a strong command of financial matters. The next chapter therefore offers a director-level briefing on key finance and accounting concepts.

CHAPTER 16

A Primer on Finance Essentials for Directors

Companies around the world have been working to create high performance boards, usually with directors coming from diverse backgrounds. Nevertheless, accounting and finance drive a significant proportion of board decisions. Directors are therefore expected to have a strong grip in these areas – but as we saw in Chapter 14, financial illiteracy on corporate boards remains widespread.

This chapter provides an essential foundation in finance and accounting from a board-level perspective. It is intended for directors who are not financial specialists. It aims to show board members the fundamentals of how to read financial reports, interpret between the lines of financial statements, implement a desired capital structure, apply valuation techniques, make better M&A decisions, and oversee risk.

Directors who are well-versed in finance can have a great impact on a board's effectiveness. They can understand what drives a company's performance and foresee the likely strategic outcomes of board decisions. It becomes easier for them to resist management fads such as financial and accounting engineering and excessive borrowing. And they are better placed to detect fraud, or avoid M&A pitfalls that can destroy value. Financially literate boards and directors don't suffer from misconceptions, but instead make wise decisions about what creates long-term value.

Reading Financial Reports

Board members do not produce accounting documents, but approving them is part of their responsibility. In short, financial statements show us the money: where it came from, where it went, and where it is now.

The conceptual underpinnings of corporate reporting:

A **balance sheet** shows what a company owns and owes at a specific point in time. It provides detailed information about a firm's assets, liabilities, and shareholders' equity at the end of the reporting period. It does not directly show the flows into and out of the accounts during the period.

The following formula is the most fundamental principle of accounting: ASSETS = LIABILITIES + EQUITY. In other words, the left-hand side of the balance sheet reflects what the organisation invests in (the assets), and the right-hand side shows how it finances itself to fund these assets (the liabilities, notably debt and equity). Overvaluation of assets and undervaluation of liabilities are classic elements of financial fraud that board members should watch out for.

An **income statement** shows how much money a company earned and spent over a specific time period. To understand how income statements work, we start at the top with the sales made. This is also referred to as the 'top line'. Then we go down, and at each step, we deduct certain costs or operating expenses associated with earning the sales. At the bottom, after deducting all of the expenses, we learn how much the company actually earned or lost during the accounting period. This is the literal 'bottom line' of the statement.

Note that profit does not necessarily correspond to money made. Indeed, some elements of the income statement, such as depreciation, are notional amounts ('non-cash items') and thus do not affect the cash position. Also, some balance-sheet items are not reflected in the income statement even though they affect cash positions. These include working capital elements such as inventories, accounts payable owed to suppliers, and accounts receivable that are due and still unpaid by customers.

A **cash flow statement** reports a company's inflows and outflows of cash. It shows whether the business stayed positive or negative based on the cash flow exchanges with other companies over a specific period. This is very important because a company needs cash on hand to pay its expenses. It is vital to understand that profits do not correspond to cash. Depreciation affects profits but not cash. And working capital or capital expenditures affect cash but not profits directly. Thus, a good approximation of cash flow is to reinstate the depreciation taken out from profits and to subtract changes in working capital and capital expenditures.

While an income statement can tell us whether a company made a profit, a cash flow statement shows whether it generated cash. Profits can be notional, but cash is a more substantial economic reality. The cash flow statement shows changes over time rather than absolute amounts at a point in time, and is thus a strong indicator of the health of an organisation. The bottom line of the cash flow statement shows the net increase or decrease in cash for the period. Board members should pay close attention to cash flow statements, because they correct the accounting distortions of income statements and provide a more realistic picture of whether an organisation makes money.

Understanding Ratios to Analyse Operating Strategies

Ratios are calculated from financial statements. They turn accounting data into valuable information, helping directors to understand operating details, measure progress toward goals, and benchmark with competitors in the same industry. From the perspective of shareholders, bankers, regulators, and analysts, ratios also measure a company's successes or failures. Directors need to receive regular reports and monitor the company through financial ratios.

Growth ratios. Organic or internal growth stems from a strategy, the natural growth of the market, or the creation of a new market through new product development. External growth occurs entirely through acquisitions.

Sales Growth = the percentage growth in sales from one period to the next CAGR

$$(\text{Compound Annual Growth Rates}) = \left(\frac{ending\ value}{beginning\ value} \right) \frac{1}{Number\ of\ years} - 1$$

Profitability ratios are among the most used and the most important accounting ratios. They are measures of performance in generating profits. Of course, profits are more meaningful when they require fewer assets to generate them (and thus cost less capital). They are also more meaningful when they require fewer sales. Thus, profits are typically related to other financial-statement items. Note also that profits (also called net income or earnings) can sometimes be simplified into items higher up the income statement, such as EBIT or EBITDA which ignore taxes or depreciation, for example.

EBIT (Earnings before Interest and Tax)

EBITDA (Earnings before interest, taxes, depreciation and amortisation)

ROIC (Return on Invested Capital) = (EBIT * (1 – Tax Rate)) / Invested Capital

ROE (Return on Equity) = Net Income / Shareholder Equity

ROA (Return on Assets) = Net Income / Total Assets

- Note that if we consider the relationship Assets = Debt + Equity, then ROE and ROA can be inferred from each other once we know the leverage of the company (its debt level).

Profit Margin = Net Income / Sales

Gross Profit Margin = (Sales – Cost of Goods Sold) / Sales

EPS (Earnings per Share) = Net Income / Number of Shares

Operating efficiency is as strong a driver of profitability as margin is. A good measure of efficiency is the asset turnover, i.e. how much sales are produced by $1 of assets.

Asset Turnover = Sales / Assets

Note that these ratios typically relate to each other. One well-known relation is the so-called DuPont decomposition: ROA = Margin × Asset Turnover. In other words, the Return on Assets is driven as much by margin (here Net Income/Sales) as it is by efficiency. Thus a 1% efficiency gain is equivalent to a 1% margin gain.

Leverage ratios look at the extent to which a company has relied on borrowing to finance its operations. A high leverage ratio may increase a firm's exposure to solvency risk and business downturns, but may also lead to higher returns for equity holders.

Debt Ratio = Total Debt / Total Assets

Debt – to – Equity ratio = Total Debt / Equity

Interest Coverage Ratio = EBIT / Financing Costs

Liquidity ratios indicate a company's ability to pay its current obligations. In other words, they show the availability of cash and other assets to pay all its bills on time.

Current Ratio = Current Assets / Current Liabilities

Quick Ratio = (Current Assets – Inventory) / Current Liabilities

Many other ratios can be calculated, notably for operations, client engagement, and employee retention. Manufacturing defects, for example, is an indicator of whether a company should anticipate increasing customer complaints and returns that can ultimately hurt business. Directors need to know what the company's customer churn and retention rates are, because firms lose their advertising and marketing investment when customer dissatisfaction rises and customers leave. Board members should also be aware of the company's employee churn rates, because constantly hiring and training new employees is expensive and can negatively impact a company's image.

Interpreting Between the Lines of Financial Statements

What might management hide? What do auditors look for?

Management often has an incentive to manipulate the company's financial statements. Directors should know what auditors look for, and also be aware that auditors do not always catch manipulation. There are several basic types of financial statement fraud:

Sales manipulation. Sales are vulnerable to misrepresentation. Common ways to manipulate sales include recording them before they are actually earned, or making up sales that do not exist. The timing of recognition of sales (and expenses) is also a key issue. A classic manipulation is to push sales into the business system (for example to storage owners, dealers, or independent representatives), thereby accounting for them internally.

Expenses manipulation. This can include capitalising normal operating expenses. Other methods include shifting current expenses to a future period to boost current earnings, or moving future expenses to the current period in order to create a 'bottom' and then increase future earnings.

Incorrect asset valuation. Overstating inventory, fixed assets, and accounts receivable inflates company assets. This can include not recording the full expense of raw materials, not writing off unsellable inventory, or misreporting current inventory. Failing to record depreciation expenses of fixed assets is also fraudulent.

Hidden liabilities. Manipulating liabilities can include not recording accounts payable or keeping certain liabilities off the balance sheet. Complex related-party or third-party transactions do not usually add value, but can be used to conceal debt off the balance sheet. Omission of warranty and product liability could also be a way to hide liabilities.

Improper disclosures. These can include misrepresenting the company and making false representations in press releases and other company filings. Some disclosures might be intentionally confusing and not understandable. Other improper disclosures include hiding significant events, management fraud, or changes in accounting policy or auditors.

Globally, the four most common financial-statement frauds are revenue/accounts receivable frauds, inventory/cost of goods sold frauds, understatement of liabilities or expenses, and overstatement of assets.

How to Identify Red Flags in Financial Statements

A director should be vigilant about anything in a company's financial statements that raises a red flag. For example, if the firm's leverage ratios are too high, this indicates that it is taking on too much debt. If this is accompanied by falling sales and margins, the company may not be in a sound financial situation. For very cyclical businesses, a combination of these red flags could be a significant concern.

If a company has years of declining sales, it is losing momentum for long-term growth. Cost-cutting could help with profitability, but a company with consecutive years of declining sales needs to revisit its growth strategy. On the other hand, rapid sales increases are also a red flag. Between 1996 and 2000, for example, Enron's sales increased by more than 750%, from $13.3 billion to $100.8 billion. Sudden and unexplained changes in sales could be a red flag, as could sales to unknown entities and sales through complex transactions.

A trend of declining profit margins could mean that management is sacrificing profitability for growth. Be aware that an economic downturn could lead to lower margins naturally. Companies need to maintain healthy profit margins to cover operating expenses and the costs of delivering products and services.

Another red flag could be raised if management proposes to extend the depreciable lives of assets. Reducing depreciation expenses could overstate income. In the 1990s, for example, Waste Management Inc. avoided depreciation expenses by assigning and inflating salvage values and extending the useful lives of the garbage trucks that the company owned. A management team that overestimates the lives of assets may well be using other accounting tricks too.

Directors should be aware of 'other' items on the financial statements. These could come under 'other expenses', 'other assets', or 'other liabilities'. It raises a red flag if these 'other' items are large relative to the overall business. Board members need to find out what they are. How often do they occur? Why doesn't management specify them clearly? Are managers hiding secrets? Apart from the 'other' categories, companies also hide problems with 'restructuring', 'asset impairment', and 'goodwill impairment'. Inconsistent expenses trends could signify manipulation, so directors need to investigate any anomalies.

It is a red flag if sales increase together with customer returns, because management could be resorting to manipulation through 'bill and hold' sales. Here, the company creates the impression of a sale by billing the customer, but it never ships the goods. In the following accounting period, the company could report that there was a customer return. Doing this allows management to report higher sales in the current period. Directors need to dig deeper if this happens.

Increasing sales without a corresponding growth in cash flows could be another accounting anomaly. A shortage of cash could indicate rising accounts receivable or inventory, meaning that cash is tied up with customers or inventories. This red flag indicates poor management: an inability to forecast demand, or poor supply chain management.

Cash flow is difficult to manipulate and is a good sign of a healthy company. Unsteady cash flow could indicate accounting tricks, such as capitalising purchases instead of expensing them. When costs are capitalised, the resulting expense is spread over several years rather than reporting all of it in the current year. This will lead to overstated assets and income. This scheme was used in the WorldCom fraud.

Implementing Desired Capital Structure

A key board responsibility is to ensure that the company is well funded to achieve its business objectives. Its capital structure often depends on the availability of internal funds and the organisation's risk appetite. A company can choose from many different possible capital structures. Once a company has decided to seek external capital, it can decide the instruments. The two main sources of financing are equity and debt.

Equity. A company is generally formed by investors subscribing for shares in return for a claim on the firm's profits. When the company generates a profit, the directors may decide to pay a dividend to shareholders. Profits retained can be used to fund future growth or future dividend payments. From the company's perspective, equity funding is relatively low risk, because there is no obligation for the firm to return the funds invested, or to pay dividends.

Stock markets allow investors to buy and sell shares in publicly traded companies. These firms gain access to capital, while investors have an opportunity to own a slice of the company and potentially gain depending on its future performance. This market can be split into two main sections. The primary market is where new issues are first offered (in an initial public offering, or IPO), while any subsequent trading takes place in the secondary market.

Debt results from borrowing money from others. It is repaid over time or at maturity, usually with interest on the loan. When a company uses debt financing, in many jurisdictions it will pay less taxes. In addition, debt appears less expensive than equity financing (although it may not be so once adjusted for risk), and does not dilute the interests of existing shareholders. Debt financing usually has covenants attached, which require the company to agree to certain conditions. Large quantities of debt could impose financial burdens on the company, and potentially put it in financial distress. Debt is thus at the root of credit risk. This is substantial for many organisations, and needs to be watched for suppliers, clients, and partners.

Some debt instruments, such as corporate bonds, can be bought and sold by investors on credit markets around the world. These debt, credit, or fixed-income markets are much larger than the world's stock markets.

Understanding Valuation Fundamentals

The discounted cash flows (DCF) method is a way of assessing, in present-value terms, a sequence of net cash flows over time, taking into account the cost of financing (or any given discount rate).

Estimating Cash Flows

The most common valuation technique is the free cash flow to the firm method. By discounting all the cash flows over the life of the project or company, we determine the value of the project or company.

FCFF (Free Cash Flows to the Firm)
= EBITDA − the annual change in working capital − taxes
− capital expenditure required by the project each year

or, expressed equivalently:

FCFF (Free Cash Flows to the Firm) =
Net Income + Depreciation − the annual change in working capital
− capital expenditure

Cost of capital, or weighted average cost of capital (WACC)

The cost of capital is the weighted average cost of equity plus the cost of net indebtedness after tax, weighted relatively according to the debt/equity ratio of the capital employed.

Example

If 75% of capital employed in a company is equity and 25% is debt, gearing is 0.33. If the cost of equity is 13.33% and the tax-adjusted cost of debt is 6%, then the cost of capital is {(13.33 × 0.75) + (6 × 0.25)}% = 11.5%.

NPV, the Net Present Value

How can a business figure out whether a new project is financially viable? Net present value (NPV) is the most used method for valuing a project or company:

$$NPV = -Investment + \sum_{t=1}^{T} \frac{FCFF_t}{(1+WACC)^t}$$

where T represents the time period (e.g. number of years considered) and t is the year considered.

NPV compares the initial costs of a project with the total value of future cash flows from that project. Because these future cash flows are worth a different amount than if that cash were earned today, a discount rate is applied to the future revenue, allowing the business to compare the future revenue to alternative investments today. The discount rate is the average cost of capital for the company (the WACC described above).

Real Options

The real options method is a way to value flexibility, future opportunities, rights, and abandonment options in investments. It is based on mathematical option-pricing methodologies and does not rely directly on discounted cash flow methods. This approach can bring valuable insights when contingencies make DCF methods difficult to use, and when decisions in the future depend on the evolution of values across time.

Market Multiples

A comparable company analysis is a process used to evaluate the value of a company using the metrics of other similar-sized firms in the same industry. The assumption is that similar companies will have similar valuation multiples.

The most widely used multiples include the following:

- P/E ratio (Price of shares/Earnings Per Share)
- EV/EBITDA (Enterprise Value or Market Capitalisation + Debt over EBITDA)

- P/EBITDA
- P/Sales (the so-called sales multiple).

Many other ratios can easily be calculated to cater for specific situations.

Making Better M&A Decisions[1]

What is synergy in an M&A deal?

Synergy is defined as a state in which two or more things work together to produce an effect greater than the sum of their individual effects. This can also be expressed as 'the whole is greater than the sum of its parts'.

Good reasons for M&A synergies include reducing costs and increasing capabilities, market pricing power, or product offerings. But although M&As can be successful, they may sometimes occur just because managers want to build empires or boost individual egos, regardless of whether synergies exist. Directors thus need to have a rational analysis to see the justifications for such deals.

What are the key decisions in M&As?

First, successful M&As need a **strategic rationale**. A merger or acquisition should be designed for growing scale and scope, redefining a business or industry, and achieving long-term competitive advantage. The rationale must be clearly communicated to stakeholders. And please remember that strategy works only if integration works: integration preparation should thus go hand in hand with early analysis.

Second, **risk analysis**. There is no doubt that acquisitions can offer growth opportunities, but they are by nature complex and prone to risk. When considering an M&A strategy, opportunity often comes with risk and uncertainty. The pricing structure should take into account the risks considered, even those as fundamental as culture risk.

Third, **due diligence** is crucial. Pre-merger planning needs to include a formal review of the targets, and an evaluation of culture, organisational fit, and other non-financial elements. The price

---

[1] See also Chapter 20.

and financing ought to be appropriate and beneficial. Pre-merger planning could also include key integration processes, coordinated decisions, efficient communication, a marketing plan, and targeted milestones. Successful M&As require active management to achieve these milestones.

Fourth, **deal negotiation**, **pricing**, and **structuring** are key. There is no acquisition that is good whatever the price, and a strong discipline in not overpaying is at the heart of a good acquisition programme.

Fifth, **merger integration** should include the new company's design, and the integration of human resources, technical operations, and customer relationships. Integration needs to be completed quickly, and should be prepared and priced in before the deal. Arguably, dedicated integration managers should ideally be involved during the deal negotiation.

Finally, boards need to conduct a **post-integration analysis**. How well did the acquisition go? Have we achieved the strategic goals? What did we learn in the process to help make the next deal more successful? Ideally, such a step will already have been planned from early in the deal negotiation.

What Do We Know About M&As Through Empirical Studies?

Larger companies and cash-rich firms typically make bad deals. Private companies make better deals than public ones.

Size matters. Acquirer announcements are negatively related to company size. The returns are more negative the larger the deal is relative to the size of the acquirer. This usually leads to integration issues later.

Mergers that focus on the core activity increase shareholder value, whereas diversification acquisitions have a bigger share of value-destructive deals.

Payment methods make a difference, revealing the discipline required in the process. Cash payments are positive for the acquirer, whereas stock-for-stock exchanges have lower returns for the acquirer. This stems from the discipline required in cash deals that use the balance sheet of the acquirer and are thus more strenuous than stock deals.

M&As involving companies with greater cultural differences perform worse. Cultural conflicts lead to managerial issues in the combined company. Culture is the number one driver of integration failure.

Overseeing Risk[2]

Regulators and other stakeholders have pushed boards to be more active in risk oversight. As we saw in Part II, failing to manage risk properly can threaten the board's reputation. Through their risk oversight role, directors can decide the risk appetite of the company, design risk policies and procedures, and monitor management's implementation of these. Grasping the language of risk helps board members to communicate better.

Although risk is a complex topic, familiarity with the following terms is a good starting point:

- **Arbitrage:** the purchase of one security and simultaneous sale of another to give a risk-free profit. Some finance professionals also call arbitrage the purchase and sale of two securities that are similar but whose risks do not cancel.
- **Basis risk:** the residual risk that results when the two sides of a hedge do not move exactly together. Basis risk is central to optimal hedging theories, such as minimum variance hedge. This risk is at the heart of the failure of hedges, and it is thus important for board members to supervise when an explicit hedging programme is in place. Any hedge presents a basis risk and directors should be aware of what the basis risk and of the principles behind this.
- **Break-even analysis:** an analysis of the level of sales at which a project would just break even.
- **Call option:** an option to buy an asset at a specified exercise price on or before a specified exercise date (cf. put option). Call options exist on financial instruments such as stocks and currencies, as well as on commodities.
- **Correlation coefficient:** a measure of the closeness of the relationship between two variables. It consists of the ratio of the covariance to the product of the standard deviation of the variables.
- **Decision tree:** a method of representing alternative sequential decisions and the possible outcomes from them.
- **Derivative:** an asset whose value derives from that of some other asset. Major derivatives include futures (traded on exchanges), forwards (traded over the counter), swaps, options, and credit derivatives.

---

[2] See also Chapters 9–11.

- **Hedging:** buying (or owning) one asset and selling another in order to reduce risk. A perfect hedge produces a riskless portfolio. However, differences between the asset to hedge and the hedging instruments, as well as changes in time horizon, make perfect hedges extremely rare.
- **Future:** a contract to buy a commodity or security on a future date at a price that is fixed today. Unlike forward contracts, futures are traded on organised exchanges and are marked to market daily.
- **Market risk (systematic risk):** risk that cannot be diversified away. The CAPM (Capital Asset Pricing Model) measures an asset's exposure to systematic risk via the beta coefficient.
- **Monte Carlo simulation:** a method for calculating the probability distribution of possible outcomes, for example from a project. It combines a large number of mathematically generated scenarios (for example, across a distribution of an input price such as an oil price) to produce a distribution of an output, such as the NPV of a project. This method can thus provide probabilities of the NPV being above a certain number depending on the oil price.
- **Moral hazard:** the risk that the existence of a contract will change the behaviour of one or both parties to it. For example, an insured firm may take fewer fire precautions.
- **Normal or Gaussian distribution:** a symmetric bell-shaped distribution that can be completely defined by its mean and standard deviation.
- **Risk appetite:** the level of risk an organisation is willing to take. It often reflects management's attitude towards risks and is thus useful for board members to supervise and (often) help define. It can be defined across the different KPIs considered for the organisation; for example, by giving acceptable bands.
- **Sensitivity analysis:** an analysis of the effect on a project's profitability of possible changes in one dimension, such as sales or costs. No project analysis today should come without it.
- **Spot exchange rate:** the exchange rate of a currency for immediate delivery (cf. forward exchange rate).
- **Spot interest rate:** the interest rate fixed today on a loan that is made today (cf. forward interest rate).

- **Spot price:** the price of an asset for immediate delivery (in contrast to the forward or futures price).
- **Standard deviation:** a classic measure of risk that consists of the square root of the variance – a measure of variability or volatility. Like all mathematical measures, it is well-defined for rather liquid assets (such as traded stocks, commodities, or currencies), and is less useful for less coherent environments. The latter include situations affected very directly by people, such as M&A integration.

Financial literacy is crucial for efficient and effective board oversight. In this chapter, we discussed six financial topics:

- reading financial reports;
- interpreting between the lines of financial statements;
- implementing desired capital structure;
- understanding valuation fundamentals;
- making better M&A decisions; and
- overseeing risk.

Boards are responsible for the integrity of the company's financial reports, so directors need to analyse and interpret between the lines of financial statements. When a company decides on financing, directors need to ensure that shareholder expectations for return on investment and bondholder expectations for repayment are both carefully managed. Desired capital structure is a balance of the pros and cons of different financing alternatives.

Understanding valuation fundamentals helps directors to make better M&A decisions. Although boards should not be involved in day-to-day risk management, directors need to communicate in risk language in order to send a message that risk management is an integral component of governance.

Board values are another essential element of governance and are fundamental in setting the tone throughout the organisation. We address these in the next chapter.

Joanne Marker and Board Values at Comfre

*T*horsten was pushing his food around his plate at Joanne Marker's dinner table. It was 25 June 2019.

'OK, spill it Thor', Joanne said.

The young man looked up at his aunt, startled.

'You said you wanted some advice?' she said.

Thorsten sighed and put down his fork. He had recently joined the board of Kloetzel & Brothers, a global financial services company, but he already had some concerns.

'How did you know when something wasn't right? Or was really wrong? On the boards you were on, I mean', he asked.

'Well Thorsten, it's like this'. Joanne put her elbows on the table and clasped her hands for emphasis. 'Board directors, they're held to the same standards as everyone else – except they're not'. Thorsten raised his eyebrows. 'They're held to even higher standards. So, whatever's going on, you need to speak up now and fight for what is right'.

'But what if they don't listen to me?' Thorsten said. 'I mean, I'm the new, young guy'.

Joanne reached across the table to her nephew and patted his hand.

'Ah. Have you tried talking to James? I mean, over coffee or lunch?' James Caspar was Kloetzel's chair.

Thorsten nodded miserably. 'Then, my dear, you might need to rethink your service to this board', she said.

'Is that what happened to you? I mean, at Comfre?' Thorsten asked.

It had been a while since Joanne had thought about the Argentinian food company where she had held a seven-month board directorship back in 1998. She had accepted the position due to her eagerness to work in emerging markets – a wish she came to realise was perhaps overeager.

'That was a case of failed due diligence, I'm afraid', she said.

'You? Not doing your due diligence? I find that hard to believe', Thorsten said.

In Joanne's second board meeting at Buenos Aires-based Comfre, she had learned that the publicly-listed company was asking the board to approve two major investments: one in a big dairy company and another in a beef farm. It was the first she had heard of the deals, and they were reaching the end of the meeting. Joanne frantically flipped through the briefing papers, wondering if she had missed something, but there was no background information on the proposed deals. She asked many questions to try to understand the strategic logic of vertically integrating, but the answers from Comfre CEO Rodrigo Martinez were too vague for her liking.

During the last coffee break of the day, another independent director, Julio Diaz, sidled up to Joanne. Away from the others, he told her that the two companies were owned by two of Martinez's brothers-in-law. Alarm bells rang in Joanne's head.

In the final discussion at that meeting, she raised the conflict of interest issue, doing her best to remain polite yet firmly voicing her concerns. The chair, Antonio Alvarez, thanked Joanne, and reassured her that the deals fully complied with Argentinian legal requirements. The board voted to approve the investments, although she abstained.

Joanne felt sick for the duration of the 13-hour return flight. A week later, after going through Comfre's numbers in more detail, her discomfort was turning to alarm. She called Diaz to ask him what he thought about her emerging hypothesis. They looked at the figures together and discussed their concerns, both of them increasingly convinced that something was really wrong.

For days, Joanne tried reaching Alvarez, but his secretary kept informing her that he was unavailable. With a heavy heart, she prepared her resignation letter and printed it off. She called Diaz to inform him of her decision, and he confirmed that he would be doing the same the following day. They decided they would each make a final attempt to reach Alvarez to discuss their concerns.

The next day, Joanne turned on the news to see that investors had responded negatively to Comfre's proposed deals, and that the company's stock price had taken a dive. She again dialled Alvarez's number but there was no reply. Then the phone rang. It was Diaz. He told her that Comfre was being investigated for accounting fraud.

After dinner, Joanne tried to catch up on other work. But she found herself wondering over and over why she hadn't enquired earlier about the ownership of the Comfre group – and wondering whom she could have asked to better understand the context. Finally, she gave up trying to work and turned on the TV, to catch the end of the late-night news. She caught her breath when she saw the images of Alvarez being arrested in Buenos Aires for alleged accounting fraud.

***

'You'd better know what kind of board you're on sooner rather than later, Thorsten dear', Joanne said.

The young man nodded, and pushed his plate away.

'I think I need to schedule a call with James', he mumbled, wiping his mouth.

17

Board Leadership and Values

Corporate governance does not exist in a vacuum, but in a social context, and that alone demands that governance systems not be divorced from a sense of purpose and values. In addition, governance builds on a number of disciplines – law, regulatory policy, control, economics, management, and leadership – all of which are influenced in one way or another by moral philosophy. Today, the intensifying calls for good governance have once again underlined the fundamental importance of values, ethics, and morality in social and public action.

As boards continue to reel from spates of corporate scandals in all contexts and economies, and increasingly make the front pages of newspapers for the wrong reasons, a painful realisation has dawned on them. Yes, the metrics, documents, and other instruments of board activity and power may appear formidable and well-structured. Yet these may prove to be powerless and wholly ineffective when ethical breaches lead to corruption and the destruction of shareholder and social value on an unprecedented scale.

When the media later dissect the boards of collapsed companies, the most distressing part of the story was often the apparent normality, even banality, of their pre-scandal activity. There were nomination and governance committees distributing reports and updates, and in many cases a large proportion of the directors were independent, including luminaries from other industries, apparently unconflicted, and even from academia.

In February 2017, the board of Unilever, the Anglo-Dutch household goods and food manufacturer, rejected a $143 billion takeover offer from Kraft Heinz. The proposed heavily leveraged bid would have been one of the largest deals in corporate history. In withdrawing its bid, Kraft cited a lack of strategic merit. Yet what derailed it within less than 48 hours was the clash of corporate values the two companies represented.

With a history spanning 130 years and roots in the health crises of Victorian England, Unilever has come to be recognised as a leader in sustainable business. It has been committed to reducing its environmental footprint and acting as a force for social good. Its Sustainable Living Plan, introduced in 2010, now informs every aspect of Unilever's global operations. So do the company's corporate social responsibility programmes: instead of coalescing around a CSR label, they have been embedded in all of Unilever's business targets.

Kraft Heinz is run by private equity firm 3G Capital, famous for growing its business through acquisitions followed by aggressive cost-cutting and heavy job losses. Unilever shareholders, 70% of whom are long-term investors, were also sceptical about the bid. Meanwhile, the UK's largest trade union, Unite, described Kraft as 'predatory' and said that any deal would lead to job losses among the two companies' combined UK workforces of nearly 9000.

In the first quarter of 2019, Kraft Heinz wrote down the value of some of its brands by $15.4 billion. It also posted a $12.6 billion loss for the fourth quarter of 2018 and confirmed that the US SEC was investigating its accounting practices. By contrast, Unilever, like its European peers Nestlé and Danone, is increasingly focusing on new niche brands and healthier products.

Quality Boards Live and Breathe Integrity

The cumulative effect of recent corporate scandals has been to place integrity at the front and centre of a board's mandate. Whereas a company's management needs to comply with rules and guidelines, including ethical guidelines, a board of directors is expected to aim higher. A board is in a good position to be the natural guardian of a consistent set of values that emanate from deep-seated and strongly internalised beliefs. And safeguarding these values goes hand in hand with embracing integrity.

The appeal to integrity is not merely an abstract moral exhortation. Smaller or larger conflicts of interest abound in board work. Dealing with them with awareness and integrity becomes essential. In an increasingly uncertain business environment, the old, practical 'give and take', with a tangible sense of reciprocity between parties, may not be enough to win the trust and loyalty of employees, investors, and customers. This also requires honesty, a sense of openness, and a willingness to listen to and accommodate the other party's needs. And it requires compassion, rather than just rules, policy, and clear precedents. Reinforcing an organisation's relationships takes a lot of trust, and more often than not a heart.

Integrity is often seen as a strong driver of a board's success. The understanding of the term, and what it means in practice, will vary from organisation to organisation. But most will agree that having integrity means doing the right thing regardless of whether or not it is popular, attracts publicity, or results in immediate gains. When divorced from integrity, individuals' and organisations' intellect, resourcefulness, and action may quickly become self-serving, devoid of meaning, and even toxic for their relationships with the outside world.

Which and Whose Values?

More than any other part of an organisation, the board understands that values morally underpin every action and initiative the firm undertakes. The board must be clear that values are not paperwork to be sorted out or boxes to be checked in a questionnaire. Rather, they make us human and connect to our deeply felt need to do good and contribute.

This may sound very lofty and hard to grasp. But we should remember that values lie at the heart of corporate culture – itself a blueprint of values, beliefs, rules, and patterns of behaviour that provides the organisation with a coherent way of looking at the world. Progressive boards have upheld the notion that business is, and must be, ultimately about people. From this vantage point, organisations are recast as deeply value-laden spaces where humans learn together and share their successes as well as failures.

Encouragingly, the discussion of values in business is not nearly as distant from the real world of contracts and performance targets as one might assume. At a time when business competition and service delivery are being pervasively disrupted, organisations can no longer rely on the output of top-down, bureaucratic, impersonal operation centres to delight customers and fire their imaginations. For this, they need employees who give the best of themselves and of their talent, creativity, and dedication. This rarely happens when companies rely solely on the old tools of hierarchy, obedience, or monetary compensation. Rather, it is a sense of shared values that inspires employees' most collaborative and imaginative efforts.

People are not drawn to innovate and create, and to break down silos in their company, simply because they receive a paycheck every month. They do so because they feel recognised and respected for who they are and what they believe in. The best organisations recognise the potential value of their culture as a potent asset, a consistent boost to their brand equity, and a magnet for talented individuals with integrity. In the long term, a vibrant company culture rooted in clearly defined and publicly upheld values is possibly the most powerful instrument for attracting and retaining talent.

Other stakeholders also increasingly demand that organisations demonstrate honesty, openness, loyalty, and a passion for contributing to society. Although this may of course play out differently depending on the company's purpose and DNA, the underlying consistency of expression and integrity of action will not go unnoticed. In the present economic, political, and social environment of a 'trust deficit', relentless uncertainty and change, these externally facing values are crucial to a company's reputation.

An effective board helps to define the company's guiding values and aspirations and ensures that these circulate throughout the organisation – including at the day-to-day operational level. In recent years, the emergence of new approaches such as the core values method has offered practical ways to build and renew culture in

In the wake of the #MeToo movement that started in the US against sexual abuse of women (and sometimes of men), and quickly gained traction across the globe, several large corporations and their boards have had to grapple with the fact that bad behaviour by their top management or directors can negatively impact the business. Leslie Moonves, who ran CBS for more than 20 years as CEO and chair, was forced to resign by the company's board in September 2018 for alleged past sexual misconduct. As part of the settlement agreement that ousted him, Moonves was forced to give up $34.5 million of stock awards. The CBS board reacted quickly once the scandal broke in summer 2018 and launched an independent investigation into the allegations. But it was also strongly criticised for not having addressed the problem sooner.

an organisation. This puts boards in a stronger position than ever to examine the company and raise questions such as:

- What is the ultimate purpose of our collective effort?
- What aspirations are we pursuing?
- What is the impact of our undertaking on society?

All too often, however, today's organisations thrive on stability, predictability, and control, and are committed to a bureaucratic model according to which companies and their employees perform their tasks in a machine-like way. This view has become entrenched to the point where it is rarely challenged, despite the obvious limits it imposes on the richness of organisational life. Viewed through this lens, people become easily replaceable and in some contexts very nearly obsolete.

Unsurprisingly, therefore, statements of a company's values, including its vision and mission, were often drafted by a few representatives of senior management with support from the PR or marketing communications departments. A neat one-page document listing these values was then placed behind glass, framed, and hung on the wall.

Strong boards today know that this won't do. More importantly, they understand that values can never be dictated by 'someone at the top'. A firm is a live, dynamic organism, teeming with rich and complex discussions, conversations, and narratives. Often, the best place to learn what makes the people in the firm tick is in the informal spaces by the office water-cooler or its social media equivalent, where employees exchange information, speculate about future outcomes, voice their hopes and grievances, and jointly try to make sense of the reality around them. Yet for decades, this 'bottom-up' narrative remained completely hidden from the organisation's official views and perspectives, which were dominated by management and its 'black and white' structures and processes.

Modern boards have grasped that the intersection of values prioritised by employees, management, and customers should serve as the basis for developing a shared vision of 'who we are' and 'what we stand for'. This vision then informs the company's mission, strategy, and policies, right down to everyday work practices.

Boards are expected to have a vision for their organisations – one that recognises the company's purpose, inspires pride in its employees and confidence among customers, and sounds genuine and accessible to investors. Vision and mission are still relevant in articulating shared purpose and direction. They are also useful for making abstract ideas practically relevant, tangible, and action oriented.

Most importantly, the values that have been captured as part of a shared vision need to be practised, lived, and celebrated. It is not enough to write them down. To quote a modern-day management thinker, Henry Mintzberg, 'We cannot take for granted that the production of rules and regulations, organisational charts, roles and responsibilities, held together by chains of command and lines of authority will allow human values and judgment to flourish'.[1]

Board Values vs. Organisational Values

Of course, boards will struggle to safeguard and oversee the 'values' conversation within their organisations if they have never taken the time before to reflect on the culture and values of the board itself. Here, the directors' personal values – which we already discussed in Chapter 3 – can serve as a simple yet productive starting point.

A passionate, committed board understands that it cannot simply find values in literature or copy them from a PowerPoint presentation. Instead, it will reflect and actively draw on values that its members have developed and honed over their many years in corporate leadership and public service. The board's values will then resonate with those of the individual directors, which are shaped by unique sets of individual accomplishments, visions for the industry and organisation, ethical outlooks, and moral beliefs.

Describing the board's collective values in a succinct manner will not always be easy. But the main contours of the ethos – of what is permissible and what is not, what the board believes in, and why these beliefs are non-negotiable – should be discernible to everyone, if not for how they are defined then certainly in the way they are projected and practised.

The board is responsible for articulating its culture and promoting values as benchmarks of the beliefs and behaviours inside an organisation. When a company has determined its vision, mission,

---

[1] Mintzberg, H. (1979). *The Structuring of Organizations*. Pearson.

and values, it is essential that the board demonstrates leadership to communicate, endorse, and implement them.

Reflecting this new board remit, the role of the chair has expanded in a similar direction. In addition to conducting board meetings in a focused and organised manner, the chair is now looked upon as a source of moral authority, particularly in times of crisis. His or her visible public stance on ethics in the context of corporate vision and values statements can contribute to dispelling the widely held perception that business is at best ethics neutral or even devoid of ethics.

Effective boards understand the importance of values, communication, and vision in building a successful company. They also recognise their own role in striving toward this goal. Put simply, boards are designed and equipped to build credibility and trust in ways that executive teams cannot. The best boards also set positive precedents and contribute to defining new standards and practices of global governance.

Family Values in Business

In general, family-owned companies have consistently shown a heightened sensitivity to defining and promoting their values. Many have actively negotiated a creative tension between family and business values, aiming to put forward a third category of 'family business values'. Some family companies have chosen to subsume their business organisation within an overarching, family-centric structure, recognising that the family needs to prosper before the business can grow as well.

Taking a far-sighted position on an ethical question, even though it may hurt short-term profitability, is an important aspect of a board member's responsibility. And it is crucial for instilling values throughout an organisation. Through daily practice and use, such values can visibly link the priorities of the leadership team with the day-to-day activities of the organisation. And the board and the company will have a solid foundation of integrity as a result.

For large companies in particular, upholding the organisation's values in the governance of its subsidiaries can sometimes be challenging. This is what we discuss next.

CHAPTER 18

The Intricacies of Subsidiary/Holding Governance

Larger organisations in particular may have tens or even hundreds of wholly- or partly-owned subsidiaries, which raises the question of how to govern them. Simply put, should they be governed at subsidiary level or at group level? And how does the role of the director change as a result? Interestingly, these questions arise in 100%-owned subsidiaries, as well as in those where the group has a majority stake or even a large minority holding. This chapter reflects on the diversity of best practices from different environments in the hope of inspiring further governance evolution in this area.

The issue of subsidiary/holding governance is becoming even more important for three reasons:

- the rise of national interests;
- increasingly engaged financial actors;
- the dynamics of business transformation.

As countries around the world increasingly seek to assert their national interests, their regulators and governments are asking for governance decisions to take place in their country and not at international headquarters. They have thus started imposing decision powers at national governance level, including in banks and insurance companies. National interests must now be protected in many areas, such as financial stability, health, and food safety. Regulators are asking for national subsidiaries to have effective boards, not just boards on paper.

As a result, subsidiaries of international groups must often go beyond complying with national laws. They must also ensure that governance, strategic decisions, and the management of any failures all protect that country's national interest. These issues therefore need to be considered at national or local level as part of a decision process. Group governance can no longer simply be imposed at national level. National boards of international groups are thus becoming more significant.

Second, previously passive financial actors, including sovereign wealth funds, increasingly regard governance as a key risk. They are therefore becoming more engaged in nominating or influencing board members, leading to what can effectively become a subsidiary/holding relationship, albeit at the other end of the spectrum to the fully owned subsidiaries of many groups. These financial actors are so proactive, creative, and resourceful that they are helping to redefine subsidiary/holding governance.

Finally, and most importantly, business transformation has shaken traditional organisational structures. Companies confronted with the reality of natural selection need to evolve and innovate. Often, this entails self-cannibalisation or diversification, which are best achieved in external but controlled entities. One classic example of this is Nestlé and Nespresso. Similarly, Russia's Sberbank developed its IT capabilities by creating an external entity. This was so successful that it became the largest player in the country; Sberbank then reintegrated it. Ant Financial and Alibaba are another good example. Firms may also need to separate previously joint activities in order to be able to sell or restructure that business more easily.

The art of subsidiary governance is to balance alignment with the holding company or group with the independence of a subsidiary's decision-making. This balance will vary depending on context. For example, the oil majors keep a tight rein on their subsidiaries, joint ventures, and production-sharing agreements. The boards of these entities have strict rules to follow, directors are direct employees of the owner, and decisions are clearly brought back to group level whenever something critical happens. The group tightly controls structures (including the shareholder agreement, board organisation, and committees) and also culture (as reflected in board practices, the notion of independence, and the style of board discussions).

At the other end of the spectrum, many financial actors, including sovereign wealth funds, tend to take a slightly looser approach. For example, the International Finance Corporation (IFC), the investment arm of the World Bank group, nominates independent external directors to be board members of its investee companies, sometimes even when the IFC holds a large stake. Similarly, Temasek, the sovereign wealth fund of Singapore, mostly uses independent directors and allows quite a bit of freedom of structure in its subsidiaries, even the fully owned ones. In the latter case, shared culture will typically ensure a certain level of consistency between the fund's overarching objectives and the decisions of its subsidiaries.

In subsidiary governance, the two main levers for adjusting the intensity of control or independence are structures and culture.

Structures

Some groups have embedded strong structures in their subsidiary governance. These can emanate from the original shareholder agreement. For example, board representation, or structures such as committee choices and chair nominations, can be clearly set out in the structuring of the organisation. In some family businesses, the representation of different family members across the group's various subsidiaries provides a basic structure. My team and I work with a family where the siblings and their children hold board positions in different subsidiaries according to their own skillsets. In addition, the siblings sit on the group board along with independent directors.

Some of the most sophisticated structures for subsidiary governance are found in the oil and gas industry. For example, I work with a national oil company that has more than 100 subsidiaries. The group proceeded by mapping these subsidiaries in terms of their strategic importance and the governance influence that the group has (some are joint ventures with strong foreign partners). The group then mapped board decisions across three dimensions:

- Long-term value, typically including strategy and capital expenditure decisions.
- Short-term performance, including the annual budget, operational organisational matters, and individual performance.
- Organisational health, including HSE (Health, Safety and Environment) responses, risk reviews, and board effectiveness.

HOLDINGS GOVERNANCE MAP

KEY DECISIONS	DIRECTOR'S POSITION TOWARDS OWNER — REPRESENTATION	DIRECTOR'S POSITION TOWARDS OWNER — INDEPENDENCE	OWNER CONSULTATION CONTACT — GROUP CEO	OWNER CONSULTATION CONTACT — ASSET MANAGER	OWNER CONSULTATION CONTACT — OTHER RELEVANT CORPORATE
LONG-TERM DIMENSIONS					
Business Plan (& changes)	▨		✓	✗	
Major CAPEX (above X threshold)			✓	✗	
Dividend and/or changes to related policies		▨	✓	✗	
Capital Structure	▨				✗
M&A and divestures at Subsidiary level		▨	✓	✗	
Changes in by-laws					✗
Changes in key policies (e.g., HSE)					●
YEARLY CONSIDERATIONS					
Annual Budget	▨		✓	✗	
Major client supply/pricing agreements				●	
Business and Financial KPIs				●	
Budget deviations (threshold specific)				●	
Capex deviations (threshold specific)				●	
Changes in Organisational Structure				✗	
Major restructurings/layoffs		▨		✗	●
N-1 executive change			✓		
BUSINESS HYGIENE					
Approval of Audit and Risk Reports					●
Disclosure reports (Financial, Audit, HSE)					
CEO appointment, removal or change; CEO succession plan	▨		✓		✗
CEO review and compensation					●
Changes in Governance (e.g., new sub-committee)		▨			●
Company HR policy (e.g., compensation policy)					✗
Changes in director's role					
Subsidiary board member nominations			✓		✗

POSITION
- ▨ BOARD MEMBER DECISION WITH OPTIONAL CONSULTATION
- ▨ SHAREHOLDER DECISION WITH BOARD MEMBER INPUT
- ▨ BOARD MEMBER DECISION WITH MANDATORY CONSULTATION

CONSULTATION PROTOCOL
- ✓ APPROVAL
- ✗ RECOMMENDATION
- ● INPUT

Figure 18.1   Holdings Governance Map

Within these categories, about 25 typical decisions are mapped. A decision is then taken as to whether the owner representatives on the board should be proactive in representing the group, or whether the directors should have the responsibility to choose. A director who proactively represents the owner might engage in mandatory consultation with the group at the appropriate level – such as an asset manager within the group or an individual responsible for governance.

The structure thus allows for a complete mapping of the group's engagement at subsidiary level, depending on the nature of the subsidiary, the group's willingness to engage, and the type of decision considered. It also illustrates the duality of ownership representation on these boards, as some decisions are taken fully independently while others require direct group representation. The clarity brought by the system is valuable.

Culture

Another way to tune subsidiary governance is through the culture embedded within boards and within directors themselves. This is a strong driver of success, as organisations such as Temasek have shown. Indeed, culture may appear to be the best driver of successful subsidiary governance, or even investee governance. This happens when truly independent directors share the same fundamental values – notably integrity, a sense of purpose, and responsibility – and the same overarching national or organisational objectives, and then decide freely what is right for the organisation.

The challenge for the group is thus to drive a well-aligned culture across subsidiaries while preserving the spirit of independence that is fundamental to good governance. This is often quite difficult. More tightly controlling groups risk having a small number of like-minded directors who lack the diversity and competitiveness of their peers in a more open group. Best practices thus include fostering a natural selection process among board members themselves, with those most able to combine alignment and independence rising further faster.

To help develop alignment, a group should organise regular sessions that bring together directors from different subsidiaries. These gatherings should focus on key dimensions such as essentials of governance effectiveness, as well as other timely issues such as cybersecurity or geopolitics, for example. Ideally, the sessions will use multiple formats and shapes (lecturers, speakers, panels, and brainstorming groups), and take place throughout the year to ensure engagement and continuous education.

In some contexts, these culture elements have become very solid. Think, for example, of the role of the party in the governance of China's state-owned institutions – including through the professionalism of Huijin, the Chinese sovereign wealth fund department dedicated to the governance of financial institutions.

There is a risk of driving the subsidiary governance process too much through culture and not enough through structures. The risk is that the homogeneity of board members will make governance less effective, especially when creativity and innovativeness matter. It is thus important to welcome some disruption and encourage a true diversity of perspectives when governing subsidiaries. This can be done within the framework of common values that are well appreciated by all involved.

By establishing the right structures and culture, groups and organisations can fine-tune subsidiary governance to their purpose. The key is to balance independence and alignment. The most engaged groups determine the level of alignment they want at each subsidiary and then create it through these two levers. And in the next chapter, we discuss how boards can enhance entrepreneurial leadership.

CHAPTER 19

Fostering Entrepreneurship from the Board[1]

The legacy of Apple co-founder Steve Jobs is that of a genius, an innovator of the most creative and visionary kind. But in 1985, the company's board let Jobs go after he got caught up in a fight with then CEO John Sculley. Sales of the second-generation Mac, the Macintosh Office, had been disastrous. Jobs argued for a discounting strategy, but Sculley was firmly opposed, convinced that this would result in an unacceptable loss. The board sided with the CEO and said that Jobs was too disruptive to the company.

Thirty years later, Sculley spoke of his regret. 'I came from corporate America. There it was kind of secular, there wasn't the passion that entrepreneurs have', he said. 'I have so much respect now decades later for founders, for the belief and passion and vision that they have. So to remove a founder, even if he wasn't fired, was a terrible mistake'.[2] Sculley added: 'I really blame the board. Because I think the board understood Apple before I came, they understood Steve. They knew what my experience was and what it wasn't. And I really believe there could have been a solution to keep me and Steve working together, because we were really good friends up until that point'.[3]

---

[1] Parts of this chapter were developed in an unpublished article with Sophie Coughlan and Peter Wuffli.
[2] http://uk.businessinsider.com/john-sculley-admits-steve-jobs-never-forgave-him-before-jobs-died-2015-5.
[3] http://www.forbes.com/sites/randalllane/2013/09/09/john-sculley-just-gave-his-most-detailed-account-ever-of-how-steve-jobs-got-fired-from-apple/.

The conflict between Jobs and Sculley exemplifies the tension at the centre of many boards. With the proliferation of regulation across sectors and an increased focus on compliance, directors dedicate considerable attention to overseeing risks. But in effectively managing short-term downside risk, boards may be stifling innovation and entrepreneurial leadership. Good corporate governance helps to ensure high-quality decisions that enhance a firm's performance over the long term. And in many industries today, entrepreneurship is central to the corporate renewal needed for long-term success.

By undermining entrepreneurship, therefore, boards may be failing in their real responsibility. Would a new Jobs avoid being fired today? Maybe not. In the hope of charting a more harmonious way forward, this chapter explores where the tensions are, how good governance can enhance entrepreneurial leadership, and the main levers for practical implementation.

'Best Practice' Governance vs. Entrepreneurship

Have regulatory and governance standards stifled entrepreneurial leadership? Danish inventor Thomas Lund thinks so. In the early 1980s, Lund founded Dansk Teknologi at the age of 32. His mission was to stimulate innovation in product development, manufacturing, and production systems, in areas such as nitrogen oxides (NO_x) reduction, offshore drilling technology, flight catering, hospital products, analysis instruments, and digital dosing pumps. Dansk Teknologi has worked with the boards of many leading Danish multinationals and other global companies, and several of its products have received international awards and have worldwide patents. Lund himself has served on the boards of several leading organisations, including the Grundfos group, the Poul Due Jensen Foundation, and the central board of Danish Industry. And he has suffered the isolation of being entrepreneurial on a large company board. 'At many companies, boards kill innovation', Lund says.

In deterring innovation, boards are threatening what is often the lifeblood of business value creation. Although today's widespread public scepticism toward business leaders, and especially those in the financial industry, is understandable, we should avoid damaging entrepreneurship and long-term value creation in the process.

The trend toward more detailed and formalistic regulation reflects a belief that risks can be 'organised away' with appropriate rules. Yet this approach ignores the fact that failure is an inherent and necessary part of capitalism – which is itself based on a natural selection process – and of real long-term business value creation. Directors must therefore seek to strengthen entrepreneurship at board level and develop a greater and smarter appetite for measured risks.

Boards Should Actively Encourage Entrepreneurship

What are the distinguishing features of a company's culture, strategy, or behaviour that make it entrepreneurial in nature? And how can boards best support the development of such attributes – or at least prevent them being suppressed – in the organisations they govern?

To address this, scholars have developed the concept of an organisation's entrepreneurial orientation (EO).[4] This consists of five components: risk-taking, or the firm's willingness to commit resources to ventures whose outcome is uncertain; proactiveness, or the ability to anticipate future opportunities in terms of both product development and industry disruption as well as customer insights and markets; innovativeness, as reflected in the types of products and services the organisation introduces to the market; competitive aggressiveness, or how directly a company attacks its competitors and pursues target markets; and autonomy, or how independently an individual or team initiates an idea and follows it through.

Much has been written about the correlation between entrepreneurial orientation and company performance,[5] and about how firms can enhance their EO. But there is far less literature on the role of boards in encouraging entrepreneurship in well-established firms.

This is a pity, because boards can support management in several ways to give companies a more entrepreneurial mindset. First, directors can help to build a culture of innovation and autonomy;

---

[4] See for example Miller, D. (1983). The correlates of entrepreneurship in three types of firms. *Management Science* 29(7): 770–791; Lumpkin, G.T. and G.G. Dess (1996). Clarifying the entrepreneurial orientation construct and linking it to performance. *The Academy of Management Review* 21(1): 135–172; and Covin, J.G. and D.P. Slevin (1991). A conceptual model of entrepreneurship as firm behavior. *Entrepreneurship Theory and Practice* Fall: 7–25.

[5] See also Urban, B. and J. Barreira (2010). Empirical investigations into firm technology orientation and entrepreneurial orientation. *International Journal of Innovation and Technology Management* 7: 329–351.

for example, by role-modelling constructive dissent and asking the right questions regarding cross-department initiatives. Second, boards can help management to build incentive structures that encourage ownership and collaboration; for example, by sharing accountability across departments for success. In addition, by demonstrating real passion for the business and investing their own resources, directors can help to foster a culture of calculated and committed risk-taking. Finally, board members' experiences from other industries can be vital in identifying potential disruptions to the competitive space.

ENTREPRENEURIAL ORIENTATION FROM THE BOARD

Dimension	Characteristics	Implications for the Board
Innovations & Autonomy	Time & space for experimentation	Define dashboard of innovation KPIs, shared across departments
	Cross-functional, diverse teams spanning boundaries	Role model a culture of constructive dissent and boundary-spanning
	Openness to discussion and opposing views	Balance of independent and executive directors
Ownership & Proactiveness	Sufficient resourcing / space allowed	Incentive structures which encourage collaboration among the leadership team (shared accountability for success, e.g. R&D Marketing)
	Shared accountability / recognition for success	
	Engagement and initiative	
Passion & Risk-taking	Energy and fun	Some resources allocation for uncertain reward
	Lack of orthodoxy	Role modelling passion
		Directors having 'skin in the game'
		Supporting culture-building initiatives
Competitive Aggressiveness	Identifying competitive space to occupy	Offering perspectives from other industries
	Targeting competitors' consumers	Identifying potential disruptions

Figure 19.1   Entrepreneurial Orientation from the Board

Innovativeness and Autonomy

Large organisations must cross typical corporate boundaries in order to innovate. Companies that encourage interaction across departments, for example, help their employees to understand more fully how different parts of the business work together to deliver to the customer. Such exchanges also allow people to collaborate and build on one another's ideas. In addition to providing forums for interaction, entrepreneurial firms realise that giving employees some degree of autonomy, in the form of time to explore and pursue innovative ideas, can lead to value-creating initiatives.

Founded in 2002, Australian software company Atlassian is a leading provider of collaboration, development, and issues-tracking products for teams. The firm had its IPO in 2015 and was valued at $30 billion in the spring of 2019, following years of strong sales growth.[6]

Atlassian gives its employees space to experiment: 'You have to give people the time and latitude to think creatively', says its co-CEO Mike Cannon-Brookes. Twice a year, the company runs 'Shipit' days, during which teams form and agree on what they think is the most important problem to fix. Each team then has 24 hours to come up with a possible solution. Projects are voted upon in successive rounds until a select few remain. If a solution seems worth developing further, then there is a cross-silo team that has already worked together and is ready to go. One of the benefits of the process is that it allows for creative disagreement, because different teams may think of different ways to fix problems. What's more, the best idea wins, not the one that is owned by the best-connected individual or favoured for other political reasons. Previous Shipit days produced JIRA Service Desk (an enterprise helpdesk software) and Confluence (an enterprise team collaboration software), which now account for a large proportion of the company's sales.

Another approach, often used by larger companies, is to use external sources of innovation to reduce organisational risk in developing new ideas and products. In 2001, for example, Procter & Gamble introduced Connect+Develop, a crowdsourcing platform that has since led to many new products. One of them is P&G's $1-billion brand Febreze, which began as a product to refresh household textiles. As the business developed, P&G saw the potential to grow the brand by broadening into air care more generally, and collaborated with external companies to develop additional Febreze products.

---

[6] https://www.cnbc.com/2019/05/09/atlassian-shares-hit-record-after-goldman-recommends-buying-the-stock.html.

Passion and Risk-Taking

To inspire and capture the best ideas from people, companies need to create an environment that stirs their employees' passions. Boards can play a useful role in this process. Directors who demonstrate real commitment and take personal risks for the company – not least in a financial sense, so that they have 'skin in the game' – help to build a company culture in which a sense of ownership can flourish. Board members also need to support management to build this kind of ownership culture.

Consider the case of Zappos CEO Tony Hsieh, who rescued the online shoe and clothing company from certain disaster in 1999. He revived the firm, building annual sales from virtually nothing to $1 billion. And by pledging to create a culture that empowered employees and made customer service a central priority, Hsieh built Zappos into a unique brand, resulting in the firm's inclusion in Fortune's 'Best Companies to Work for' list. 'Positive office culture assures you of passionate employees, outstanding performance and the ability to attract the best talent,' Hsieh said.[7]

Innovations included a yearly Culture Book (available to anyone interested in its content), a Face Game (in which users score points based on their ability to correctly identify fellow employees), nap rooms, a petting zoo, a bowling alley, karaoke, and other events. Each employee was also challenged to make at least one improvement every week to help Zappos better reflect its core values – including 'be humble', 'do more with less', 'be passionate and determined', and 'create fun and a little weirdness'.

But a growing conflict between Hsieh and the Zappos board ultimately forced the sale of the company to Amazon in 2009 for more than $1.2bn. The board viewed what it called 'Tony's social experiments' as PR stunts that were distractions for the business, and pressured Hsieh to focus less on employee happiness and more on selling shoes. Worried that the board might fire him and destroy the company culture, Hsieh approached Amazon, which he believed better understood Zappos' culture. Today, Hsieh continues to run the company in his own unique way.[8]

---

[7] Hollender, Jeffrey (2013). Lessons we can all learn from Zappos CEO Tony Hsieh. *The Guardian*, 13 March 2013. http://www.theguardian.com/sustainable-business/zappos-ceo-tony-hsieh

[8] Hsieh, Tony (2010). Why I sold Zappos. *Inc Magazine*. 1 June 2010. http://www.inc.com/magazine/20100601/why-i-sold-zappos.html.

Boards have an important role to play in bringing passion to a company, but can only perform it if the boardroom culture encourages open exchanges between directors. As we have seen in this chapter, board members may be overly sceptical and inject excessive doubt, suffocating new ideas as they emerge. Building trust at board level is therefore essential if directors are to bring 'crazy' ideas and creativity, and help fan emerging entrepreneurial fires within the company.

Mergers and acquisitions are another area where boards need to balance entrepreneurial instincts with prudent risk assessments. We will look more closely at this in the next chapter.

20

The Board's Oversight Framework for M&As[1]

Companies are looking beyond industry boundaries and national borders for external growth opportunities. While merger and acquisition (M&A) activity is cyclical, deals themselves have become increasingly complex and sophisticated. This is stretching the abilities of boards, and is compelling directors to devote more time, focus, and dedication to M&A oversight. M&A decisions are among the most important that a board must make. And for many directors, the M&A process is one of the most challenging, frustrating, and dangerous.

Decisions to approve or reject offers are closely watched and criticised by investors, public authorities, and other stakeholders. The directors of the acquiring company may face disapproval for paying too much and leaving money on the table, and must weigh concerns about empire building or egos. They also face mounting pressure from employees, suppliers, customers, the media, and regulators, all of which could be affected by an M&A deal.

In a fast-moving situation, directors are supposed to make all the most important decisions in a very short period of time. Their personal interests are also at stake, because directors of both the acquirer and target companies will often lose their board seats as a result of a deal. The M&A process is a stress test for boards – if anything goes wrong, the directors may be liable for damages for

---

[1]This chapter was initially written as an article with Abraham Lu.

M&A BOARD ORIENTATION

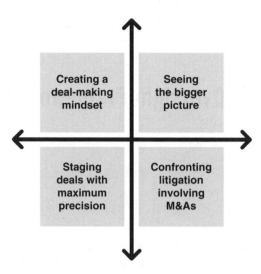

Figure 20.1   M&A board orientation

breaches of duty or other alleged transgressions in making the deals. Even when legal liability is less of an issue, the reputational stakes are high. In short, directors are vulnerable when overseeing M&A deals.

This chapter presents an M&A oversight framework for board members. Given the high-stakes role that directors play, deals have to be well conceived and structured, and implemented with discipline. When boards fail in their M&A oversight and succumb to deal mania, the process becomes even more stressful. But the four-stage approach outlined in Figure 20.1 can help directors make better M&A decisions.

Creating a Deal-Making Mindset

M&A deals can start with a simple phone call. In April 2015, Royal Dutch Shell's CEO Ben van Beurden explained how the company's acquisition of BG Group came about. 'I called [BG Group Chair] Andrew [Gould] up and we had a very good and constructive discussion about the idea and it very quickly seemed to make sense to both of us', van Beurden said. In under a month, the two companies arranged a $70 billion oil megamerger.[2]

---

[2] Zhdannikov, D. and K. Schaps (2015). Sunday telephone call sparked $70 billion Shell-BG deal (8 April 2015). Reuters.

Such a phone call may appear to be a sudden event with too much information and urgency. But it may not seem so sudden to experienced directors – they conceive of deals all the time, including preparing to buy or sell the business the next day if the price is right. A board with a deal-making mindset will not struggle to make the case for how a certain transaction will fit with the company's strategy.

Boards with strong M&A DNA have institutionalised the merger and acquisition process, possibly with an M&A committee. The task of this committee is to supervise the company's M&A strategy, challenge management's thinking on potential transactions, and analyse potential mergers, acquisitions, investments, or disposals.

Such a board is always prepared for transactions, and has current knowledge of how specific deals can create value. Stakeholders, including shareholders, are encouraged to propose deals that might be beneficial. Dry runs are typically organised, with investment bankers presenting a proposal. The deal flow is structured and analysed by looking at the type of acquisitions or buyers that the organisation could target, and possibly mapping them into a matrix. Furthermore, simulated discussions, outside of real transactions, are encouraged.

A quick consensus on the board regarding a deal typically reveals a lack of preparation. Discussions need to be rich and tense, or else the board will certainly fail. Acquisitions are complex, and directors should challenge them. 'Boards must have the diversity of knowledge necessary to grasp the full implications of management's recommendations and to remain independent judges of them', Gould says. 'I am a firm believer that all boards should have their own body of industry specialists amongst the other skills that boards require'.[3]

Contrary opinions can typically be levered into a better deal. To have such opinions, a board needs to have the means and structures to collect adequate information. For example, one director may stress regulatory risk. This led Syngenta to negotiate a large break-up fee with both Monsanto and ChemChina, its potential buyers, in the case of regulatory problems – something that enhanced the overall value of the deal. Good board work on acquisitions will be structured, will require much information and specialisation, and will lever constructive dissent.

---

[3] Andrew Gould HPB presentation at IMD, May 2016.

Seeing the Bigger Picture

When considering a merger or acquisition, executives and deal advisors are often caught up in the idea of the deal itself, and come close to being enamoured with the transaction (or sometimes hating it!). An active board should be willing to focus on the big picture and investigate the deal's assumptions more deeply in order to reassess all the challenges, risks, and opportunities.

This big picture could be a corporate strategic shift, a stream of similar transactions to support one strategy, or simply an industry trend. Deals driven by a bigger strategy often succeed.

The board's big picture could also relate to the geographic, macro, economic, governance, technological, regulatory, or societal environment.

Staging Deals with Maximum Precision

The board's comprehensive and objective oversight can help management to follow a disciplined process at every stage of a transaction. Figure 20.2 below illustrates the six phases of an M&A deal.

Strategy Fit Review

The board needs to understand clearly why the deal is being proposed. With a majority of M&A deals well demonstrated to be

China's largest business property developer, Dalian Wanda Commercial Properties, a $40 billion company, has signalled a major shift in strategy in recent years. Knowing that China's real estate market could have an uncertain future, Dalian Wanda decided to reduce its reliance on property sales and make forays into 'alternative, income-generating businesses away from the property market'.

The company became an aggressive acquirer in pursuing this strategy. It bought the US cinema chain AMC Theatres in 2012; British yacht maker Sunseeker International in 2013; Infront Sports & Media and the World Triathlon Corporation in 2015; and Legendary Entertainment for $3.5 billion in 2016. From a strategic shift perspective, the company successfully expanded overseas to diversify away from China's property market, even though it then faced pressures to scale back this foreign expansion.

A BOARD M&A PROCESS

Figure 20.2   A board M&A process

destroying value, directors need to be convinced that this particular deal is different. They should ask questions such as:

- How was the deal sourced and what alternative deals are being considered?
- What are the potential and unique benefits?
- What is the key driver of the deal: to strengthen core business, acquire a technology, establish market presence, or gain market share from competitors?
- How realistic are the underlying assumptions about synergies? (Synergies are typically highly overvalued by executives and advisors alike. Integration needs to be thought through from the start.)
- Does the culture of the target align with that of the acquirer? (Culture clashes are the number one cause of integration failure.)

The board has a responsibility to be independent, create an open discussion environment, encourage debate, and keep dominant individuals in check (such as the CEO or a particular board member).

In this way, everyone can contribute openly to the strategic fit analysis. This is particularly important when a CEO puts his or her job on the line if a deal is not approved – raising the question of why they are so motivated to transact.

Some deals have been ripe with conflicts of interest. These include Glencore's 2013 acquisition of mining company Xstrata, when Xstrata management was financially incentivised to sell, and the Glencore CEO sat on the Xstrata board. Glencore had begun investing in Xstrata in the 1990s, to leverage the benefits of controlling production in addition to trade.

Risk Analysis

No matter how diligently the board works, there are always information gaps and uncertainty. M&As can create tremendous value, but most of it is never captured by acquirers. And although there is no doubt that acquisitions can offer growth opportunities, such deals are by their nature complex and risky. In any M&A strategy, opportunity is accompanied by risk and uncertainty.

Deals often have financial risks. Boards therefore need to assess the sensitivities of net present values to growth rates, input prices, and discount rates. But directors' risk analysis must go well beyond this and cover human dynamics too. Egos and office politics typically prevent objective debate within the leadership team, advisors make deals for fees and are not accountable for the results, and leadership differences may exist between the acquirer and the target. Human factors could also lead to other risks, such as a flawed strategic rationale, pricing discrepancies, financing flaws, and poor post-acquisition execution.

'My observation from both near and far is that the human failing is by far the most critical element in badly judged large M&A transactions. The ability to retain the power of the CEO role and the degree of intellectual humility necessary to execute it properly is not given to many people', Gould writes. 'Hubris is an occupational hazard for leaders, it feeds on isolation, and business leaders can deceive themselves and distance themselves from reality . . . It is important to point out that hubris syndrome can be acquired during the exercise of power and may disappear once the individual has left the position of influence'.[4]

---

[4] Andrew Gould, Chair BG, in IMD High Performance Boards presentation.

These days, regulatory barriers are considered to be one of the biggest threats to global M&As, with 71% of executives in one survey blaming competition regulators for their failed deals.[5] A record number of deals are being blocked or abandoned as a result of antitrust hurdles – including Comcast's $45bn offer for Time Warner Cable, which was abandoned after regulators raised concerns that the deal would create a monopoly. In addition, the US authorities have blocked some M&A deals on national security grounds in recent years. In March 2018, for example, US President Donald Trump blocked a proposed $117 billion buyout of US chipmaker Qualcomm by Singapore-incorporated BroadCom.

Regulatory concerns vary by sector, according to the above survey. In the energy, mining, and natural resources industry, executives cited environmental regulations as their biggest concern when considering future deals. In the telecommunications, media, and technology sector, meanwhile, data protection and cybersecurity regulations are the top concerns. During deal structuring, it has become commonplace to include heavy penalties – often on the bidder – if the transaction is not subsequently approved.

In general, the risk of integration failure is the top M&A concern for boards, as capturing synergy is one of the biggest risks. To make integration work, boards have to communicate constantly with stakeholders, stabilise the morale of their respective companies, supervise the integration of structures and processes, and approve specific initiatives to achieve the strategic objectives. Some boards shed the decision responsibility and opt instead for co-CEOs, co-Chairs, or two headquarters. A good example of this was the Lafarge Holcim merger of two proud competitors, which involved a delicate balance of power. But such a practice usually does not work in the long term. Either one company comes to dominate the other, or the two firms work separately rather than as one unified entity.

Due Diligence

Due diligence is a critical process to validate accounting and technical information and the acquisition rationale, in order to obtain a true understanding of the target company and how the transaction

---

[5] Smith Freehills, H., FT Remark, and MergerMarket (2016). Beyond Borders: The Future of Dealmaking. April 2016.

might advance the buyer's intended strategy. For larger transactions, management should present the board with a report describing the scope, timeline, and resources for each due diligence phase, along with the due diligence results of each phase.

A thorough due diligence process could include commercial and operational matters; legal, financial accounting, and tax issues; employee benefits and human resources; the US Foreign Corrupt Practices Act; reputation, integration and synergy, and insurance; and environmental and engineering factors. Boards should oversee the entire process.[6]

Due diligence should address not only the financial side of the deal, but also non-financial aspects related to its technological, operational, and reputational dimensions. Regarding the tangibles, boards need to devote sufficient time to any possible issues related to intellectual property and technology before these cause damage. But directors also need to do their non-financial due diligence and look at the intangibles – including the compatibility of culture, the reaction from stakeholders, and the morale of employees.

In driving non-financial due diligence, a board can ask various questions. What if stakeholders do not like the deal? What will happen to the morale of the employees of both companies? What if the highly specialised people and top talents do not believe in the deal? How can all the intangibles be managed? The board must undertake a thorough, well-documented investigation before acting.

Deal Structure and Pricing

Boards should be especially vigilant when evaluating the financial aspects of a deal. How much value will truly be created, and is the premium paid worth it? And who is pricing the deal? Investment bankers are typically conflicted, but internal teams may have their own motivations as well. Sometimes many elements are hidden in a complex structure, using partial share and options deals, or a staggered payment scheme such as earnouts. Although these can reveal a smart risk management strategy that alleviates overpricing risk, they can also hide a certain complacency: it is always easier to pay in shares than in cash!

---

[6] Deloitte (2016). M&A: The Intersection of Due Diligence and Governance. May 2016.

In addition, boards should consider all the alternatives to acquisitions – such as joint ventures, organic growth, alliances, and partnerships – as well as the reason why the acquisition is more promising, and not only more stimulating emotionally.

While Monsanto's offer set a benchmark for valuing Syngenta, pricing could become a secondary consideration for ChemChina. The company's investment in Syngenta was widely seen as a way to secure food supplies for China's huge population and have access to Syngenta's intellectual property and cropcare technology. Unlike Monsanto, ChemChina had no incentive to dismantle, reintegrate, and sell parts of Syngenta to extract synergies, thus making it a more credible partner for the company's employees and society at large.

Integration

Before approving a deal, directors need to review the integration plan and assess its realism. What is the timeline? How fast can the target company be integrated? What are the expected problems? Who will lead the integration? Ideally this person will already be involved in the pre-deal and deal process. Company culture is a particularly sensitive integration issue, and thus differences and compatibilities are high on the board's deal risk map. People, and which key positions to retain, are also an important consideration. Both culture

---

Companies need to have strong in-house structuring and pricing skills. Otherwise, they will put themselves in the hands of others and risk overpaying directly or indirectly (through a poor structure, for example). Vodafone's $183 billion takeover of Mannesmann in 2000 was the biggest cross-border bid in history. In total, Vodafone paid 56 times earnings, a 72% premium to Mannesmann's closing share price. Five years later, Vodafone announced that it was taking a goodwill charge of $40 billion. The company admitted that the record post-acquisition write-down was due to overpayment. This deal destroyed significant value, largely because the flawed valuation was done by outsiders.

Boards should be aware that, regardless of the sophisticated financial models used in pricing, valuation is always relative. Value is measured in the eyes of the beholder. What may provide value to one acquirer or target may not provide the same value for others. At the same time, there is no deal that is good enough regardless of the price. Overpricing often causes the acquirer to fail, because it reveals a lack of discipline – and not only financial.

and people should therefore be part of the integration KPIs. And the board should be updated regularly on the progress of the integration against these and other indicators.

Companies often underestimate the timing and cost involved in completing an overseas integration. In some jurisdictions there are significant employment entitlements, requiring a complex consultation with the affected employees. Such factors could become obstacles to successful integration. Thus, those responsible for leading the integration will ideally already be involved at the pre-deal negotiation stage.

Post-Integration Analysis

Finally, boards need to review regularly the integration after acquisition along a series of questions:

Do we have a strong process for tracking deal success?

Are we achieving the strategic goals?

Have we focused on the right issues?

Ideally, such a step will already have been planned from an early stage of the deal negotiation.

Confronting Litigation Involving M&As

In the M&A process, board directors are vulnerable to litigation in many legal environments – not least in the US, where nine out of ten M&A transactions are legally contested by investors.[7] A board's failure to complete all the required homework on a deal, including obtaining adequate insurance coverage, could result in significant damage to the deal and the company. The five examples below illustrate how litigation typically arises when boards fail to handle deals properly.

Conflicts of Interest

Conflicts of interest continue to dominate the discussions in M&A litigation. Typical conflicts include the involvement of a large

---

[7] Cornerstone Research (2015). Shareholder Litigation Involving Acquisitions of Public Companies. February 2015.

shareholder in the deal, management negotiating employment and compensation packages during the deal, and advisors' dealings on all sides. Boards that fail in their oversight here could be sued for breaching their duty of care.

In 2011, Barclays Capital and Del Monte Corp. agreed to pay the food company's shareholders to settle a case that raised a conflict of interest. The Delaware Court of Chancery found that the advisor, Barclays, helped with the buy-side financing and failed to disclose its relationship with the target. It also found that Del Monte's board failed to provide the oversight that would have checked Barclays' misconduct. Del Monte paid $65.7 million of the settlement, while Barclays Capital paid the remaining $23.7 million, according to the court filings.

Lack of Disclosure

In M&A deals, class-action lawsuits are often filed, alleging that boards have failed in disclosure – for example, concerning the existence of the M&A negotiations, the deal terms, or other material information about the transaction. This could cause a dilemma for the boards of target companies. If the disclosure is too early, shareholders could allege that they were injured by the premature announcement; but if the disclosure is too late, shareholders could claim that they were injured because they sold their shares before the merger announcement and the subsequent large price increase.

Lawsuits can also be brought against the acquiring company. These might allege that the board failed to disclose the M&A negotiations, or the deal's future prospects and effect on the acquiring company, in a full and timely manner. These suits can involve huge potential damages for companies on both sides of M&A deals.

Hostile and Friendly Takeover

The directors of a target company who resist a hostile takeover could be sued. Shareholders could allege that the board members breached their fiduciary duty and denied them the opportunity to profit from the high offer price.

The directors of a target company who approve a friendly takeover could also be sued. Disgruntled shareholders could allege that the company was being sold for too little, and that the directors made a bad decision.

Pre-acquisition Mismanagement

After an acquisition, the new company may sue the previous directors and executives of the target company, claiming that they mismanaged the business prior to the deal. This is problematic for the prior directors and board, since they no longer control the company and may have no insurance coverage.

Post-acquisition Mismanagement

After the acquisition, the board and directors of the acquiring company can be sued in connection with their management of the target firm. This might happen when the new management team has little experience of operating in a particular industry or market.

Boards need to take an increasingly sophisticated approach to the M&A process. Yet the main principles are simple:

- creating a deal-making mindset, with strong due diligence and risk analysis;
- seeing the bigger picture;
- staging deals with maximum precision, including structuring, pricing and integration;
- confronting litigation involving M&As.

Boards and directors are crucial to helping their companies capture value during the M&A process and reduce the risk of failure. I encourage every board and director to consider the four principles above when preparing for their company's next M&A transaction.

In this chapter we saw how corporate culture can often be crucial to the success or failure of an M&A deal. We now return to the issue of boardroom culture, and to the key relationship between the chair and CEO.

Joanne Marker Confronts Failing Board Culture

*M*ay 2018: *Joanne Marker was attending her first board meeting at JenJolt, a software services company providing outsourcing services to major corporations. She had become increasingly interested in the dynamic nature of the competitive landscape, and was keen to explore how IT could be a strategic lever in her industries of expertise.*

With her knowledge of the markets, and with her global network in some of JenJolt's potential spheres of interest, Joanne was excited to explore ideas for different alliances that she felt were promising for growth. Her meeting documents were highlighted, and she had detailed notes questioning some of the assumptions behind the scenarios presented in the board briefing.

Joanne had arrived at JenJolt HQ at 7.40 a.m., after flying into San Francisco the previous night. She had talked to a few other early arrivers over a cup of coffee. At 8.00, she sat down and waited. The others continued to stand, eating pastries and making jokes that sounded like they might be golf-related. All the other seven directors were 40- to 50-year-old white men, many of whom had gone to the same Ivy League business school.

She re-read her notes while she waited. The chair, Stephen McElvoy, entered the room at 8.10, together with CEO Jerry Morgan. The two were laughing as they sat down in the two vacant seats. Joanne looked around, but all around her were smiling faces. She seemed to be the only one irritated by this ten-minute delay.

Just after the mid-morning break, Joanne raised her hand. McElvoy nodded at her.

'A question: Will Jerry be staying for the whole meeting?' she asked. There was silence for a moment.

'Well, that's what we usually do – no secrets here!' McElvoy clapped Morgan on the shoulder. 'We're just trying to help Jerry, who's doing a fine job. It's not easy, we know. And we all appreciate what he's doing here'.

Joanne looked around the table, but no one would meet her gaze.

'OK then', she said.

She then asked Morgan some pointed questions about the markets he had entered, the strategic alliances he had created, and why he wasn't targeting different geographies. In her view, his answers were unsatisfactory. But when she looked at the other directors, they didn't make eye contact.

November 2018: Two JenJolt board meetings later, Joanne forced herself to speak up. McElvoy nodded at her, unsmiling. He had already come to dread her questions.

'I would like to request that the board have a discussion without Jerry present', Joanne said. 'It's nothing personal', she said to Morgan. 'In my experience it's good practice to have a conversation without the chief executive present'.

Morgan flushed and stood, despite the protests of the other directors that this wasn't necessary.

'Sure, Joanne. No problem', Morgan said, winking as he exited the room. 'I've got tons to catch up on before lunch'.

McElvoy stared across the table at her.

'So, what is it you wanted to say, Joanne?'

She explained her concerns about Morgan: that he had failed to identify a number of competitive threats and was racking up dangerous levels of debt with his acquisition plans.

The other directors defended him. 'Give him some time, Joanne. He's just ramping up', said Alex Lincoln, another independent director.

'And just how much time do you want to give him, Alex?' Joanne asked. 'When is the cut-off, would you say? I think JenJolt is in a critical situation, and we need to act now'.

'What about 12 months – this time next year?'

'Too long', Joanne said. 'Six, max. He'll have run the company into the ground in a year'.

'That's a bit harsh on Jerry', said Will Jones, another director. 'Give him a chance!' Others came to the CEO's defence too.

'Gentlemen', she said, 'I can see I am the only one who thinks that a change in leadership is a priority for this company's survival'.

After returning home late that evening, Joanne pressed the send button, emailing McElvoy her letter of resignation from JenJolt's board. He replied immediately: 'I am sorry to lose you Joanne. But don't you think you are over-reacting?' he wrote.

March 2019: Joanne opened The Wall Street Journal *to the Business News section for her morning update. The headline jumped out at her: 'Departure of Morgan from the helm of JenJolt'. The article detailed how the board had closed ranks and was refusing to confirm or deny if Morgan had been fired. But the journalist reported that an unnamed source had attributed Morgan's departure to being the result of 'a rampant acquisition spree and spiraling costs, combined with little ability to deliver on promised growth'.*

The article also questioned the forthcoming announcement of annual results by the company.

21

The Chair–CEO Relationship

The partnership between the chair and CEO is the critical catalyst to ensure that the four pillars interact to promote board effectiveness. A healthy relationship between the two may differ in form depending on the company, its situation, and the personality of the individuals – but the essential preconditions are trust and role clarity. It is vital that both the chair and CEO clearly understand their respective roles, which need to be both distinct and additive. In practice, this means that the chair and CEO do not overlap in the work they do. Rather, each performs a unique function, building upon the efforts of the other, to jointly enhance the quality of the board's work.

The chair and CEO must meet regularly to communicate and review issues, opportunities, and problems. Furthermore, their relationship needs to be one of openness and integrity, and be underlined by a clear division of responsibilities. Before looking at the nature of their relationship, it is important to define their respective roles.

The Role of the Chair

The chair is responsible for the leadership of the board. This entails ensuring the effective operation of the board and its committees, in conformity with the highest standards of corporate governance. He or she sets the board agenda, which should be primarily focused on strategy, performance, value creation, and accountability, and ensures that issues relevant to those areas are considered by the board. The chair must make sure that the board determines the nature and extent of any significant risks that the organisation is willing to embrace in implementing its strategy, and also that directors review the effectiveness of the company's risk management and internal control systems on an ongoing basis.

Facilitating constructive debate and decision-making, and generating productive board dynamics, is another of the chair's key roles. This includes building in adequate time for discussion of all important agenda items (and strategic issues in particular). And it involves devoting attention to complex or contentious issues, making sure that non-executive directors in particular have sufficient time to consider them. Part of the chair's role in promoting meaningful boardroom exchanges is to secure accurate, timely and clear information for directors, especially regarding the organisation's performance.

Building links between the board and management, including through appropriate delegation of authority, constitutes an important component of the chair's role. (We will discuss board–management relations in more detail in the next chapter.) Promoting effective relationships and communications between non-executive directors and members of the executive committee is critical in order to enable a productive exchange. Here, the chair needs to secure access to senior management without intruding on the CEO's responsibilities.

It is vital that the chair continually monitors the board's composition, balance, and diversity (in terms of competencies, perspectives, and gender), and plans the succession for board and senior management appointments. When new directors and committee chairs join, the chair needs to arrange comprehensive, tailored on-boarding programmes and induction processes for them. Ensuring the effective establishment, composition, and operation of committees is critical, as is making sure that committee chairs are held accountable.

The chair is responsible for proper disclosure in the annual report of information regarding the organisation's governance perspectives and the board appointment process – including a description of the board's policy on diversity and gender, any measurable objectives it has set, and progress on achieving these.

The disclosure should also include a description of the search and nomination process.

Board education is also within the chair's sphere of responsibilities. He or she must ensure that directors continually update their skills, knowledge, and familiarity with the organisation, in order to contribute fully on both the board and its committees. This includes regularly reviewing and agreeing individual training and development needs with each director, as well as addressing the needs of the board as a whole.

The chair has the task of monitoring board performance and effectiveness, via a formal annual evaluation of its main committees and individual directors, as well as an externally facilitated evaluation perhaps every two years. These evaluations should consider the balance of skills, experience, independence, and knowledge among the directors, how well the board operates as a unit, and any other factors relevant to its effectiveness. More importantly, the chair acts on his or her views, as well as on the results of the performance evaluations, by recognising the board's strengths and addressing its weaknesses. Where appropriate, he or she proposes new board members or seeks the resignation of existing directors.

The chair also has a role in ensuring effective communication with shareholders, host governments, and other relevant stakeholders, and in making sure that the views of these groups are understood by the board. When proposing the re-election of directors, the chair confirms to shareholders that, following a formal evaluation, these individuals continue to perform effectively and demonstrate clear commitment. In addition, the chair needs to check that the organisation is maintaining a dialogue with its principal shareholders about the remuneration, governance, and strategy of directors and senior managers.

An effective chair maintains a harmonious and open relationship with all executive directors, providing advice and support while respecting their executive responsibility. As we will see later in the chapter, supporting and advising the CEO in strategy development and other matters is an important element of the chair's role.

Great chairship uses many dimensions, summarised in the figure underneath, which captures golden rules inspired by great chairpeople.

5 GOLDEN RULES
INSPIRED BY GREAT CHAIR

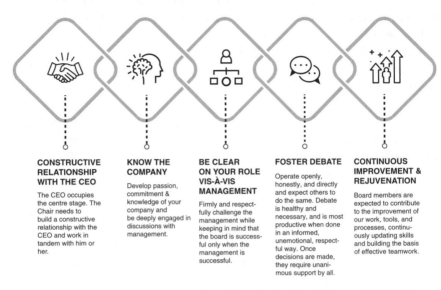

CONSTRUCTIVE RELATIONSHIP WITH THE CEO

The CEO occupies the centre stage. The Chair needs to build a constructive relationship with the CEO and work in tandem with him or her.

KNOW THE COMPANY

Develop passion, commitment & knowledge of your company and be deeply engaged in discussions with management.

BE CLEAR ON YOUR ROLE VIS-À-VIS MANAGEMENT

Firmly and respectfully challenge the management while keeping in mind that the board is successful only when the management is successful.

FOSTER DEBATE

Operate openly, honestly, and directly and expect others to do the same. Debate is healthy and necessary, and is most productive when done in an informed, unemotional, respectful way. Once decisions are made, they require unanimous support by all.

CONTINUOUS IMPROVEMENT & REJUVENATION

Board members are expected to contribute to the improvement of our work, tools, and processes, continuously updating skills and building the basis of effective teamwork.

Figure 21.1   Five Golden Rules Inspired by Great Chair (such as Risto Siilasmaa, Hsieh Fu Hua, Beat Hess, Rolf Soiron, Christoph Franz, Michel Demaré, and Others)

The Role of the CEO

The CEO is the leader of the organisation, managing it within the authorities delegated by the board and implementing the strategy. In most cases, the CEO develops the key content of the strategy process, such as competitive analysis and proposals, and ensures effective co-creation of key strategic recommendations with the board. He or she ensures that previously agreed corporate strategy actions are well reflected in the business.

In conjunction with the chief financial officer, the CEO develops an annual budget and funding plan consistent with agreed corporate strategies, and presents it to the board for approval. This should include developing processes and structures to ensure that capital investment proposals are thoroughly reviewed, associated risks are identified, and appropriate steps taken to manage these risks.

The CEO drives the culture of the organisation through role modelling, principles, incentives, and other means. As such, a key function of the chief executive is to ensure business is conducted in accordance with sound principles. Furthermore, he or she is responsible to the board for the organisation's performance in line with agreed business plans, corporate strategies, and policies, and keeps it updated on progress in this regard.

In addition, the chief executive plans human resourcing to ensure that the company has the people and capabilities it needs to achieve its plans. This includes overseeing a healthy talent pipeline and ensuring that robust management succession and development plans are in place. This HR strategy should be presented to the board from time to time. It entails developing a structure and establishing processes and systems to ensure the efficient organisation of resources. The CEO also leads the top management team, including through the development of performance targets and appraisals.

Communication is also important, because the CEO is the public face of the company. Part of his or her job is to develop and promote effective communication with shareholders and other relevant stakeholders. For example, financial results, business strategies, and, where appropriate, targets and milestones need to be communicated to investors.

Chairs are Increasingly Active

Although all effective chairs perform similar functions, they tend to have different individual styles of acting and interacting. Today, it is increasingly common for chairs to play a more active role in the organisation, while not overlapping with the CEO's executive style.

The active chair is a key player in driving boardroom culture and setting the direction of the organisation together with the board. He or she ensures that the board not only understands the business and its customers, but also impacts the organisational culture. Visibly present, the active chair sets a tone of integrity and clearly defines what this means in practice.

By regularly working in the business (at least one or two days a week, and more often three or more), he or she participates in the supervision of the firm's operations. An active chair challenges strategic thinking, co-creates the organisation's strategy with the board and management, and closely monitors the execution of business plans. In-depth oversight and review of the CEO, as well as in-depth oversight of management and the talent pool, is key for the active chair. He or she spends a great deal of time and energy coaching and advising the CEO and senior executives, and serves as an active liaison between the board and management.

The active chair is a dedicated leader of the board who takes its performance extremely seriously and works tirelessly to discipline and energise it. By constantly scanning the external world, he or she develops the board's stakeholder knowledge. He or she also serves as the company's representative in key stakeholder relationships, as well as when crisis strikes.

Chair–CEO Dynamics – the Hallmarks of a Productive Relationship

As we saw at the start of this chapter, a healthy relationship between a CEO and chair is characterised by significant trust, frequent and open communication, and yet not too much closeness or dependence. The chair is a visible actor and is deeply familiar with management's operations, though is not actively involved in their execution. In addition, the chair clearly communicates the boundaries of what constitutes acceptable ethical behaviour and intervenes when these are crossed. During a crisis, the chair steps up and takes a leadership role by supporting the CEO (or firing him or her and managing the succession if needed) and communicating externally.

In a healthy relationship, the CEO respects the chair's input and seeks his or her guidance on key strategic and risk-related matters. The chief executive proactively supplies the chair with necessary information, and demonstrates accountability by reporting against the agreed strategy, as well as flagging key risks as they arise.

There are several simple indicators of a healthy relationship between the chair and CEO.

- **A clear and well-planned board agenda,** with timely and relevant information supplied by management, which does not place an undue burden on the organisation. Meeting minutes document actions and who is responsible for them.
- **Consistent and respectful messages** from the chair and CEO to management with regard to strategy and risks.
- **Mutual respect of boundaries and roles.** The chair does not consult with senior executives without first asking the CEO's permission; similarly, the CEO doesn't talk to individual directors without first aligning with the chair.

- **Regular communication** between the CEO and chair. This gives the chair access to relevant management information and systematic updates on key events and pipeline issues. And the CEO is able to execute strategy with a free rein.
- **Clear trust** between the chair and CEO, as demonstrated by mutual support for strategic decisions made in the boardroom and in the organisation. Trust is easily revealed by each assuming good intentions from the other on all interactions.

Warning signs for possible dysfunction in the chair–CEO relationship include:

- **Unreasonable requests.** A chair who demands extensive, detailed financial analysis or in-depth reports on operational issues may lack trust in the CEO. This results in a considerable cost to the CEO and management in terms of the energy required to supply the information, and generates stress and ill will. As the CEO senses the lack of trust, he or she becomes more defensive and may begin to suspect the chair's motives. The overall effect is to undermine trust between the two.
- **Operational interventions.** A chair who starts intervening directly in the organisation's operations and issues directives to management often signals a lack of trust in the CEO's leadership. Alternatively, the chair may just be used to being in a leadership role, and may feel that he or she is more competent than the CEO. A lack of discipline in maintaining this important boundary undermines the CEO's authority in the organisation.
- **Lack of consistency on strategic direction.** If the chair and CEO express different visions of the organisation's strategic direction and key risks, this spells trouble in their relationship. A lack of alignment will necessarily lead to disagreement about how to mobilise organisational resources, not to mention differing expectations with regard to CEO accountability and reporting.
- **Indecision by the board.** If the board cannot come to a decision, this may signify that it is receiving inadequate information from management, or that the chair is not productively

facilitating the conversation. If information is the problem, this could indicate a breakdown in communication between the chair and CEO.

- **Board members directly approaching management.** When communication between the chair and CEO breaks down, directors may be frustrated and approach senior or even junior managers to try to find out what is going on. This can make the CEO defensive and undermines his or her trust in the chair's ability to restrict board members to their proper role.

- **Lack of respect for the CEO from the board.** If directors fail to listen to the CEO, or make comments that show a lack of respect for his or her opinions or competence, this can signify a key disconnect in the CEO–chair relationship. The chair needs to defend the CEO and ensure that he or she is properly supported; failing to do so quickly kills trust and goodwill.

- **Lack of respect for the chair from senior executives.** The chair is the boardroom leader and the lead governance actor of the organisation, and as such merits respect from executives, as well as senior and junior staff. If senior executives make jokes in the boardroom at the chair's expense, and the CEO does nothing to stop it, this denigrates the importance of the chair's role. Ultimately, this undermines the authority of both the chair and the board.

Tests of the Chair–CEO Relationship

In 1993, Maersk Mc-Kinney Moller stepped down as CEO of Maersk after 28 years, and was succeeded by Jess Soderberg. Moller handed over the chairship to Michael Pram Rasmussen in 2003 but remained active in the group's decision-making and activities, frequently going to its Copenhagen headquarters and travelling around the world to represent Denmark's largest privately owned enterprise. Soderberg was fired in 2007 due to mistakes made after Maersk's €2.3 billion takeover of P&O Nedloyd, the world's third-largest container line at the time. Nils Smedegaard Andersen was then hired to replace him.

A crisis situation involving an integrity breach can also strain the relationship. The chair may be tempted to blame the CEO, suspecting him or her of improper conduct – or of not maintaining sufficiently firm boundaries in this respect. Or a director may have a (real or perceived) conflict of interest. In this case, the CEO may suspect the chair of cronyism or not being sufficiently diligent in screening the board members.

When the relationship between chair and CEO is put to the test, both need to remember their roles and their duty to serve the best interest of the company. In such situations, it helps if both are personally resilient, do not succumb to stress as a result of external pressures, and do not over-react emotionally. One way to reduce the tension, and to re-establish productive exchanges, is to have a pre-agreed protocol according to which the CEO and chair agree to abide by certain principles before reacting. For example, they could agree that in times of crisis, they should be immediately available to speak to one another – in person if possible – and that their first exchange will be devoted only to asking questions and not expressing judgements. In this way, they will seek to understand the situation before evaluating the events and potential outcome.

Maintaining integrity, and not succumbing to psychological needs or indulging in self-deception, is critical in such situations. Mature, self-aware individuals with integrity will reflect on their own role in contributing to the healthy functioning of the chair–CEO relationship. And even if they are dissatisfied with the consequences for them personally, they will fulfil their duty toward the board and the organisation at all times.

Even in the best chair–CEO relationship, there are situations that put the pair to the test. Succession, for example, is often a sensitive topic. The CEO's succession is the responsibility of the chair or the relevant board committee. However, when the chair raises this issue with the CEO and asks for information regarding the leadership bench strength among the senior executive team, it can create tension in the relationship. Such discussions may provoke resistance from the CEO, who may consciously or subconsciously feel that the chair is seeking to replace them. Likewise, when the CEO discusses the chair's retirement and succession, the chair may feel a similar deep sense of rejection – especially if he or she (usually an experienced and powerful individual with a track record of success) is coming to the end of his or her career.

Case: Boardroom Tension with Employee

At a major global investment bank in London, during the first boardroom meeting of the year, the Chief Talent Officer was invited to present the results of the latest employee engagement survey. She reported that there was a disconnect between the culture espoused by the company versus the behaviour that was being rewarded and practised by its senior leaders. The bank had been going through a growth period during which there were many programmes focused on culture and work–life balance, but increasingly senior staff were being pressured to deliver financial results. Thanks to their extraordinary achievements, staff had legitimate pride. And jokes were circulating about the 'amateurishness' of the non-executive board members who were not investment bankers. In concluding, she addressed the chair, whose name was Peter Lyre, saying: 'Employees are starting to wonder if the information we have is the truth. No pun intended,' she laughed. Silence fell in the boardroom, all eyes of the directors going first to the chair and then to the CEO. How should the chair react? Was this a play on his name? Should the CEO intervene? Or minimise his involvement?

The Ideal Attributes of a Chair

Increasing regulatory pressures, demands for effectiveness, expanded accountability, and higher social expectations require chairs to be far more involved than they traditionally have been in the past. The chair can no longer be a distant individual, but instead needs to be fully committed to understanding the organisation's issues and devoted to its success. Chairs who possess the following 'ideal' attributes will be more likely to succeed in this mission:

- **Character and courage:** The chair must be seen to be an honest broker, a straight-talking, open-minded leader focused on doing what is right for the long-term health of the organisation. He or she should be forthright and not hesitate to speak his or her mind, but also should not rush to judgement.
- **Consensus-building:** The chair must keep all sides productively engaged and focused on the important issues. This means having a good sense of what needs to be done and, at the same time, not being easily side-tracked by others' attempts to dilute negative results, exaggerate good outcomes, or engage in debates over unimportant matters. The chair encourages constructive dissent in order to build a true consensus.

- **Relevant experience:** Effective chairs understand the CEO's job of building and managing a strong and cohesive team. Having had experience of running an organisation, chairs can establish effective processes for the oversight and support of the CEO and top management team.
- **The ability to be an external spokesperson:** There are times when the chair has to be a credible spokesperson for the organisation – such as in a crisis. He or she needs to be well-versed in such a role and remain focused on the relevant message in order to avoid portraying the organisation in a bad light in the media and/or with regulators.
- **Dedication and commitment to board work:** An effective chair is willing to do the homework by going through the details as well as understanding the broad concepts, and prepares thoroughly for board meetings. These activities may require additional time; for example, to understand what is not in the meeting materials.

These attributes will enable the chair to cultivate and foster respect and trust from the CEO, which is necessary to build a positive and constructive relationship. This is in turn essential for ensuring best-practice governance of the organisation. The CEO is also key to ensuring this partnership works effectively. The two need to recognise the importance of this relationship, understand their respective roles and responsibilities, and do their part in making it work.

A healthy relationship between the board and management is also crucial for effective governance. And it is to this issue that we turn in the next chapter.

22

The Board–Management Relationship

Observing boards' decision-making is an exciting and relatively new undertaking. In the past, researchers found it difficult to study directly the mechanics of board activities. This precipitated the growing interest we see today in considering and analysing the board on the strength of its decision-making capacity and characteristics.

Of major importance in this context is the issue of the board's relationship with management. Today's active boards seek to play a distinctive and additive role in the organisation. What's more, the nature and quality of their communication with management is critical in defining and achieving a sustainable business culture. There are two main aspects of the board–management relationship: supervision and support.

Supervision

In its supervisory role, a board works to ensure that management is making sufficient effort in critical strategic areas, such as managing risks and responding to competitive threats. The focus on compliance that was typical in the past has proved insufficient in today's competitive globalised environment. As a result, boards have become more directly and deliberately involved in charting their companies' strategy. They have emerged as a source of extended vision, helping to contextualise and interpret many of the opportunities and challenges facing the organisation.

In maintaining a clear view of the company's strategic differentiators, the board has an important role to play in drawing out relevant and necessary information from management, and in the process challenging and testing it. How far the board can go in 'interrogating' the management is a gauge of the trust and goodwill that has been established between the board and the executive team, and also depends on the quality of the questions that the board asks.

With more directors having become involved in strategic decisions in recent years, boards increasingly want to have a say in how management goes about complex new initiatives, including change processes. In this context, it is no longer rare to see the board put forward its own sets of metrics and incentives. Just as a strong board needs a regular dose of internal dissent to remain healthy, boards are embracing the need to challenge management views and proposals in areas that have long-term repercussions for the organisation's well-being.

The board's supervision of management initiatives also implies follow-up, and in particular monitoring implementation progress. This may take various forms. For example, the board may task management with preparing an implementation plan for specific recommendations that the board has endorsed. Action items have become a key board process that starts immediately after the board meeting itself (usually within 48 hours). Minutes, on the other hand, are prepared at more length as they have legal weight, and are presented a few weeks before the following meeting for adjustment. Periodic monitoring reports, annual or otherwise, will then provide details on action points included in previous implementation plans, especially if these actions are still outstanding.

The board should be able to review and comment on the design and results of specific programmes, but also to conduct thematic reviews of management issues and initiatives on a regular basis. Technology can facilitate many of these processes, particularly if it combines self-evaluation features with project management and also collaborative and work-sharing software capabilities. When tackling complex, multistakeholder undertakings, the board may choose to be creative in fulfilling its supervisory role by devising custom time-tables, roadmaps, dashboards, and other tools that help visualise and measure progress as well as follow-up.

Peter Cuneo became CEO of Marvel Entertainment in July 1999 with the company in dire financial straits and its corporate culture depressed. He turned the company around, and ten years later it was sold to Walt Disney for more than $4 billion. Cuneo credited Marvel's active board for helping to make the turnaround possible.

'In order to execute this turnaround we knew we had to be supported and surrounded by the brightest, most aggressive minds we could attract', Cuneo said. 'The individual members of Marvel's board were encouraged . . . to be much more involved in the business than merely attending quarterly meetings'.[1] He noted that the board played the role of a trusted advisor for Marvel's senior executives on current and future business developments, but never made decisions for them.

Marvel Cinematic Universe has become one of the biggest movie franchises in history, with over a dozen box-office hits. In 2019, the Marvel movie 'Avengers Endgame' earned an astonishing $1.2 billion in its opening weekend.

Support

In addition to their role as auditors of company performance, boards also have an advisory role to play. Directors' expertise should help management in making important strategic decisions. In particular, setting organisational strategy has emerged as an area where effective boards have performed an advisory, collaborative role.

Along the way, it has also become commonplace for board members to search outside the organisation for relevant trends and data (see also Chapter 5). Directors are conscious of the dynamics of disruptive change, which inspires them to examine how familiar issues play out in different industries, segments and markets.

Working out and recognising their own role and use of authority has been a continuous challenge for board members around the world. To begin with, the dual roles of supervision and support come with different time horizons. Boards therefore need to balance them carefully.

The tension between supervision and support has sometimes been recast as a tension between accountability and organisational development. Directors who settle fully into an accountability role

---

[1] https://www.forbes.com/2010/02/01/peter-cuneo-marvel-leadership-managing-turnaround.html#387e1ea76fa1.

may become unlikely to play a robust developmental role. Nonetheless, much of this tension can be diffused when the board is energised by the organisation's mission. Such boards are in a good position to exercise adequate controls while providing independent viewpoints – a powerful combination that can mitigate many types of management behaviour, including overconfidence and excessive risk-taking.

Blurring the Board–Management Relationship

Board members have a responsibility to know, and understand in detail, the backgrounds of key executives in the firm. High performing boards tend to nurture and invest in each director's relationship with top executives, often using tools such as *dual coaching*. Similarly, a key priority for the CEO should be to build a strong relationship with the board – formal, informal, professional, human, and social. The CEO would be well advised to know about the board members' occupations, businesses, and families. He or she needs to listen and ask questions consistently and be seen to attach real value to the board's opinions.

So far, so good. As long as boards and management teams embrace the relationship in all its facets and social complexity, they will have a healthy, robust foundation to build on, right? Not always. In reality, there are many ways in which the difference between the roles of the board and the management team can become blurred.

For instance, company founders, family members, and alliances with board members that are based on these relationships, may exert a strong positive or negative influence on the culture of the organisation. Through his or her sheer knowledge of the company, a CEO may have overwhelming influence on board decisions. This immediately creates an imbalance of power.

In addition, there is a powerful 'birds of a feather' phenomenon in business that chips away at the distinction between board and management roles. Many directors are themselves current or former CEOs. Consciously or otherwise, the fraternising instinct may be tough to resist. This can lead to a sense of misplaced solidarity and patience, even with a CEO who has clearly long outlived their usefulness.

Similarly, ex-CEOs on the board often accept dated solutions and strategies that are oblivious to the realities of today's marketplace, let alone that of the future. This is because their judgement and acumen have been compromised by an overwhelming sense of familiarity, past achievements, and the feeling of what it was like to be the top executive in their old organisation. When mixed together, these perceptions can give rise to an unyielding, even if not openly articulated, need to protect the CEO.

Conversely, in some organisations, CEOs wield considerable power over the board, and can greatly influence the process of selecting directors. In many cases, dominant CEOs will prefer board members similar to themselves – not just in terms of demographic characteristics such as ethnicity, social background, and gender, but also in terms of personality type – and may exercise this bias in the director recruitment process.

Research has shown that the longer the CEO's tenure, the more likely he or she is to have allies installed on the board. And some of them will support the chief executive's decisions no matter what. This trend has been further amplified by the arrival of the 'celebrity CEO'. For many years, there has been a tendency among corporations to recruit larger-than-life, charismatic chief executives, typically from outside the company, and to bring them in amid frenzied media attention that shouts if not 'saviour' then certainly 'superhero'.

The trouble with overbearing, overconfident, and narcissistic CEOs is that they sincerely believe they are creating shareholder value even as they are destroying it. Many of them are enthusiastic risk-takers, pushing through dramatic ramp-ups in spending on mergers and acquisitions, capital investment, and research and development. In the long run, these behaviours will interfere with management's ability to stay in touch with organisational reality, thus preventing real learning and change.

For example, Fiat Chrysler Automobiles in 2014 initiated a civil lawsuit against its former Australia CEO whom it accused of breaching the law and his contract by giving cars to celebrities and inflating contracts to benefit his financial interests. For his part, the former local CEO denied breaching his legal duties and said the Chrysler Asia Pacific CEO and other senior company officials had approved his actions. It is then hard to decipher what is healthy and what not.

Writing Governance Codes Is Easier Than Changing Behaviours

Boards that do address the issues of learning and change are often particularly hopeful that revising governance codes will produce meaningful shifts in the way their directors interact with top management teams. What many boards fail to realise, however, is that for all their good intentions, writing something down is not the same as implementing it in daily communication and action.

Through the write-up of hundreds of pages of codes and manuals, a board may aim to change an organisation by conducting an in-depth internal survey, mapping out the roles and responsibilities of the board and management, and rating different areas for effectiveness and importance. The changes may be first drafted by one director and then sent to all the other board members for amendments, with the final text then discussed and agreed – word by word – by the board as a group.

But this does not guarantee real progress, nor that the quality of the relationship between the board and management will ascend to a new level. All too frequently, despite greater lucidity on paper, only minor changes may be observed in practice. Tellingly, strong top executives tend to resist and resent even soft challenging and questioning of self-edited performance targets, strategic thrusts, results, or succession plans.

This is not to say that all exercises and initiatives aimed at specifying more clearly the roles and domains of the board and management are doomed from the start. On the contrary, there is great value to be derived from tasks such as detailing existing areas of responsibility, outlining perceived 'missing' areas, clarifying decision authority in specific scenarios, defining the respective roles of the chair and CEO in setting agendas, and documenting perceived roadblocks. But this value will only present itself when the board recognises these exercises for what they are – departure points in a long and demanding process of individual and group adaptation, change, and commitment.

On high performing boards, a big part of that commitment comes from understanding that creating sustained business value requires a strong CEO. Such a chief executive needs to be matched with an equally strong board that is ready and willing to engage with them dynamically. This is a very different power equation from the one we described earlier in this chapter, where a weak board protects an underperforming CEO out of a false sense of solidarity and identification.

To balance the CEO's influence, directors should re-examine the board's composition with the objective of bringing in knowledgeable, independent, and skilled members who can act as counterweights to the chief executive and provide oversight of the corporation. Directors can also help to restore the board's influence by using their own human capital – such as their status as a former CEO, or their experience on a board compensation or auditing committee. All these undergird the social nature of the decision-making process that takes place in the boardroom.

In theory, independent directors should enjoy more decision-making influence and power than dependent board members. However, empirical research has uncovered little evidence that the dependent/independent distinction is significant in relation to influencing the board's decisions and its relationship with the CEO.

Crucially, and regardless of the organisation's performance, the board should under no circumstances waver in its ability to observe and judge management's behaviour objectively. Once the board finds itself seduced by the company's perceived power and success, its capacity for discharging its duties will likely become compromised. Boards of directors are important monitors of corporate behaviour, and can rein in opportunistic action on the part of top management by providing incentives for it to pursue appropriate goals. Overbearing executives are increasingly seen as a *result* of the corporate system, in addition to performance systems and structures, power allocation, and managerial beliefs. In many organisations, the absence of challenge or resistance from shareholders and other stakeholders, including the broader financial community, may have encouraged management's illusion of grandeur and vast control.

Finally, today's boards have a tangible and growing role to play in managing the organisation's relationship with stakeholders such as governments and the broader public – a topic we will cover in greater detail in Chapter 27. Successful companies run by overconfident leaders may be exciting to watch – but at some point, stakeholders are likely to demand mechanisms that will mitigate the downside risk of narcissistic CEOs. Those checks are expected to come from the board, particularly as twenty-first-century boards become more diverse and independent. And effective diversity is the theme of the next chapter.

CHAPTER

23

Effective Diversity

Diversity is Good . . . But Why; and When?

The assertion that diversity is good has become a mantra in business. Many studies demonstrate the advantages of diversity for companies in search of new ideas, observations, strategic directions, and competitive advantage. Organisations may derive tangible *task-related benefits* from diversity, because having a variety of expertise enables a firm to assign each part of a task to people with the relevant knowledge. Diversity also has *innovation-driving benefits*, because people with different perspectives see things differently. This can lead to creativity and a questioning of assumptions, and ultimately to new synergies.

However, diversity also comes with downsides, because it raises barriers to alignment. These include *communication-related barriers*. People's different frames of reference mean that words and actions can have very different significance: this makes communication less efficient and can lead to conflict that may be difficult to resolve. Other barriers arising from greater diversity are related to *identity and trust:* we find it harder to identify with and deeply trust people who are different from us.

When there is a strong need for innovation, and shareholders represent divergent views, diversity is a key strategic advantage. But the situation is different when there is a single shareholder with a clear view of what needs to be accomplished, and when the need for innovation is limited – for example, where a private-equity firm has taken ownership of a company and is seeking to turn it

DIVERSITY AT THE BOARD LEVEL

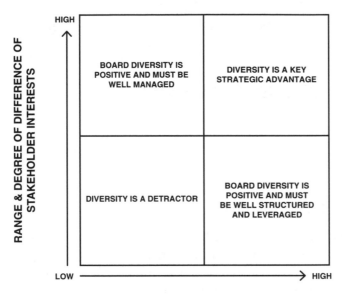

Figure 23.1   Diversity at the Board Level

around. In that case, board diversity can lead to time being wasted on conflict and difficult communication, detracting from the discipline required.

In order to tap fully into the benefits of diversity, boards need to manage this process well. That itself calls for a significant investment of energy and time and requires a dedicated and skilled chair. Ultimately, diversity is a choice (see Figure 23.1).

Diversity as a Considered Choice

In previous decades, when corporations did choose to become more diverse, it was as a result of a powerful external push – and in many cases, a jolt delivered by momentous, structural changes in the marketplace. One such milestone came about in the 1990s, when a number of US multinationals started generating more than 50% of their revenue from international markets. Suddenly, the user of their products in the US Midwest was no longer their typical customer. Predictably, this gave rise to widespread interest in understanding, communicating with, and marketing to other countries.

The Bursa Malaysia Berhad stock exchange stated in July 2014 that effective January 2015, every listed issuer was required to disclose in the annual report its diversity policy, covering the Board of Directors as well as the workforce, in terms of gender, age, and ethnicity. This is part of Bursa Malaysia's enhanced disclosure requirements which aim to complement previous initiatives launched to inculcate diversity in the boardroom and workplace. A few years earlier, the 2012 Malaysian Code on Corporate Governance recommended that boards should establish a policy to formalise their approach to boardroom diversity. Nominating committees, in particular, have been encouraged to take the necessary steps to ensure that recruitment exercises draw on diverse pools of candidates. Boards should then explicitly disclose in their annual reports their diversity policies as well as specific targets and measures taken to meet those targets.

Today, it has become mainstream to say that a board's composition should more closely resemble the make-up of the company's stakeholders. This entails having directors with diverse objectives, social and economic agendas, communication channels, and preferred technologies. In this chapter, we focus on five dimensions of diversity – gender, culture, personality, age, and social background – and look at how a strong chair can manage these to make a board more effective.

Gender

The debates regarding gender balance in the boardroom have zoomed in on many of the obstacles to understanding and practising diversity and have brought several questions to the fore. Should boards of directors as well as C-suites strive to fulfil self-imposed gender quotas? And are certain types of societies better predisposed to opening the boardroom to greater numbers of female directors?

In many societies around the world, women are still in the process of entering the workforce in more substantial numbers – a key long-term prerequisite for their assuming corporate leadership positions. In addition, research has suggested that diversity, including gender diversity, has been shown to produce more pronounced positive effects in countries with stronger shareholder protection[1] – because this motivates the board to draw on the diverse knowledge, experience, and values of each director.

---

[1] Post, C. and K. Byron (2014). Women on boards and firm financial performance: a meta-analysis. *Academy of Management Journal* 58(5): 1546–1571.

In 2019, Amazon appointed a black woman to its all-white board of directors amid increasing pressure on the company to diversify its leadership team. Rosalind Brewer, Starbucks' chief operating officer, became the fourth woman and the only person of colour on Amazon's ten-person board. Firms face growing demands from shareholders and activist groups to add more women and people of colour to their board. In 2018, BlackRock, the world's biggest asset manager, asked companies in its portfolio with fewer than two female board members to disclose their attempts to increase board diversity.

Much effort has been made in academia, the media, and elsewhere to correlate female representation on boards with companies' financial, operational, or strategic performance. This constitutes a laudable attempt to identify a 'selling point' for advocating more female directors, although the findings so far have been mixed.

In a 2015 MSCI study, companies with at least three female board members outperformed others in overall returns on equity by an average of 36%. A similar study in 2018 by MSCI showed that companies with diverse boards (three plus female directors over three years) and leading talent management practices experienced growth in employee productivity that averaged 1.2 percentage points above their industry medians. This growth rate exceeded that for firms with just a diverse board and for firms with only strong talent management.[2]

Such findings have led more institutions to view gender diversity as a yardstick for making investment decisions. For instance, a number of asset management firms have launched funds which invest specifically in companies showing high levels of gender diversity on boards and in senior leadership. One such investment fund is the Street Global Advisors' Gender Diversity Index ETF, which was launched in March 2016 and seeded with an initial $250 million from the California State Teachers' Retirement System (CalSTRS).[3]

More fundamentally, however, boards should challenge the validity of the underlying research question. It is truly necessary to place a burden of proof on female executives and proponents of greater gender diversity? Is a greater female presence on boards only desirable if it comes with a guarantee of demonstrable and consistent improvements in a company's quantitative indicators? Do women

---

[2] https://www.msci.com/documents/10199/4bd5f3bb-e5a4-4993-9c2a-4b44423ba4a2.

[3] www.businesswire.com/news/home/20160307005890/en/State-Street-Global-Advisors-Launches-Gender-Diversity.

need to be 'better than men' before they gain more equitable representation in the boardroom?

The business community must revisit these simple yet deep-seated issues with more clarity and integrity if it is committed to long-term improvements in corporate governance. It is also possible that gender diversity creates different *distributions* of performance (for example, by truncating downside risks on large transactions or integrity issues) rather than levels of performance.

Culture

The growing diversity of nationalities represented on corporate boards has likewise posed complex questions and raised practical obstacles to boards' long-term performance, as well as to day-to-day operations. What is obvious is that for all the incessant talk of globalisation, a truly global culture remains conspicuous by its absence.

To develop an understanding of other cultures, we need to be able to examine our own. The tricky thing about culture is that it is very much the software running through the human brain – and, much like real software, it is invisible (see Figure 23.2). At an individual level, culture is about mental programming and conditioning, the bulk of which takes place in childhood and school. This early-life process leaves every individual with a set of fundamental assumptions about themselves, others and the world. According to cross-cultural communication studies pioneer Edward Hall:

> Culture hides much more than it reveals, and strangely enough what it hides, it hides most effectively from its own participants. Years of study have convinced me that the real job is not to understand foreign culture but to understand our own. I am also convinced that all that one ever gets from studying foreign culture is a token understanding. [To study another culture] is to learn more about how one's own system works.[4]

At a minimum, the opportunity to learn about one's own cultural profile, habits, and emotional triggers will strengthen one's confidence and boost self-acceptance. Crucially, this teaches us that others may be very different in terms of their cultural backgrounds – and that is okay.

---

[4] Hall, E. (1959). *The Silent Language.* DoubleDay.

CULTURAL ICEBERG

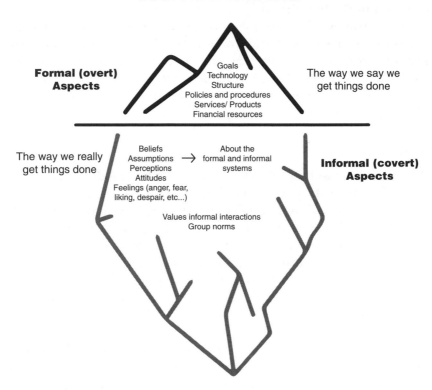

Figure 23.2   Cultural Iceberg.
Source: Based on data from Stanley N. Herman, TRW Systems Group 1970

Personality

Personality is an important aspect of diversity. While there are many ways to differentiate between personalities, one increasingly popular theory is the Big 5, according to which there are five different dimensions of personality. The NEO PI-R, for example, is gaining acceptance as a personality tool. It defines the five big dimensions as being emotionality, extroversion vs. introversion, openness, agreeableness, and conscientiousness; each of these five dimensions has six subdimensions or facets. (For a more detailed description of the NEO PI-R, see Chapter 7.)

Diverse personalities can bring great benefit to the boardroom by stimulating debate and challenging perspectives. However, because this is a less obvious element of group diversity, it can sometimes be poorly managed and become dysfunctional. Often, too, diversity of personality is uncomfortable and therefore unconsciously resisted. Some personality dimensions might even result in the emergence of an in-group. For example, if the chair is fast-paced in meetings, he or she might become highly impatient with directors who are more methodical. And at lunch, the chair may unconsciously choose to sit next to someone who resembles them on this dimension, thereby becoming closer to that person and building up trust. It is therefore particularly important that the chair is aware of personality differences and the challenges these may present in boardroom discussion.

Figure 23.3 below shows a board mapping of personalities. The CEO (an Italian from Sicily) had a high score on the emotionality dimension, while the British chair was at the other end of the spectrum. While both were high-performing individuals, this difference created difficulties in communication that had become excruciating. When well managed, the combination of a resilient chair and a sensitive CEO can be wonderful: the heightened sensitivity of the CEO helps the organisation tackle challenges and threats, while the chair offers a safe psychological base. But when poorly managed, that combination becomes a threat to the organisation.

Age

Age diversity has become increasingly important for boards in the context of innovation. The demands put forward by innovation – particularly the need to think about and anticipate trends in the market – require boards to display diversity of thinking and have the right mix of directors who will make innovation part of every board discussion.

The business risk of not understanding innovation has become more acute than ever. Toyota, for example, made changes to its organisational structure, including its boardroom, in both 2016 and 2017. It cited the need for quick judgement, decisions, and action through *genchi genbutsu* (onsite learning and problem-solving), because 'the changes the company faces require a different way to think and act'.

INDIVIDUAL NEO PROFILES OF A BOARD

EMOTIONALITY	Resilient	Responsive	Reactive
N1 Worry	0 33 Unworried; calm; unconcerned	43 58 68 Usually calm, sometimes worrying	100 Worrying, tense, apprehensive
N2 Anger	0 33 Even-tempered; slow to anger	58 68 Seldom angry, but can be provoked	100 Quick to anger, hot-blooded
N3 Moodiness	0 33 Optimistic; contented; no blues	43 68 Sensitive to losing, but recover well	100 Self-blaming; pessimist; blues
N4 Social concerns	0 33 Socially confident, self-assured	58 68 Gets embarrassed, then get over it	100 Sensitive to embarrassment, shy
N5 Self indulgence	0 33 Resists temptation; stoic	58 Sometimes yield to temptation	68 100 Easily tempted; self-indulgent
N6 Sensitivity to stress	0 33 Resilient to stress and crises	43 68 Experiences stress, but can cope	100 Sensitive to stress & pressure
EXTRAVERSION	Introvert	Ambivert	Extravert
E1 Warmth	0 33 Reserved; distant; cool	43 58 68 Moderate engagement	100 Attached; affectionate; warm
E2 Outgoingness	0 33 Loner; prefer privacy	43 58 68 Mix well, but enjoy privacy	100 Sociable; prefer company
E3 Assertiveness	0 33 Non-assertive; passive	43 58 68 Comfortable in foreground	100 Dominant; speak up; leading
E4 Activity level	0 33 Slow-paced; inactive; laid-back	43 58 68 Ordinary pace and energy level	100 Active; energetic; fast-paced
E5 Excitement seeking	0 33 Conventional; avoid risks	43 58 68 Enjoy moderate stimulation	100 Seeking pleasure, thrills, adventure
E6 Positive emotions	0 33 Serious, sober, lacking enthusiasm	43 58 68 Neither serious nor cheery	100 Cheerful; light-hearted; joyful
OPENNESS	Preserver	Adaptor	Explorer
O1 Imagination	0 33 Down to earth; focused; realistic	58 68 Occasional daydreamer	100 Imaginative; abstract, creative
O2 Aesthetic sense	0 33 Prosaic, unmoved or bored by art	43 58 68 Moderate interest in art	100 Artistic, aesthetic, stylish
O3 Depth of emotions	0 33 Discount own and others' feelings	43 68 Accepting of feelings	100 Interested in own and others feeling
O4 Willingness to experment	0 33 Habitual, like routine & familiar	43 58 68 Try new things incrementally	100 Experimental; seeking novelty
O5 Intellectual curiosity	0 33 Practical; here and now	43 58 68 Moderate interest in abstraction	100 Inquisitive; theoretical; curious
O6 Tolerance for diversity	0 33 Conservative; dogmatic	43 58 68 Middle of the road	100 Liberal; unconventional; tolerant
AGREEABLENESS	Challenger	Negotiator	Conciliator
A1 Trust in others	0 33 Cynical; sceptical; suspicious	43 58 68 Cautiously trusting	100 Trusting; forgiving; accepting
A2 Candor	0 33 Guarded; cautious; political	58 68 Tactful but open	100 Frank; open; straight-forward
A3 Consideration for others	0 33 Self-absorbed; high self-interest	43 58 68 Giving if asked	100 Considerate; helpful; nurturing
A4 Compliance	0 33 Competitive; head-strong; fighter	43 68 Can compete if necessary	100 Cooperative; compliant; peaceful
A5 Modesty	0 33 Self-promoting; seen as arrogant	43 58 68 Feel equal to others	100 Self-effacing; humble; modest
A6 Sympathy	0 33 Hard-hearted; rational; justice rules	43 58 68 Caring for others selectively	100 Soft-hearted; merciful; sympathetic
CONSCIENTIOUSNESS	Flexible	Balanced	Focused
C1 Sense of competence	0 33 Unprepared; inefficient; unsure	43 58 68 Quite well prepared and confiden	100 Self-confident; planned; resourceful
C2 Orderliness	0 33 Disorganised; unmethodical	43 58 68 Sometimes disorganised & untidy	100 Neat; tidy; organised; meticulous
C3 Sense of responsibility	0 33 Unreliable; bending the rules	43 58 68 Follows the rules most of the time	100 Stick strictly to the rules; reliable
C4 Need to achieve	0 33 Easy-going; unambitious	43 58 68 Relaxed about success	100 Driven; ambitious; enterprising
C5 Self discipline	0 33 Distractable; procrastinating	43 58 68 Quite focused, but can waste time	100 Finisher; workaholic; self-pacing
C6 Deliberateness	0 33 Hasty; snap decisions	43 58 68 Makes considered decisions	100 Cautious; deliberate; thorough

Figure 23.3   Individual NEO Profiles of a Board

As boards recognise the need to accelerate innovation, they have also been more receptive to appointments of young members whose background may greatly expand the board's collective experience and expertise. One of the board members at private Swiss bank Vontobel, Björn Wettergren (born 1981) is an engineer MBA and founding family member whose previous roles spanned banking, venture capital, and human resources. This illustrates the bank's commitment to adjusting its board structure as digital technologies – the cloud, robotics, advanced analytics, cognitive computing, and artificial intelligence – reshape its service delivery.

Social Background

Social background is another critical dimension of diversity. The 2016 Brexit referendum in the United Kingdom highlighted long-standing tensions and distrust between 'big business' and employees. As part of her campaign to become Prime Minister, Theresa May revisited the theme of workers playing a larger role in the boardroom, as a way of overcoming the legacy of boards reproducing the same elite, narrowly defined social and professional circles. May suggested it was time for employees to have more input in the way businesses are run.[5]

The experience of Northern European, particularly Scandinavian, economies that placed employee representatives on boards as far back as the 1970s shows that this is a long-term project that requires a cultural change to be successful. Shifts in the power balance – and the ensuing power struggles – are inevitable. So are issues of confidentiality, because sensitive information may easily be channelled to the workforce. And like in the early days of any diversity initiative, there is always the risk of going through the motions by appointing token representatives whose voices may or may not be heard.

Having directors with diverse social backgrounds is helpful for ensuring a wide range of viewpoints (and therefore for preventing blindspots). But if this diversity is not well managed, it may result in tensions that can lead to governance failures – as in the case of Hull House.

---

[5] http://recruiter.e4s.co.uk/2016/08/01/employees-boardroom/.

We Have Embraced Diversity . . . Now What?

At a practical level, board members will develop a deep appreciation of how to capitalise on their team's diversity. In particular, they
will learn to understand the strengths that reside in individual directors' competencies, and how these can transfer, multiply, and inform
new areas of the organisation's activities and competitiveness. For
example, many companies that expanded into central and eastern
Europe during the 1990s later built on this experience and their
newly acquired skillsets by formulating an expansion strategy for the
Asia-Pacific region in the 2000s. In doing so, they drew on their executives' knowledge and expertise gained in emerging markets, and
internalised it as a powerful differentiating factor in the company's
future strategy.

In the long run, pursuing diversity becomes a journey and a learning process. As on all journeys, companies and organisations that are
overseen by inspired, visionary boards will not hesitate to take risks,
adopt contrarian approaches, and push the envelope. They will
challenge and redefine existing narratives of diversity by creating
new role models; nurturing diverse talent through mentoring programmes; and pursuing alternative paths to excellence in diversity.
Much of this will entail deep thinking about what the source of the
company's competitive advantage will be in ten years' time.

Well-defined objectives and outcomes are a crucial element
of any organisational effort aimed at strengthening commitment
to diversity and then managing that diversity effectively. Board
members must be able to show, rather than just feel, their new
outlook on diversity – whether it relates to gender, culture, or
other attributes. Their knowledge must translate into a skill set,
and the behaviour that this drives should become automatic and
take the form of a habit. From there on, board members and
executives should be able to measure their progress and growth
toward excellence.

They say a little knowledge is a dangerous thing, and the same is
true of diversity. Many boards have succumbed to the temptation of
approaching diversity in a mechanical way – by checking boxes, or
filling stated as well as unstated quotas. True, even going through the
motions like this may be better than doing nothing, as it may at least
produce modest results. But as copious research has shown, diversity can only be a powerful predictor of a company's performance

ESG Measures for Investment

Diversity is just one aspect of 'responsible investing', guided by measurable sets of environmental, social, and governance (ESG) principles. These considerations include environmentally friendly products, effective use of technology, and building equitable workplaces.

Indicators such as the executive/employee pay ratio, the level of transparency in reporting balance-sheet data, or the absence of tax-avoidance schemes are no longer 'nice-to-know' nuggets of information. Rather, they provide a substantial gauge of a company's health, sustainability, and long-term growth prospects.

when it is understood and managed well. Boards that are superficially diverse but have failed to address, reflect on, and mobilise that quality will soon face issues of miscommunication and resentment as directors report overwhelming feelings of being 'thrown together'. In this scenario, diversity turns into a liability as the board underperforms 'normal' homogeneous teams by a wide margin (see Figure 23.4).

THE IMPACT OF DIVERSITY ON BOARD PERFORMANCE

Figure 23.4   The Impact of Diversity on Board Performance.

Source: Adapted from J.J. DiStefano and M.L. Maznevski: Creating value with diverse teams in global management. *Organizational Dynamics*, Vol. 29, No 1; and research by C. Kovachu.

The Chair's Role in Building and Nurturing Diversity

It is a recurring theme in this book that the chair has an important role to play – and the task of integrating diverse board members into a high performing team is no exception. The board chair leads the way in embracing inclusiveness and diversity. He or she is conscious of the need to do more than just respond to demographic trends in the outside world.

To start with, models of building consensus are largely determined by culture. According to Lewis,[6] the American style of arriving at a consensus can be characterised as structured individualism, as senior and middle managers make individual decisions. UK directors are likely to be more comfortable with casual leadership, while Scandinavian executives will fall back on the principle of *primus inter pares* – in other words, 'the boss is in the circle'. Depending on their cultural make-up, boards in other countries may lean toward autocratic, top-down styles or a combination of hierarchy with group agreement. Once consensus has been built, the question of who is accountable arises. In some cultures, it is the individual manager; in others, it is the boss. In Asia, one could argue that the entire team is collectively accountable.

Leadership styles are strongly defined by culture too. Depending on the particular cultural context, leaders may demonstrate and look for technical competence; place facts before sentiments, and logic before emotion; and be deal oriented, with a view to immediate achievements and results. Alternatively, they may choose to rely on their eloquence and ability to persuade; inspire through force of personality; and complete human transactions emotionally. Or they will dominate with knowledge, patience, and quiet control; display modesty and courtesy; and create a harmonious if paternalistic atmosphere for teamwork.

Boards can only bridge differences if they understand what these are. Building diversity is an ongoing process whereby collectives create their own world of meaning, and where directors integrate new meanings and add new dimensions to themselves. Ultimately, they learn about themselves and about the need to understand others,

---

[6] Lewis, R.D. (1996). *When Cultures Collide.* Nicholas Brealey Publishing.

recognise the inherent contradictions, and learn to embrace other people's realities.

Chairs can do a lot of good work in this area – not only in educating the board, but also in setting the tone for management and the entire organisation. The company should visibly advance from aspiring to diversity awareness to achieving and disseminating sensitivity, understanding, and knowledge. Once these become widespread, the organisation and the board may be truly able to celebrate diversity as a key part of their identity and achievement.

A board chair who is committed to growing diversity in the organisation will encourage others to understand very clearly who they are; to recognise the 'spectacles' or filters that colour their perceptions; and to seek common ground in all situations. Board members will learn to switch their cultural gear in order to improve interaction. And as they invest time and patience into building trust across a diverse board, they will take differences in decision-making into account.

Many types of exercises help bring a board with a diversity of perspectives towards more shared views. This helps build constructive dissent, which is itself at the heart of good governance. For example, one we use is the board history exercise. Board members are encouraged to share (and draw!) their experience of the most significant moments in their tenure at the company. This allows to build a common view of the past based on diversity of understandings, which by itself helps reconcile views to the future.

Diversity brings specific expertise to a board, as well as increased potential for innovation. Poorly managed diversity, however, can be disruptive by hindering communication and eroding mutual trust. A strong board will thus develop processes to manage diversity well. Even well-established boards should have a systematic board composition oversight, with regular assessment of required capabilities (from expertise to familiarity) and a current composition matrix. And as we will see in the next chapter, boards also need to have a detailed overview of the organisation's executive talent pipeline.

Table 23.1 The Board History Exercise

The exercise starts by a short individual talks, in which board members identify their personal views, before engaging smaller groups (say three or four) into a group task which brings these views together.

Individual Task

Identify the three most significant events that happened in your company for *your time period*.

Restrict your choice of events to those events that hold significance for your company today and continue to influence the company:

- Something that happened externally: changes to industry, markets, political shifts, new regulations.
- Changes in company boundaries: mergers, acquisitions, sell-offs, new product-markets.
- New management philosophy or introduction of a new process, technology, or IT system.
- Change in leadership (hiring, retirement, etc.).
- Event 1: _____
- Significance: _____
- Event 2: _____
- Significance: _____
- Event 3: _____
- Significance: _____

Group Task

- Group members share their individual list with others.
- Select one significant event per group member.
- Finalise your list.
- Make sure the group has a balance of EXTERNAL and INTERNAL events.
- For each event, draw a picture or icon.
- Each group member should get prepared to give a brief description of their event

The exercise closes by a presentation of the different posters/pictures. These can become part of board folklore . . .

CHAPTER 24

The Talent Pipeline

Talent has become a critical resource and an integral component of a company's overall business strategy. The governance discussion has therefore also shifted to focus on human capital, and on talent oversight as part of strategic planning. In particular, a company's ability to build its pipeline of effective leaders has become a strategic consideration. This is often referred to as leadership 'bench strength' – the capabilities and readiness of potential successors to move into key professional and leadership positions.

Although issues of human capital and capabilities are not new to board agendas, a board's oversight mandate has often been seen primarily in terms of risk governance, ethics, and corporate responsibility rather than talent. And when boards did play a part in issues related to talent, their involvement typically focused on appointing, mentoring, and monitoring the performance of the CEO, alongside board composition, tenure, and appointments.

The Board's Responsibility for Talent Management

Now that corporations have universally recognised talent as the key ingredient in their success, and acknowledged that the 'war for talent' rages on unabated, where does that leave the board? What is the board's responsibility in terms of the organisation's talent management?

Depending on the specific issue, boards get involved at different levels. At the basic operational level, many boards are doing more of what they have been doing for years: they are expanding their oversight of management's activities related to talent acquisition, development, retention, and employee engagement throughout the organisation. Directors may be expected to examine talent supply and demand data as part of capital investment and business strategy reviews on an annual basis, or even more frequently. This includes developing learning paths for high-potential individuals across the organisation. As in other areas of governance, the board acts to foster high productivity and performance.

But in the new people- and talent-focused landscape, there is more to be done in the boardroom than supervising longstanding hiring procedures. Proactive boards will identify key positions within the organisation's leadership (it may be a handful of posts or a couple of hundred). They will actively learn about the talent pipeline that is in place to fill different types of positions, especially should a particular role need to be filled urgently in the future. With top jobs, such as that of CEO, the board will recognise that recruiting for the C-suite is commonly coordinated at a global level. Effective boards will have a succession plan in place, as well as a set of predefined metrics to gauge the new CEO's job performance and its effect on the company's results and reputation.

In addition to procedural considerations, the board should have an instinctive, almost visceral appreciation for the type of leader the company needs at present, as well as in a few years from now. The ideal candidate's professional experience, industry background, leadership style, and track record, and to some extent even nationality and personality, must be a good fit with the current juncture in the company's growth, and also with the challenges ahead. Does the firm need someone who will tread lightly and respect the delicate consensus that has been established within the organisation over the years? Or has complacency set in, meaning that the company needs a leader who will shake things up and disturb the old order? Or will the new CEO's main task be to keep tabs on spending and restore financial discipline?

Whether the company is aiming for radical transformation, a return to profitability, aggressive expansion, or another scenario, the new CEO chosen by the board must be a solid fit for what lies ahead – even if the short-listed candidates come from different industries or countries.

In February 2017, luxury fashion retailer Barneys named Daniella Vitale, the company's chief operating officer, as its new CEO. Her predecessor as chief executive, Mark Lee, said that the company had put a succession plan in place in 2012 for Vitale to become the CEO in 2017.

Lee had himself mentored Vitale when they worked together at Gucci and then at Barneys. By the time Vitale became CEO, she had plenty of leadership experience in the company, and had worked in several different parts of the business.

From Succession Plans to Transitioning Leaders, Boards Have a Role to Play

By the same token, today's global executives expect the transition process to be nurturing. In their minds, the most valuable personal development is challenging and experiential: it broadens skills, builds expertise, offers the opportunity to work in other countries and cultures, tests judgement, gives autonomy, and promotes visibility.

Companies can provide systematic support to help improve the success rate of leaders in transitions. According to Michael Watkins, 'Organizations can help transitioning leaders to leverage the time prior to switching jobs by providing them with information, access and coaching support to diagnose the situation they are walking into, the relationships they need to build, the resources they need to secure and the expectations they need to set'.[1] This is a radical departure from the long-established practice in organisations of matching a person's evidence-based qualities with those of the job to be performed. This approach was built on an obsession with proof and written documentation, as if writing up an activity actually made it happen.

Transitions into new leadership roles typically test an executive's mettle from day one, with pressure to diagnose, strategise, delegate, and communicate effectively. Success or failure during the transition period is a strong predictor of how the executive will fare overall in the job. Promotions, by contrast, often challenge the new leader to learn to delegate and communicate differently.

Once the leader has obtained insight into the key learning goals, he or she can work towards speeding up every transition. Leaders then need to focus on identifying the best sources of intelligence.

---

[1] Narasimhan, A. and J.L. Barsoux (2014). *Quest.* IMD Publishing, p. 88

Obviously, they will consume the available documentation and analyses about the business. But this is usually far from being sufficient. Real insight comes from identifying the people who can provide more fine-grained insight into why things are as they are, enabling the leader to look at the business with the eyes of a historian.

It is critical to understand how the organisation got to the state it is in today. If serious problems were not addressed early enough to avoid a crisis, then why? What does this say about the culture and politics of the company, and about the competence and courage of its leadership? If bad decisions were made, how did that happen? What does this say about decision-making processes and team dynamics?

The New Talent Dynamic: Culture, Values, Community

As well as identifying key positions and the talent pipeline that is available to fill them, boards shape talent dynamics within their company at a much more fundamental level: that of overseeing and defining the organisation's culture. This reflects the trend of regarding talent as a key asset and therefore an intrinsic part of the risk culture of an organisation.

In Chapter 17, we examined organisational culture as a source of coherence and continuity that helps employees make sense of what goes on around them. We noted that in the twenty-first century, a company's culture – which stems directly from people's values and beliefs – can make or break the firm's fortunes in areas such as talent attraction and retention, brand recognition, and reputation with stakeholders. We also showed that the main forces driving a successful organisation ahead – innovation, creativity, and imagination – tend to thrive in an environment of 'us and them', where a sense of shared values trumps any organisational, bureaucratic, or even monetary considerations. In addition, the need to develop new products, enter new markets, or combat new competitors also dictates the demand for specific types, profiles, and cohorts of talent.

In many situations, organisations simply do not possess enough strategic knowledge regarding talent development. The board is then in a strong position to provide leadership and guidance on the entire gamut of talent-related considerations. These include nurturing a talent-friendly corporate culture, establishing robust talent pipelines, developing sound and transparent recruiting and performance monitoring mechanisms, and having succession plans for filling the roles of top executives, especially in a crisis or following the sudden departure of top talent. Increasingly, boards expect to monitor strategic talent management areas such as HR strategy, organisational culture, employee engagement, succession planning, and development.

Much of the board's expanded sense of commitment to looking after the talent pipeline comes from the evolving view in the business community of leaders and leadership. In the past 50 years, the leadership debate has migrated from exceptional individuals having 'the right stuff' in terms of a scientifically determined leadership skillset, to a much more distributed and dispersed take on what constitutes leadership and where it resides. In consequence, many organisations and their boards have broadened their definition of talent in ways that allow them to target and capture the leadership potential throughout the workforce.

As a result, boards no longer see succession simply in terms of reporting the number of potential candidates within an organisation. Directors are looking for more visibility into executive management successors and asking for greater rigour regarding the professional development of succession candidates, including exposure to these individuals at board level. In addition, boards have been facilitating a broad-based shift in focus from individual to organisational learning. They have also sought out opportunities to meet with senior management personnel below the top level, thus getting a direct view of the talent pipeline.

As firms cast a wider net in building a diverse boardroom, a growing number of directors now come from professional accounting and legal firms, or build on previous roles as general counsels and HR specialists. That makes them more likely than their peers to understand issues related to executive talent (such as succession planning) and non-executive talent (such as employee engagement). In addition, and unlike in the past, a growing number of directors and chairs attend breakfast meetings with young staff. This gives them a better understanding of young employees' motivation for joining the company, as well as a glimpse of the firm's emerging talent 'DNA' that will shape its future identity, competitiveness, and innovation.

As well as conceiving the natural habitat of talent within the organisation infinitely more broadly than in the past, companies are also abandoning the deep-rooted top-down approach to talent management that allowed for very little employee engagement. Instead, with the aim of unleashing talent 'hidden in plain sight', employees are given more control of their personal and professional development. In particular, talent has come to be seen not only as a key competitive differentiator, but also as a magnet for new talent – because talent attracts talent, because talent can recognise other talent, and because talented people want to join winning, motivated, and high performing teams. This is where boards need to exert influence throughout their organisation and nurture a mindset of 'we shall become whom we have hired'.

To avoid the intensifying pressures of product commoditisation, and to tackle disruptive change in its industry head on, a company must be able to deliver unique customer value. That can only be created by employees who bring a full measure of their initiative, imagination, and zeal to work every day. Unfortunately, there is not much room left in strait-laced, bureaucratic, top-down organisations for higher-order, intrinsically human qualities such as passion, ingenuity, and self-direction. The machinery of bureaucracy was invented in an age when human beings were seen as dispensable – the weakest link in the production chain of command. Multiple layers of bureaucracy may have been designed to facilitate an organisation's processes and to keep things moving – but in reality, they inevitably take over and start to dictate. This puts a firm limit on which part of themselves individuals are allowed to bring to their jobs.

Meanwhile, many organisations have begun to pursue the opposite goal, of replacing hierarchy with community. It is within a community that humans are drawn to work together and share a sense of purpose, and where economic need is no longer the be all and end all. In a community, the opportunity to contribute is not bounded by narrow job descriptions. Control is peer-based rather than coming from a boss. Emotional satisfaction, rather than financial gain, drives commitment. In sum, workplaces that have self-organised as communities may act as genuine and powerful amplifiers of human talent and capability. The modern-day workforce seeks out organisational designs that are based on

Board-like Roles as Preparation for Board Membership

Steve Vamos, who joined the Telstra board, had been chief executive of two multinational subsidiaries operating in Australia (Apple and Microsoft) and was able to experience the board-like role of running regional operations for both companies, governing a number of Asia Pacific subsidiaries and others around the world. He learned 'the art of the boardroom' to make important points through careful and thoughtful questions, and to express views to management without being directly instructive.[2]

respect for the ability and wisdom of humans at work, without the daily battle against the isolating and alienating effects of rigid, hierarchical management.

A board should also be aware of its own potential talent issues, especially as demands on its organisational skills and overall abilities increase and as its composition changes. Today's boards need directors who are independent of management; who have more time to devote to board service; and who have expertise in risk, global trends, talent, technology, sustainability, and social media. In addition, boards may require improved communication, education and development, coaching, and mentoring skills, and, perhaps, more experience with regulatory agencies.

As managers move through transitions and develop into organisational leaders, they eventually become part of the talent pool for the board. Board-like roles (running business units or regions) are good preparation for executive directorships. Even for the most talented and experienced leaders, the role of executive board director is a very different function and responsibility.

In addition to talent management, boards must also pay increasing attention to the challenges and opportunities presented by social media. The next chapter assesses these and suggests ways for directors to increase their effectiveness in the digital age.

[2] www.afr.com/leadership/how-not-to-behave-in-the-boardroom-20150601-ghe5va

CHAPTER 25

Boards and Social Media[1]

Certainly not a specialist of social media myself, I have discovered how much board members can learn from stepping out of their usual and sometimes dated ways. The extra effort to understand the evolution of the social and business environment through the social media lens is immensely rewarding and the tools available truly productive. Better learned individuals such as Estelle Metayer,[2] whose lectures and insights have inspired this chapter, can guide us towards better mastery of content.

In general, boards spend little time thinking about social media, and many directors are still accustomed to more formal and structured sources of news and information. But social media is increasingly a way of life and is fundamentally changing the way people interact and communicate – including by democratising the world's information and revolutionising the way we do business. As of the first quarter of 2019, Facebook had 2.38 billion monthly active users. Daily in 2019, 500 million tweets are posted on Twitter and 5 billion videos are viewed on YouTube.

---

[1] Many of the ideas in this chapter are based on the work of Estelle Métayer, and I would like to acknowledge my intellectual debt to her perspectives and thinking.
[2] President of Competia and serial board member of talent, with a tech and social media slant towards stewardship principles. One of the many truly exceptional board members full of passion and integrity who have inspired this book.

Social media is not only a way to share information, but also a forum for conversations among consumers and activists that can derail and destroy company reputations. Social media are transforming the context the business works in, such as employees to management relations. Even further, for the astute board member, social media present a fantastic source of information on the company, its context, the competitors, and the landscape at large. Board members should use social media to listen to what customers, employees, and other stakeholders are saying about the organisation – but they should probably not be creators of social media content themselves.

JP Morgan's Failed Foray into Twitter Q&A

In late 2013, JP Morgan announced a Twitter Q&A with its vice-chair, creating a hashtag #AskJPM. Having received a barrage of negative and sarcastic comments, the bank cancelled the event before the Q&A could go live. This has since become an oft-quoted example not only of misguided social media strategy but also of a major corporation supposedly unaware of and disconnected from its current public image.[3]

Although some industries are more affected by social media than others, most organisations are impacted in some way. CEOs still tend to be afraid of social media, often feeling that they do not have the time, or that it is somehow not relevant to them. Companies can be rather unsophisticated when it comes to formally gathering data from social media and using these for corporate strategy, operational plans, and risk management. Directors and executives don't always ask for this information – nor do they rely on it for decision-making. But board members and senior management can no longer overlook the effect that social media can have on a company's reputation, or the speed at which isolated digital rumblings can turn into a tidal wave of discontent.

In March 2010, Greenpeace posted a graphic video on YouTube claiming that Nestlé used palm oil in KitKats, and was thus contributing to the destruction of orangutans' habitats. Nestlé asked YouTube to remove the clip, citing copyright infringement; environmental campaigners told CNN the copyright infringement claim

---

[3] https://econsultancy.com/blog/63901-the-top-16-social-media-fails-of-2013/.

> The #MeToo movement against sexual harassment and sexual assault started to go viral as a social media hashtag in October 2017, following sexual abuse allegations against Hollywood film producer Harvey Weinstein. The movement has not only implicated individuals, but also cost several businesses substantially.
>
> Streaming service Netflix reportedly lost $39 million for severing ties with actor Kevin Spacey,[4] who played the lead character in the famous Netflix production 'House of Cards'. In January 2018, hotel and casino company Wynn Resorts lost $3.5 billion in market value after the emergence of sexual harassment allegations concerning CEO Steve Wynn.[5] And in the following month, shares in fashion retailer Guess tumbled almost 18%, and the company's market value fell by more than $250 million in a day, after model Kate Upton accused the firm's co-founder Paul Marciano via Twitter of using his power to 'sexually and emotionally harass women'.[6]

was 'a pretext for stopping the word being spread and an apparent attempt to silence us'. Greenpeace reposted the video on Vimeo, and many other users reposted it. On 20 May 2010, only ten weeks later, Nestlé announced it would stop sourcing the unsustainable palm oil. This was a victory at minimal cost for Greenpeace and social networking.

At present, most companies are slowly coming to grips with the task of finding optimum tools and systems for scanning, analysing, and evaluating relevant social media content. Directors are learning how to ask the right questions, acquire the necessary capabilities for the organisation, and attract suitable talent for making sense of its digital footprint.

Why Boards Should Understand Social Media

Boards need to understand social media for several reasons:

- **To manage reputation risk.** In April 2017, United Airlines stumbled with its social media response following the forcible removal of a passenger from one of its flights. The airline initially would not admit it had made a mistake. Its CEO later had to apologise, losing face and some credibility in the

---

[4] https://money.cnn.com/2018/01/22/media/netflix-kevin-spacey-cost/index.html.
[5] http://fortune.com/2018/01/29/steve-wynn-stock-net-worth-sexual-misconduct/.
[6] https://www.reuters.com/article/us-guess-stocks/guess-shares-slump-after-model-kate-upton-tweets-about-exec-idUSKBN1FL6BK.

process. United's share price tumbled as well. The airline later settled the lawsuit that the passenger had filed.

- **To avoid blind spots.** Social media can help boards to pick up early signals. Different businesses have different cycles. A number of tools allow companies to scan social media and detect where rumours are coming from, enabling them to quantify the level of urgency.
- **To increase knowledge in ethical ways.** How intimately do you want to know your employees or your customers? Glassdoor is giving access to employee perspectives often differentiated from corporate surveys. It may offer intriguing insights revealing moods and sometimes facts. Target, the US supermarket chain, has been able to identify when its customers were pregnant, often before the women had made it public, through an analysis of their purchases. But should the firm have used this information for marketing purposes? Boards should be having ethical discussions about the use of private data.
- **As a source of independent intelligence,** by using sites such as socialmention.com and other social mentions sites. When BlackBerry announced that it was pulling out of the consumer market, it could have avoided the backlash had it used sysomos to conduct a generational analysis. This would have demonstrated the differences in the product's reputation between age groups and the potential liability of simply taking it away. Many companies, including Nestlé, have set up social media command centres to get a better sense of what employees or other key stakeholders are saying about the firm and its products.

By now, board members increasingly understand that social media may serve as a digital red flag, pinpointing trouble before it acquires serious magnitude and ramifications. With continued advances in data analysis, social media may also be harnessed for its predictive power, highlighting problems and dissatisfactions that are bubbling under the surface and can be dispelled through simple, timely, and effective interventions.

The key thing to note is the speed at which information is shared on social media, which means that situations can escalate quickly. Under stress, it is difficult to think clearly and react appropriately. Companies therefore need to have a clear checklist of what to do in a social media crisis.

Mozilla's Failure to Engage

In March 2014, OkCupid.com, a popular online dating site, called for a boycott of Mozilla Firefox to protest against the world's second biggest web browser naming a gay marriage opponent as chief executive.

Brendan Eich, a founder of Mozilla and creator of its technology, had made a $1000 donation to opponents of gay marriage in 2008. OkCupid sent a message to visitors who accessed its website through Firefox, suggesting they use browsers such as Microsoft's Internet Explorer or Google's Chrome. Mozilla was slow to react.

'We didn't act like you'd expect Mozilla to act', wrote Mozilla Executive Chair Mitchell Baker in a blog post. 'We didn't move fast enough to engage with people once the controversy started. We're sorry.' A few days later, Eich stepped down.

Besides crisis prevention and management, a good sense of what is brewing on social media can yield powerful insights into customer needs, perceptions, and satisfaction. In addition, smart organisations can cultivate a loyal digital audience by engaging with customers via social media and responding to their concerns. Effective social media engagement can also give a great boost to the company's brand visibility and credibility, both online and offline.

What Boards Should Do

While many boards today are still largely cut off from social media, this is rapidly changing. Boards need to take three steps in particular to get up to speed.

Getting It Right: Directors Don't Post, They Listen!

Social media is now a primary source of information. It is better for directors to refrain from proactive communication unless a solid protocol has been established by the board. Nonetheless, tools such as Hootsuite allow board members to easily track the organisation and its competitors or substitutes. Also, many tools allow a better understanding of rising trends. Thus, social media has become a source of independent intelligence. For example, www.socialmention.com or meltwater social can help boards understand the landscape, notably in consumer goods markets. A debate on what tools are used by the different board members (and seeing holes and complementarities), and possibly a short session by a digital specialist from the firm on the most interesting opportunities, is worth engaging with.

Ask Questions

The board should ask hygiene questions covering issues such as:

Social media policy
- Do we have a social media policy for employees?[7]
- Is this policy part of the employment contract?
- Does it define how the employee engages in social media, whether in his or her own name or that of the company?
- Is it clear who owns the intellectual property (see the article 'Lawyers, guns and Twitter: Who owns your Twitter account')?[8]
- Are employees receiving coaching and training?
- Is there a budget to support these initiatives?

Information gathering
- Which sources are we listening to? Does the list include review sites, blogs, Twitter and Facebook, as well as consumers' forums? Does it include LinkedIn and Google+?
- Is the company systematically gathering and analysing social media information to assess reputational risks?

Crisis management
- Do we have a response plan in case of digital crisis? And who is managing it?

Figure 25.1 provides an illustration of a social media early crisis protocol.

Occupy the Space

The cost of ignoring the digital world during a crisis can be seen in BP's failure to address the Deepwater Horizon oil spill on social media. The space was soon occupied instead by an imitator posting false news. Thus, a key question for any organisation in today's social

---

[7] Examples of social media policies can be found at http://socialmedia.biz/social-media-policies/.

[8] http://www.searchenginejournal.com/lawyers-guns-and-twitter-who-owns-your-twitter-account/10612/.

SOCIAL MEDIA COMMENT AND RESPONSE PROTOCOL

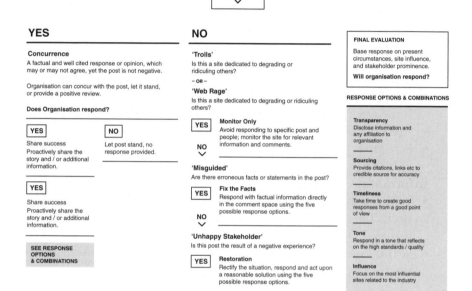

Figure 25.1   Social media comment and response protocol.

Source: Based on data from Shaun Holloway, MBA, Director of Information Technology at Association of College and University Housing Officers – International.

media world is: Are we occupying the space? The ability to occupy the space may well depend on engaging employees well beyond their usual responsibilities. This in turn will require the organisation to have a culture of engagement on social media through strong and proactive policies. While the Nestlé well-documented example of proactive management requires resources of large scale, a simple social media policy and a culture of social media engagement, fine-tuned by a daily practice in the organisation, can foster a transparent and engaged culture that will be resilient to external shocks. And in the next two chapters, we focus on the board's engagement with investors and stakeholders.

CHAPTER 26

Boards and Investors

There is a trend toward increasing engagement and advocacy by shareholders who expect to have greater access to boards. More generally, environmental, social, and governance (ESG) dimensions have become important factors in investments. This has been accentuated by greater technology-enabled exchanges of information between boards and shareholders.

Information Design and Capital Raising: Crowdfunding

The proliferation of new approaches to raising capital has resulted in higher quality and transparency of information available to investors. From private equity to crowdfunding, the 'closed shop' way of interacting on investment decisions is becoming a thing of the past. Instead, accurate and timely – often real-time – information is made available, thus delivering on the promise of digital technology. It has had a powerful effect on levelling the playing field between institutional and private investors, as well as between active and potential investors.

The Oculus VR is a virtual-reality headset that puts players into their favourite games. With over $2 million raised in 30 days through crowdfunding, the Oculus team went on to raise additional investment capital and was acquired by Facebook. The $2 billion acquisition was controversial and many crowdfunding backers that contributed to the Oculus campaign expressed their desire to benefit from the company's success since they were the first supporters of the company.

The impact of the transforming shareholder role has been felt on many fronts, including in the form of institutional shareholder-led initiatives regarding the composition of boards. There have also been regulatory changes in response to shareholder demands. These include 'say-on-pay' rules, where investors vote on executive compensation, as well as a requirement that shareholders approve dilutive transactions. Demands for shareholder engagement are likely to continue to intensify.

Investors vary from institutional shareholders and pension funds, which often use asset management firms to manage their portfolios, to activist investors, who are more directly involved. Boards can actively frame the dialogue with major shareholders through ongoing, high-quality communication, and by engaging with them on key issues such as strategy, succession planning, and emerging risks.

One prominent board member, who also owns a sizeable stake in a large-cap pharmaceutical company, told me privately that he feels more powerful in shaping a firm's direction as an investor than as a board member. Investors exert strong influence by directly communicating their concerns, withholding votes from directors, waging a proxy contest to elect an alternative board, voting against company proxy items, or sponsoring proxy items of their own. These generally relate to compensation, board structure, anti-takeover protections, and bylaw changes. Or, of course, shareholders can simply start selling their shares.

Types of investors:

- activist investors;
- institutional investors – required by US Securities and Exchange Commission regulations to vote all items on the proxy and to disclose their votes to investors;
- blockholders;
- pension funds.

Investors differ by:

- objectives;
- time horizon;
- size;
- activity level.

In January 2019, Olympus took steps to speed up reform of its much-criticised governance by welcoming a foreign activist investor to its board. As part of a shake-up of its leadership team, the Japanese company announced that it was inviting Robert Hale, a partner at leading shareholder ValueAct Capital Management, to become a director. The unusual move may be a belated reaction to foreign investors' criticism of how Olympus dealt with accounting improprieties earlier in the decade.

The Move toward Increasing Shareholder Engagement

In the US, the main thrust of shareholder democracy is that directors should be more accountable to shareholder concerns; for example, regarding excessive compensation, risk management, and board accountability. Elements of shareholder democracy include majority voting in uncontested board elections, brokers being disallowed from voting in uncontested elections, the right of investors to nominate directors ('proxy access'), and 'say on pay' votes by investors concerning executive compensation.

Shareholder advocates believe that plurality voting lowers the quality of governance by insulating directors from investors. They advocate a stricter standard of majority voting, whereby directors must receive 50% of the votes to be elected. The impact of majority voting on governance is unclear. Dissenting votes are often issue-driven and not against the director personally – shareholders may vote against directors on the board's compensation committee in protest at the CEO's pay, for example. This might inadvertently result in the removal of directors with important strategic, operational, or risk qualifications.

In Europe, the European Shareholder Rights Directive (formally known as the Long-Term Shareholder Engagement and Corporate Governance Statement) aims to contribute 'to a more long-term perspective of shareholders which ensures better operating conditions for listed companies', by:

- increasing the level and quality of engagement of asset owners and asset managers with their investee companies;
- creating a better link between pay and performance of company directors;

- enhancing transparency and shareholder oversight on related-party transactions;
- ensuring reliability and quality of advice of proxy advisors; and
- facilitating transmission of cross-border information (including voting) across the investment chain, in particular through shareholder identification.[1]

More and more boards are pursuing fuller and more effective engagement with shareholders. Online voting and participation is increasingly common: Intel typically collects hundreds of shareholder questions throughout the year via a message board, for example. In a similar vein, Pansoft Company Ltd., a China-based software developer, supplemented its 2012 annual shareholder meeting in China with a virtual meeting accessible to shareholders around the world. This practice has now expanded.

Overall, however, real shareholder engagement in publicly-traded companies remains light. True, ESG factors have moved to the forefront. But there is still a long process for investors to understand the real intricacies of governance described in this book, and for them to become truly active players in this regard. At the same time, boards need to remain engaged with many other stakeholder groups besides investors. This is the theme of the next chapter.

---

[1] http://eur-lex.europa.eu/legal-content/EN/TXT/?uri=COM%3A2014%3A213%3AFIN.

27

Managing Stakeholders

The economic and social upheavals of recent years have revived the old debate over the extent to which companies serve the interests of shareholders as opposed to stakeholders. Maximising shareholder value has been the prime focus of business ever since the birth of the corporation. Those who uphold this view may argue that the different groups that have a stake in the performance of a business often present conflicting agendas, and that these agendas will in any event be best served by keeping a close eye on the company's bottom line.

Many company directors share this outlook. They consider the firm's interactions with stakeholders such as governments, regulators, media, and the wider public as primarily a distraction from the business activities that the organisation was set up to perform. In extreme cases, boards may have an outright negative perception of some stakeholders, such as non-governmental organisations. Directors may view NGOs as at best not having a direct relationship with the company; and at worst, as representatives of groups that are innately anti-business and typically a source of nuisance and opposition to a company's operations, as well as to its broader interests and general well-being.

Lafarge and its Post-Tsunami Efforts in Aceh, Indonesia[1]

Cement maker Lafarge's plant in Aceh, Indonesia was destroyed in the 2004 tsunami that wrought devastation on Northern Sumatra. On the back of its immediate rescue, recovery, and other humanitarian efforts, the company was quick to announce plans to invest $90 million in rebuilding the facility.

Lafarge framed this initiative as part of its broader commitment to support economic recovery in the tsunami-affected region, and in line with the aid plan the company had drawn up for its employees, sub-contractors, and local communities.

The Lafarge Group also launched a programme to rebuild 500 homes, a school, and a mosque in a village about a mile away from the factory, which was almost destroyed by the tsunami. In parallel, the company undertook to rebuild several other schools and mosques across the Aceh province, as well as to deploy mobile medical assistance teams.

In carrying out these plans at a time when the local community found itself at its most vulnerable, Lafarge teamed up with three NGOs:[2]

- Atlas Logistique, a French NGO coordinating the rebuilding programme on site;
- Habitat for Humanity, an international NGO, which provided building materials and also hired and trained local people to build houses; and
- Dompet Dhuafa, a local NGO, whose mandate was to facilitate relationships between local communities and the authorities, help to identify rightful land owners, and provide advice regarding local housing requirements and cultural sensitivities.

Shareholders vs. Stakeholders: A Definition

Whereas the definition of a shareholder has remained virtually unchanged for centuries, the concept of stakeholders has gone through many shifts over the past few decades. This has been largely in tandem with changes in the dominant discourses on business and management. Today's discussions of the roles, mandates, and expectations attached to corporations are firmly rooted in the paradigm of 'business in society'. In this perspective, a company's goals and activities cannot be divorced from the impact they have – not only on stakeholder groups such as customers and employees, but also on local communities and society at large.

---

[1] www.lafarge.com/en/lafarge-confirms-its-long-term-commitment-aceh-indonesia.
[2] http://growinginclusivemarkets.org/media/cases/Indonesia_Lafarge_2008.pdf.

The stakeholder conversation is therefore increasingly relevant in the boardroom. Managing stakeholders is a complex undertaking that at times may feel like navigating a minefield of disparate perceptions and expectations. But as the spate of corporate and boardroom dramas this century has illustrated, how stakeholders see an organisation is a strong indicator of its health – particularly at critical junctures in the company's existence – and of its potential to create long-term value. Stakeholders also act as a company's moral compass, challenging it to do the right thing – on a day-to-day basis as well as in situations that are crucial to its survival.

How to Identify a Company's Key Stakeholders

Stakeholders that are critical to a company's long-term success are those that cannot be disregarded, ignored, or replaced without damaging the firm's reputation and long-term growth prospects. Typically, they include a government's law-making bodies and regulatory agencies, as well as public utilities; unions and other employee representatives; consumer associations and consumer rights advocacy groups; and influential NGOs that often set the tone and topic of debates on issues such as the environmental impact of a particular industry's or corporation's current projects.

Today, social expectations and corporate governance standards dictate that companies and boards continually elicit their main stakeholders' support, and engage them in active dialogue. Analysing different growth and risk scenarios will cast new light on which stakeholders act as gatekeepers on various frontlines and whose buy-in will be critical in executing new growth, innovation, and integration initiatives.

The Board Can Be Instrumental in Shaping the CEO–Stakeholders Conversation

Board members can exert strong influence in moulding the CEO's view of stakeholders, including NGOs. Directors can also offer considerable guidance and support as the chief executive goes about engaging with the company's stakeholders. To begin with, board

MTN Nigeria was hit with a $5.2 billion fine for failing to disconnect unregistered SIMs from the network in 2015. After a drawn-out process that involved engaging former US attorney general Eric Holder as a negotiator, the fine was reduced. Among other concessions to the government, MTN also agreed to list on the stock exchange. The listing was approved in May 2019. More generally, some have wondered whether heavy, politically motivated fines are being imposed, sometimes on the pretext of tax evasion or illegal money transfers abroad. This shows how stakeholder management can become sensitive and complex.

members tend to have a broader range of access through their network and more open perspectives than CEOs, as well as a wider sense of the organisation's purpose. The board therefore has a critical role to play in backing and inspiring the CEO's interactions with stakeholders.

Importantly, even if the organisation is entering uncharted territory in reaching out to specific types of stakeholders, the board cannot limit its involvement to just ticking boxes and complying with regulations. Instead, listening to key stakeholders gives directors a good opportunity to understand the real concerns of the company's customers, suppliers and employees, and the broader public. Many corporate disasters happened because the board was removed from what was happening on the ground. A sudden event whose repercussions may upset a firm's stakeholders – internal or external – is very likely to produce a crisis that the company will be hard-pressed to defuse.

In that context, making the stakeholders' voices heard in the boardroom can be crucial in narrowing the gap between the board's perception and reality. As we saw in Chapter 21, the chair in particular is in a strong position to represent the company in building relationships with major stakeholders, and to bring the knowledge gained back to the boardroom.

Anticipating Stakeholders' Influence and Impact

A company's strategic planning process must ensure that all stakeholder relationships are managed properly. This is particularly important for anticipating, assessing, and measuring the impact that these different groups can have on a company's direction and results. Stakeholders have their own sets of checks and balances that are likely to sound an alarm bell if the company tries to exaggerate

In March 2015, the board of South African Nuclear Energy Corporation (Necsa) suspended the CEO for disciplinary lapses, following consultations with the Ministry of Energy. The Ministry subsequently changed its position and instructed the board to reverse the suspension, which the board declined to do. The Ministry then announced the formation of a task team to investigate the board.

its accomplishments or play down negative results. In many corporate crises, it is the stakeholders that provide early-warning mechanisms by flagging the company's shortcomings and its impending or recent transgressions.

This particular role played by stakeholders becomes even more important to an organisation's sustainability and success when it concerns international operations, especially those in developing countries. In these environments, stakeholders such as NGOs often compensate for underdeveloped legal, regulatory, and ethical frameworks. On the downside, cultural, historical, linguistic, and other barriers tend to be firmly entrenched. This means that situations can become fraught and dramatic scenarios flare up quite unexpectedly, more so than in the company's domestic market.

Many companies have learned from experience that maintaining the local status quo is enough of an uphill battle in itself, and are therefore reluctant to discuss how their business affects local communities. There are even more constraints to negotiate in fast-growth markets run by authoritarian governments, where national and local regulations can change on a whim.

For today's companies, properly managing relationships with their stakeholders are no longer an afterthought subsumed to a larger project of maximising returns to shareholders. External stakeholders in particular are no longer relegated to the fringes of activity and influence. Governance imperatives, growing regulatory pressures, and the public's newly articulated expectations of accountability and social responsibility, have placed stakeholder engagement squarely on the boardroom radar. The availability of new communication platforms such as social media has brought an extra level of volatility into these relationships. But it has also allowed chairs and directors to be proactive, analytical, and empathetic when addressing stakeholder needs and requirements.

Disney English: A Game-Changing Approach to Chinese Stakeholders

In the early 2000s, The Walt Disney Company encountered repeated delays and obstacles in obtaining government approvals for construction of a theme park in Shanghai, China. Executives soon realised what the key to overcoming these problems was: listening, understanding, and accommodating the local authorities' and partners' aspirations for their country, their hometown, their families, and their own professional and career development.

The company discovered that one of the most prized commodities it could offer to its partners and their communities was the opportunity to learn English. That is how Disney English[3] was born – a learning programme built around the company's own recognised curriculum, innovative technology, and involvement of popular Disney characters and stories.

Following the programme's success and rapid growth across a number of Chinese cities, Disney representatives said they were also pleased with the exposure the programme facilitated within the broader Chinese media market, which is traditionally restricted by government controls and quotas.[4]

Meanwhile, the $3.7 billion Shanghai Disney Resort, run by a joint venture between The Walt Disney Company and three firms owned by the city's municipal government, opened in June 2016.

By paying increasing attention to stakeholders and societies, and taking a broader long-term view of the organisation's activities while at the same time delivering results, boards are embracing the concept of stewardship. In the concluding chapter, we discuss the importance of stewardship and the role that boards can play in promoting it.

---

[3] http://disneyenglish.disneycareers.com/en/about-disney-english/company-overview/.

[4] http://www.ft.com/cms/s/0/4d6cfd1a-8932-11df-8ecd-00144feab49a.html#axzz4JPoQq100.

28

Stewardship from the Board

More than ever, boards need to act as a counter-balance to the short-term thinking that pervades much of the corporate world. To avoid succumbing to the pressures that drive the behaviour of many business leaders, boards must remain vigilant and define clear boundaries to guide decision-making for the long term. As such, they act as stewards, enabling the organisation to thrive and sustain growth while enhancing the wealth of its stakeholders and the well-being of the societies in which it operates. This is what we call stewardship.

Stewardship draws on notions of accountability, long-term orientation, and responsibility for protecting assets over time. With the clear objective of benefiting society with its aligned values, structures, and processes, stewardship provides a firm's leaders and employees with the clarity of purpose to generate value in the broader sense. The essential idea is that those who are entrusted with wealth of any kind have an obligation to hand those assets on in better shape than they inherited them. And the board has a key role to play as a steward of the organisation. I have explored this topic in depth with Ong Boon Hwee, then CEO of the Stewardship Asia Centre, in a separate book.

Society increasingly expects business to contribute to creating lasting and more inclusive value. At the same time, firm ownership is ever more complex and varied – including state-owned enterprises, family businesses, sovereign wealth funds, publicly-traded companies in which institutional investors hold large stakes, and so on. Steward-ship offers a way to meaningfully address both legitimate societal expectations and the complexity of ownership structures.

Stewardship encourages business leaders to shift mindsets, and to creatively engage their organisations and other societal actors to enhance wealth creation for all over time. Until recently, the dominant view was that business should focus on creating value for a firm's owners and shareholders. But along with expanding their global footprint, today's companies are being compelled to redefine their view of corporate achievement and success.

My own work on stewardship rests on a belief that the language of stewardship is critical and reflects deep values embedded in organisations' personalities. Researcher Abraham Lu and I conducted an empirical study of the narratives that companies construct and use to communicate their purpose and activities.[1] Their choice of terms – both conscious and unconscious – reflects their view of the world and their underlying values, beliefs, and culture. Using word content analysis, our quantitative study of word incidences by potentially well-stewarded companies and those less well stewarded helps to build a picture of the major differences in narrative between them.

What we found was striking: there are indeed clear differences in the way companies refer to their stakeholders and employees, as well as in the word usage related to appetite for debt or innovation and time horizon. Words are used differently by different companies, and the choices of words align well with material differences between firms. We then examined words used in more than 2500 annual reports from 872 companies with sales of $10 billion or more over several years, a study that we have now expanded to 16 000 firms across 15 years. From this, we constructed an Implied Steward-ship Index, based on the relative difference between sets of words, to compare material metrics such as investment in R&D, trends in labour, and use of financial leverage and check word use versus actual company choices. Words are strongly related to the values truly displayed by companies in regard to material choices (such as capex or R&D spending) as well as cultural attributes (such as agility or conservativeness).

---

[1] Cossin, D. and B.H Ong (2016). *Inspiring Stewardship*. Wiley.

STEWARDSHIP'S THREE DIMENSIONS

**LEADING WITH IMPACT
TO DELIVER RESULTS**

**LONG-TERM VIEW OF
VALUE CREATION**

**CONNECTION WITH
COMMUNITIES & SOCIETY**

Response Options & Combinations

Transparency	Sourcing	Timeliness	Tone	Influence
Disclose information and any affiliation to organisation	Provide citations, links etc. to credible source for accuracy	Take time to create good responses from a good point of view	Respond in a tone that reflects on the high standards / quality	Focus on the most influential sites related to the industry

Figure 28.1   Stewardship's Three Dimensions

Supported by our quantitative study, we identified three key dimensions of stewardship, as illustrated in Figure 28.1.

Building Upon a Rich Cross-Disciplinary Legacy of Thought

Stewardship has its theoretical origins in several different traditions. The notion of treating people with respect is implicit in many streams of ethics and philosophy. There is often a sense of service and duty that characterises the spiritual concept of stewardship. In a business sense, the focus is more on the sense of oneself as being responsible for something greater than simply the individual or company, and over a longer time horizon extending beyond one's lifetime. In economics, agency theory states that individuals will act in their own self-interest, and need to be incentivised or constrained to act for the benefit of the organisation. Stewardship theory, which grew out of organisational psychology and sociology, says that individuals will act to protect the assets they control on behalf of their owners and society at large, and are motivated by autonomy.

Psychological, Organisational, and Cultural Influences on Stewardship

A number of factors – social, organisational, and individual – interact to affect the likelihood of stewardship emerging in a given context. Individuals who are intrinsically motivated and are driven by higher-order needs are more likely to act as stewards than those who rely on external rewards. But stewardship is not just a matter of getting the right people – context matters too. For example, individuals may be more likely to act as stewards in cultures that place greater relative value on institutional collectivism (that is, a sense of connection to society as a whole, rather than an affiliation with an in-group such as a family unit). However, it is important to avoid generalisations, given the complex intersection of different factors.

Countries such as Singapore and Switzerland provide examples of organisational stewardship. By securing the foundations and building conducive and supportive structural conditions, they enable stewardship to flourish.

Steward Leaders Build on their Unique Strengths to Drive Stewardship

There are many business and national leaders whose personalities and legacies have come to exemplify stewardship. These leaders come from very different organisational contexts, including financial and institutional investors, family foundations, trans-generational family businesses, public agencies, and state-owned enterprises. In searching for what stewardship looks like, my co-author and I studied steward leaders at work in a variety of organisations and environments – notably in volatile and uncertain contexts requiring clear and bold direction, at inflection points, and during crises. We found a range of compelling examples from whom we can learn.

Ratan Tata's clear focus on business success combined with social and national economic impact helped to provide India with a solid domestic industrial base over the course of his tenure (1991–2012), illustrating how impactful stewardship can be in an emerging-market context. Family business Maersk had a clear long-term focus from the start, and this continues today. Founded by Arnold Peder Moller, the business grew from a shipping company into a global trade conglomerate, whose legacy was secured through its structure as well as its deeply held values.

There are many more examples of stewardship, which vary in context and form, in state-owned firms as well as in family companies or widely held publicly-traded corporations. Zhang Ruimin took Haier from being a low-quality manufacturer in 1980s China and transformed it into the world's leading white goods producer. Eiji Toyoda's unique lean management philosophy (the Toyota Way) was disruptive and paradigm shifting. Warren Buffett's unique and far-sighted investment strategy is built on a holistic and innovative method of asset selection. And when Chung Juy-yung founded Hyundai in 1946, his efforts not only led to the creation of a highly successful conglomerate, but also made a key contribution to the foundation of post-war Korea's industrial base.

Steward Leaders Deliver Long-Lasting, Meaningful, and Inclusive Impact

Stewardship requires leaders who have strong drive and a passion for the organisations they lead and the societies they live in, and who are conscious of the trade-offs required to ensure their meaningful contribution over time. Many of the steward leaders we studied had critical turning points in their upbringing, developed key values that drove them, and had people who inspired them. Whether through their internal value set or personality, they have a unique ability to create meaning through stories, build trust, and foster organisational knowledge sharing. Driven by a compelling sense of purpose, steward leaders are able to engage employees with the vision of the contribution they are making.

Well-stewarded organisations focus on delivering current performance without compromising future impact in terms of earnings. They also ensure the continuity of the capabilities and relationships that form the basis of their ability to create future value. Success for these organisations can be measured as the net positive impact on future generations in terms of economic, social, and environmental performance. They are willing to sacrifice short-term profits in the interest of securing longer-term benefits for the organisation.

Conservative financing is one way to ensure continuity of operations and resilience in the face of crisis. Our study findings reinforce this: companies scoring highly on our Implied Stewardship Index use 50% less long-term debt than firms scoring at the lower end. Safeguarding the future requires having a vision of where the company is going and making the trajectory possible by investing in capabilities such as R&D, marketing, and branding. Well-stewarded organisations are able to operate effectively over longer time horizons, enabled by a culture based on trust, and by structures that are well aligned with the company's strategy and purpose. And crucially, these organisations are supported by boards that think strategically toward the medium and long term, feeding and nurturing the succession pipeline to secure the leadership legacy over time.

Firms need to play their part in building a healthy ecosystem in which stewardship can flourish. They can do this internally, by stimulating intrinsic motivation in employees, and externally, through clear links to stakeholders and the surrounding communities, which cultivates a landscape of greater transparency and trust. Organisations that are well stewarded have a clear sense of where they are going and why, are strongly committed to creating wealth in both the medium and long term, and build governance systems that foster effective exchange and supervision among the relevant actors.

As such, stewardship is built on a virtuous spiral (shown in Figure 28.2). Steward leaders build on their own vision and purpose for the organisation to inspire their people, both through the strategy and the culture. This then contributes to societal well-being and the company's integration into society. These societal connections then

THE STEWARDSHIP LANDSCAPE

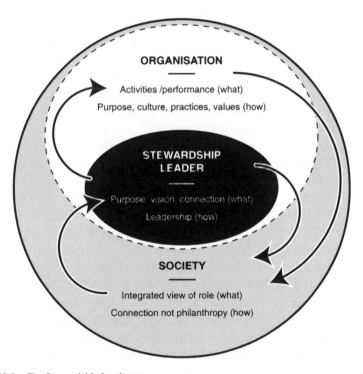

Figure 28.2   The Stewardship Landscape

help the steward leaders to scan the environment and adjust course if required, realigning the organisation to deliver on its promise. In the process, its employees and other stakeholders are inspired by its integrity. And so on.

The Stewardship Landscape

While stewardship relies on strong leaders to drive it, several other important actors ensure that management balances issues of short- and long-term strategic relevance. These actors also consciously scan for and manage risk. Effective oversight helps to keep the organisation on track, so that people perform their roles with a high degree of conscientiousness, competence, and integrity. As well as an enlightened and responsible CEO, therefore, company owners, boards, and management have their respective roles to play in ensuring that the right governance is in place.

The important relationships between the owners, the board, and the management are depicted in Figure 28.3 below. Together, all three steward the firm – safeguarding and growing values, and benefiting its stakeholders and the wider community over the longer term. As trusted and responsible stewards, they seek to hand over a thriving business and organisation that is in better shape to the next generation or to their successors.

Becoming a Steward Leader: What it Takes

Although there is no template for steward leadership, the steward leaders we studied share three key characteristics. First, they are transformational individuals who inspire their followers to excel and achieve superior performance through their charisma, inspiration, intellectual stimulation, and individualised consideration. We call this leading with impact.

Second, through a combination of prudence and care, steward leaders safeguard the future and ensure that the organisation and its stakeholders thrive over the long term. They exercise the judgement and discipline to sacrifice short-term profits for long-term gain. This enables the organisation to regenerate over time. Finally, by being transparent, accountable, and responsible, steward leaders demonstrate a deep understanding of the organisation's broader social impact to bring about positive social change.

AN EXAMPLE OF

THE KEY ACTORS IN THE STEWARDSHIP ECOSYSTEM

Figure 28.3   The Relationship of the Key Actors in the Stewardship Ecosystem

Individual steward leaders have very different personalities and ways of behaving. What they share is their ability to use their strong personal conviction to drive and sustain organisational purpose and culture, to enable decision-making and activity that is consistent and aligned, and to invest in nurturing high-quality connections both internally and externally, demonstrating their understanding of the firm's integral role in society.

Through deep self-awareness and knowledge of their gaps, steward leaders pursue a journey of lifelong learning. Building on our research, we have developed an assessment tool to help board members assess their own strengths and any areas that need to be addressed as they work to secure their own stewardship legacy. This questionnaire is intended to identify development gaps and is most helpful when used in the context of a coaching conversation; it is included in our book *Inspiring Stewardship*.

Stewardship Risks

Leaders are human and vulnerable to hubris. Dizzying rates of change mean that our ever more connected world is vulnerable to shocks, currency fluctuations, and other forms of volatility. For steward leaders and their organisations, reinvention, flexibility, and adaptability are essential. Failing to identify threats can jeopardise the very survival of the organisation and the future of all those involved with it.

Many leaders fall victim to their own success, and stay fixed in their ways. Others become enamoured with their own views, overconfident and increasingly isolated in their thinking. But steward leaders acknowledge that they are vulnerable to risks – including those related to reputation, cognitive and behavioural biases (which distort leaders' perception of reality), leadership transitions, leadership feuds, and political risks. Great stewards enhance their self-awareness and manage their own weak points, by pursuing lifelong learning and by building diverse teams to challenge them and promote a healthy counterpoint to their own views.

Boards Are Key to Fostering Stewardship

Our notion of stewardship advocates committed co-creation between owners and managers working together to build a company's future. Although some have argued that such engagement creates an excessive burden, we would counter that it is the quality of connection that needs to improve, rather than the quantity. Co-creation does not necessarily imply an additional reporting burden. In some contexts, stewardship might translate into greater focus on the quality of interaction between management, boards, owners, and shareholders. In other contexts, it might mean taking ownership and initiative to fill in institutional gaps, and to reinforce capabilities where they are lacking.

By acknowledging and building on the organisational connections that do exist, stewardship helps to build a firm's wealth over time, lifting societal players along with it. There are clear long-term financial, economic, social, and other benefits to be gained as a result. Boards have an important role to play in fostering steward-ship at the firm level. I therefore encourage you to consider what impact you can make as a steward leader – individually and collec-tively – so that we can work together to make stewardship a reality.

Conclusion

Governance is a key driver of quality success of organisations, from start-ups all the way to multinationals and beyond, including governments and countries. Boards and committees are principal actors of governance and their effectiveness.

This book was inspired by my work over many years with boards around the world. For any organisation, there are four pillars to a board's effectiveness: outstanding directors with the right focus and dedication; sophisticated information architecture, internal and external, formal and informal; the long list of structures and processes, all developed with clarity and sophistication; and healthy board dynamics and culture, based on the right values, including integrity and, accountability and constructive dissent.

These pillars of board effectiveness are nourished by the many practices developed in this book. I urge all boards and their directors to think how they can further strengthen these pillars to bring about world-class governance, and in so doing contribute to a better world.

I wish you every success in your board and governance endeavours.

Index

Page locators in *italics* and **bold** refer to images and tables, respectively.